SOCIA

NEW ORIENTATIONS
FOR
SOCIAL POLICY

ORGANISATION FOR ECONOMIC CO-OPERATION AND DEVELOPMENT

ORGANISATION FOR ECONOMIC CO-OPERATION AND DEVELOPMENT

Pursuant to Article 1 of the Convention signed in Paris on 14th December 1960, and which came into force on 30th September 1961, the Organisation for Economic Co-operation and Development (OECD) shall promote policies designed:

— to achieve the highest sustainable economic growth and employment and a rising standard of living in Member countries, while maintaining financial stability, and thus to contribute to the development of the world economy;

— to contribute to sound economic expansion in Member as well as non-member countries in the process of economic development; and

— to contribute to the expansion of world trade on a multilateral, non-discriminatory basis in accordance with international obligations.

The original Member countries of the OECD are Austria, Belgium, Canada, Denmark, France, Germany, Greece, Iceland, Ireland, Italy, Luxembourg, the Netherlands, Norway, Portugal, Spain, Sweden, Switzerland, Turkey, the United Kingdom and the United States. The following countries became Members subsequently through accession at the dates indicated hereafter: Japan (28th April 1964), Finland (28th January 1969), Australia (7th June 1971) and New Zealand (29th May 1973). The Commission of the European Communities takes part in the work of the OECD (Article 13 of the OECD Convention).

Publié en français sous le titre :
LES NOUVELLES ORIENTATIONS
DE LA POLITIQUE SOCIALE

FOREWORD

Ministers responsible for social policy within OECD countries met in Paris on the 8th and 9th December 1992 to consider a number of issues facing the social protection systems of Member countries. The main focus of the meeting was a consideration of the appropriate orientations for social policy in an economic and social climate that differs markedly from that of the past.

This report, from OECD's Directorate for Education, Employment, Labour and Social Affairs, includes the reference documents prepared by the OECD Secretariat as a basis for discussion at that meeting. It is published on the responsibility of the Secretary-General.

TABLE OF CONTENTS

LIST OF TABLES

LIST OF CHARTS

PREFACE

Public systems of social protection have been extremely successful in minimising the hardship which can result from the range of risks faced by everyone – for example illness, disability, unemployment or old age. Not only have individuals been helped. There have also been positive consequences for society and the economy. Income support and care for elderly and disabled people give other family members more freedom to work, to raise children, and, more generally, to participate in society. Public health care and education are important not only for the well-being of individuals, they also serve as investments in the productive capacity of the economy – as do programmes which provide the unemployed with income and with assistance in training and job search. Together, these and other benefits of social policy contribute to a more efficient, a more stable, and a more just society.

The risks remain, as do the programmes that have evolved in response to them. But the economic context has changed. All countries now are confronted by increasing demands on their social policy expenditures while, at the same time, they face growing resource constraints and, often, budget deficits. And the current recession has underscored the serious financial pressures affecting systems of social protection. These pressures are exacerbated by the expected increase in social expenditures because of the ageing of populations.

The result, a dilemma which is of major concern in many countries, has led to a rethinking of the objectives and of the financing of all public policies, and social policies in particular. The fundamental objectives of social protection remain the same – improving the welfare of individuals and of the whole of society. However, programmes introduced in the post-war era of rapid economic growth, and sustained with increasing difficulty during the 1980s, are now seen as insufficiently responsive to the realities of the 1990s: slow growth, persistent levels of high unemployment, increasing numbers of families with low income, inequality of opportunity, marginalisation, urban unrest and rural decline.

For example, while income support programmes enhance security, they are not intended to be long-term alternatives to employment. To the extent that these systems lead to persistent dependency on the State, they become a poor alternative to active participation and self-sufficiency. Earnings must remain the primary source of income among the able-bodied of working age – a difficult goal at a time when there are unacceptably high levels of unemployment across the OECD area. Nevertheless, maximising human potential and individual choice increases personal dignity and the resources available to the economy. Thus, collective goals can be enhanced by constructive individual actions; personal initiative, in turn, can be enhanced by providing people with a greater capacity to act in their own behalf.

OECD governments are examining their social programmes, not only to alter any unintended effects, but also to use available resources more prudently. Public authorities are reviewing the ways in which social policies can be delivered more efficiently and searching for a more effective way of providing society with social protection that is consistent with current and future needs and resources. This requires greater coherence between labour-market, education and social policies. For example, policies which aim to enhance equity and social protection should structure their incentives so that workforce participation is encouraged.

Efficiency and effectiveness in the delivery and financing of health care is a particular focus. The health status of OECD populations has improved progressively over past decades and systems of medical care clearly have contributed to this result. But there is no automatic link between improvements in health status and growth in national expenditures on medical care. Important reforms are being introduced in national health systems which can significantly alter incentive structures for payers, providers and patients, in the belief that even better results can be achieved without unsustainable increases in health care expenditures. Policies in the future also need to be much wider in scope than medical intervention alone. There is growing evidence that the health status of a population can be improved significantly by combining medical knowledge with health promotion policies. This includes encouraging people to remain fit, improve their diet, and consume less tobacco and alcohol. Maintaining good health, albeit important in its own right, is also one means of containing health care costs.

In addition, changing population structures suggest that current arrangements for the provision of retirement pensions also must adapt to this new context. Moreover, with the most rapid increase in numbers occurring among individuals of 80 years of age and over, the special needs of the larger numbers of frail elderly will require increased expenditures. We cannot shrink from providing the resources required to ensure that the needs of the elderly are met in ways which respect individual dignity and choice, but we also must be mindful of the needs of other groups. For example, despite increasing life spans, workers have been encouraged in a variety of ways to cease work earlier, often by offering early retirement pensions which are financed through charges paid by, or on behalf of, those still in employment. This tendency is now proving unsustainable: people who could continue in active life are being pushed or pulled out of the labour force, while declining numbers in the working-age population will be asked to pay more. A new balance in the allocation of scarce resources among competing needs is required.

In sum, effective social policies are essential both for the individual and for society. Though economic constraints should not be seen as a reason to underestimate the importance of social objectives, social policies cannot be developed outside the reality of budgetary considerations. Social policy, too, has an obligation to ensure that resources are mobilised more efficiently and effectively, not only because of current economic difficulties, but also for the credibility of the policies themselves as investments in society.

In December 1992, Ministers responsible for social policy in OECD countries met to consider these issues. The new orientations for social policy presented in this volume were endorsed by Ministers at that meeting. They represent a first step in the development of a framework for the ongoing assessment of social policies within a context of social and economic change. The development of an improved capacity to monitor the evolution of social policy is high on the OECD agenda.

Chapter 1

NEW ORIENTATIONS FOR SOCIAL POLICY

INTRODUCTION

When they last met at the OECD in 1988, Ministers for Social Policy accepted that, particularly in a climate of budgetary constraint, an active society in which all members have a constructive role was a primary goal for social policy. This *leitmotiv* was also influenced by the anticipation of the effects of population ageing.

Both economic and demographic pressures and constraints remain, as does the objective of full participation in society: the 1988 policy agenda is still relevant, and, although population ageing continues to be a central issue, the growing prominence of other, more immediate, concerns may extend the social policy agenda and alter priorities.

- Heightened economic and social insecurity and fissures in social cohesion have emerged. Among the symptoms, particularly visible in some urban areas, is the appearance of a culture of dependency on non-market incomes among those trapped in long-term involuntary joblessness. Where such incomes derive from public benefit payments, they burden government budgets; where they derive from illegal or criminal activities, they can be a direct threat to society and to its fabric.
- The reach of economic insecurity continues to widen as employment growth stagnates, and as unemployment and particularly long-term unemployment increase. The resulting hardship is putting systems of social protection under financial pressure.
- In some countries, the distance between the top and the bottom of the income and earnings distribution has been increasing. Many different circumstances may lead to this result, but particularly during economic slowdowns, there is the risk that life chances are diminishing for some households, particularly as the number of economically vulnerable family structures increases.

The goal of social policy is to improve societal well-being. The same broad goal is common to all areas of public intervention – from education and the labour market to the environment and the economy – whether the goal is pursued through improving the efficient operation of competitive markets, or through avoiding or correcting any undesirable effects of market forces. Social policies generally complement and support the market mechanisms through which economic progress occurs; they provide protection against personal economic insecurity which is a first step to a stable social climate and, hence, to consumer and business confidence.

There is growing awareness on the part of governments that public policies have not always led to adequate solutions to social problems. Even well-formulated policies, crafted in a circumscribed area of competence, may conflict with objectives in other domains and restrict policy success. The concern is not limited to social policies: it bears upon coherence across social, labour market, and education policies, and between these and economic policy. The extent to which responsibility can be shared – among government, collective actors in the private sector, and individuals – so that the comparative advantages of each are best utilised is also under review.

Policies rarely proceed in isolation: their effects may reinforce, diminish or thwart other desirable outcomes. The policy environment will change. The urgency of the problems which have emerged in the current economic environment, the rapidity of economic and social change, and unintended policy contradictions are leading to a broader approach to policy formulation and new orientations in social policy.

ADAPTING TO CHANGE

Notable improvements in the quality of life have occurred in this century, many attributable to collective provisions for the old, the sick and infirm, and other vulnerable groups in society. Especially prior to the 1970s, the objectives of social policy generally were met. The consequences of the oil price shocks put systems of social protection to a severe test, the results of which proved that, in most cases, these systems had been well constructed to fulfil their intended tasks. But unintended consequences also have emerged. While public measures providing protection against the vicissitudes of life enhance security, they are not meant to replace the responsibility of individuals to take initiatives on their own behalf when it is possible for them to do so. To the extent that these systems may lead to persistent reliance on the State, a poor alternative to self-sufficiency is created; policies which fail to promote the realisation of individual potential and greater personal control over the circumstances of life may hamper rather than help society.

Systems of social protection, at their inception, had a clear purpose. Everyone is at risk of a diminished capacity to work because of events beyond one's control: old age, illness or disability, or because of other events which may affect them or a family member on whom they depend for sustenance. Across families, the ability to manage such events differs. For some, the loss of earnings or the consequences of caring for an ill or impaired relative may be catastrophic; for the more fortunate, the resources necessary may be available. With the diminishing importance of the extended family in most OECD countries, the capacity of the family unit to cope with income disruptions or caring responsibilities has been further reduced. In the first instance, public collective schemes which replaced a portion of lost income, or provided an income guarantee in some form, served to protect against the risks of life in a more orderly, more efficient, and more equitable fashion than was possible through dependence on the family, with the charity of the community as a last resort.

Other important objectives were served as well. Two world wars left a legacy of loss and insecurity. The reconstruction process was undoubtedly aided by the social cohesion that, in large part, emerged from the security offered by systems of social protection, developed or extended to cover new groups and additional risks, in the years after World War II.

The positive consequences of social security, broadly defined, continue today. Because the elderly need not fear serious deprivation, their adult children are freed to work, raise their children, and to take advantage of opportunities and to make contributions to society that might otherwise be denied them; the unemployed are provided with income not only for survival, but also to permit time to search for a job appropriate to their skills, or to acquire new skills; public intervention in the education and support of children is an investment in tomorrow's resources, and in everyone's future; provisions for health care are an investment in the productive capacity of human resources. Together, these and other benefits of social policies contribute to a more efficient and a more just society.

But circumstances change, and public policies must adapt to the new environment. Policies that were effective in the post-war era are less responsive to the needs of the 1990s. The new context of slow growth, persistent labour market difficulties, ageing populations, increasing female labour force participation, a growing rate of marital dissolution and lone-parent families, urban decay, disaffected youth, and other changes, are leading to a re-examination of the role of social policy, and public pol-icy in general. There must be a partnership between public policy and individuals which enables and empowers people, rather than passively providing for them. Moreover, the new view extends to relationships among policy arenas. The role of social policy is not a subordinate one, relegating it to remedying the failures of other policies: there is a reciprocal responsibility between social policy and economic policy not to aggravate conditions in either domain, but to support the shared objective of improving the lives of people.

THE CHANGING CONTEXT FOR SOCIAL POLICY

Trends in Social Well-being

Repeated pauses in economic growth and the rapid structural and technological changes that have characterised recent decades have resulted in increased economic and social insecurity. High levels of unemployment, the growth in long-term unemployment and in hidden unemployment, and reductions in the stability of jobs have diminished the security of working-age families and have increased dependency on the State. Among the elderly, many remain inadequately protected. As populations age, with those who are very old increasing most rapidly, demands on the State, on communities, and on families will grow.

Notable among the positive developments is the continuing rise in women's labour force participation. In part, this reflects the increased options for self-realisation open to women, although full equality of opportunity in the labour market remains elusive in all countries. A side effect of increased independence for women has been their growing economic ability to end incompatible relationships – the positive side of changing family structures. The phenomenon of the dual-earner family is another consequence of more women choosing to work in paid employment. Less positively, however, it may also reflect income insecurity and the inability of many households to sustain an adequate level of living without two pay checks. In addition, the changing use of household time is creating new demands for services traditionally produced within the home, particularly those relating to the care of children and other dependent relatives, and an increasing need for policy directions that will facilitate a balance between work and family responsibilities.

The health status of populations continues to improve on average, although there are signs of growing divisions in health status by income level and region in some countries. Universal access to health care has been achieved in almost all OECD countries, and there is a growing emphasis on health promotion and disease prevention through healthier lifestyles. Popular expectations with respect to standards of care have risen as health status has improved. Hence, the need for more effective and more efficient health care has emerged as a result of both increased demand for quality care and cost constraints. Although the growth in health care costs has stabilized in most countries, the rise in the numbers of the very old will exert pressures on the cost of health care (and the cost of non-medical services required to maintain their optimal health status). Moreover, improvements in the state of medical knowledge, leading to reductions in the incidence of premature death from disease, may enlarge the pool of those with chronic illness later in life. To some extent, even the success of medical interventions may create expenditure pressures on health systems. However, system reforms that have taken place or which are in progress in a number of countries are intended to improve the efficiency of health care delivery, thereby reducing costs while maintaining quality.

Thus, current and anticipated expenditure pressures and resource constraints underlie the new orientations in social policy.

Unemployment and social exclusion

Employment and earnings represent the route to self-sufficiency for most individuals and families, and are the dominant source of household income among the non-aged in every OECD country. The link between earnings and self-sufficiency weakens as job insecurity increases. Nearly 30 million individuals are counted as unemployed in the OECD area. But unemployment rates by themselves do not explain the depth of individual hardship, nor its true extent.

In addition to open unemployment, many not actively looking for work would like to work but, in the present state of the labour market, are unable to do so. Labour market conditions also restrict the opportunities available to individuals to work as much as they would like: much employment is only seasonal, some part-time work is involuntary, and many women are unable to work full-time because child-care services or assistance in caring for frail elderly relatives are not available. Moreover, many people are excluded from full participation: female employment is segregated in a limited range of occupations, and older workers often find themselves excluded from opportunities.

Some individuals are more likely than others to face barriers to employment, or to adequate earnings. Women traditionally have had limited entry into higher paid occupations, inflexible working conditions that are often incompatible with the dual responsibilities of work and family, and have higher unemployment rates than men. Racial and ethnic minorities also have a disproportionate share of adverse labour market experience. Similarly, the older worker, once unemployed, has difficulties in re-entering employment, is heavily represented among the long-term unemployed, and may be pushed, involuntarily, into early retirement. And the loss of income affects not only the unemployed, but their families and the wider community as well.

There has been an alarming increase in some countries in the numbers of children who live in poor families.

For the majority of children who experience periods of family poverty, the cause is not attributable to family structure, but, more likely, to labour market and other social circumstances. Some of the increase in poor children relates to the rise in marital dissolution and lone-parent families, especially economically vulnerable lone-mother families. But this family type represents only a modest proportion of all families with children – from 10 to 15 per cent on average (with the highest incidence being one in four families with children in two countries).

Dependency on the State, persisting for indefinite periods, occurs for many individuals and families affected by economic hardship, marginalisation, and social exclusion. Although persistent dependency is undesirable for the individuals affected and for the State, social protection is important for all, particularly the most vulnerable: without it, their problems would be even more severe.

The aged: economic and demographic concerns

Historically, older age groups were heavily represented at the lower end of the income distribution in virtually all OECD countries. More recently, the elderly, on average, appeared to be at least as well off as the non-aged in most countries. This improvement in economic status, both absolute and relative to the non-aged, attests to the success of social policies towards the aged in all countries. However, less positively, the narrowing of this gap between the incomes of the aged and others has been partly brought about by a decline in the economic status of a significant proportion of the non-aged. But there are early warning signals that the relative economic status of the elderly, particularly those lacking any means additional to social benefits, may be falling in at least one country, and possibly others.

Despite major improvements in the economic position of the aged as a group, for a minority the advantages have been relatively few. Those most likely to be economically disadvantaged are older women, particularly those who are alone. Others in the early stages of old age may also remain behind. Those who retire involuntarily – whether due to ill health, labour market conditions, or other uncontrollable circumstances – may suffer an unaffordable loss of earnings. Recent increases in long-term unemployment and in long-term receipt of disability pensions suggest that the size of this disadvantaged group may have grown.

In sum, large numbers of the aged are better off than their predecessors: public benefit systems have generally improved over time; eligibility for private pensions has increased as private systems mature; and with continuing good health, some also continue to receive earnings after the customary age of retirement. But there are also significant numbers who have had relatively low prior earnings and have similarly low benefits after retirement; whose interrupted work histories because of unemployment or family needs have denied them benefits from occupational schemes; whose ill health may have curtailed their labour force attachment and affected their retirement benefits; or, for other reasons, are not adequately protected in their old age.

The ageing of populations also raises concerns. Increases in the numbers of the elderly, both absolutely and as a proportion of the population, will result in many more demands for income support, health care, long-term care, and other services – particularly with the numbers of the very old growing most rapidly. In the absence of significant increases in economic growth or other mitigating factors, the consumption of the aged will increase while contributions to their support may decline because of the reduced proportion of the population which is potentially active. Moreover, the traditional role of the family in caring for dependent aged relatives is changing as family structures change and as more women work in paid employment. Hence, improvements in the efficiency and effectiveness of social policies are urgent, not only because of current circumstances, but also in preparation for the future.

THE NEW ORIENTATIONS

The new orientations in social policy are a response to a new setting in OECD Member countries: slow growth, persistent labour market problems, social and economic insecurity, and policies (not only social policies) that have not been sufficiently effective in improving the situation in recent years. The policy prescriptions may be familiar, but it is the way in which the role of government is perceived that is new. Governments can no longer be thought of as providers of largesse, but instead, as partners that enable and empower people to take initiatives on their own behalf and to exert greater control over the circumstances of their lives. The new partnership between the government and the people, taking into account different national social traditions, is not simply an effort to shift responsibility, but to maximise human potential and the choices available to individuals, thereby increasing personal dignity and the resources available to the economy. Slow economic and social progress in past years may be explained, at least in part, by a tendency towards narrow problem-solving efforts; effective and efficient problem resolution requires a broad playing field, with co-operative efforts among government, individuals, and collective actors in the private sector, and across policy domains.

CONTRIBUTING TO SOCIAL AND ECONOMIC WELFARE

Non-inflationary growth of output and jobs, and political and social stability are enhanced by the role of social expenditures as investments in society.

Over the past two decades economic growth has not been accompanied by a return to full employment. Long-term unemployment and persistent joblessness prevail and can provoke frustration and, frequently, despair. Hence, despite considerable progress in living standards, concerns are emerging about deteriorating social cohesion.

The effective co-ordination of economic, social, education, and labour market policies is central to the reduction of structural rigidities. These reduce both social and economic welfare because they represent lost output and because of the need to invest resources in rectifying their effects.

Economic success is of little value if accompanied by failure on the social front. Strains and rifts in society inhibit economic progress by making families and individuals less flexible and more defensive. Social policy has a crucial role to play in addressing such problems.

The Role of Social Policy in the Partnership

Unrestrained market forces, in their normal selection process, exclude some individuals from the fruits of competition and from the mainstream of society. Social policies pursue the goal of improving well-being through various forms of correction to market processes. Some provide protection against risks such as the loss of income because of unemployment or marital breakdown, and against the consequences of illness and injury, while others alleviate the effects of other misfortunes and the resulting personal hardship. Systems of protection against certain risks are important to the functioning of the economy, not least because they give individuals the security necessary for them to take economic initiatives which themselves present risks. More broadly, they provide the political and social stability required for structural adjustments to the economy.

A further set of social programmes, which assist recipients at particular stages in their life cycles (students, families with children, the aged), operate through *de facto* transfers between generations. In many cases, the financing of these programmes, whether through specific levies on individuals or employers or through general taxation, in combination with the allocation of benefits, is redistributive: those with low incomes contribute less and receive relatively more than those with high incomes. As a result, social policies have made a significant contribution to reducing chronic poverty, particularly among the aged.

Policy interventions are necessary both to correct market failure and to promote their smooth functioning particularly in the provision of personal services and intangible investments in human potential. For example:

- they correct the tendency of private insurance markets to select low-risk individuals, for example those who are healthy or who have other characteristics predictive of long life;

- they correct the inability of capital markets to finance universal investments in early childhood education, in later formal education and in other forms of training, particularly in cases where the recipient of training has too few assets or income sources to be able to afford basic living expenses;
- they avoid the waste of resources on remedial services for problems which can be prevented by, for example, setting standards for safety and health in the workplace.

However, the most appropriate balance between social and economic goals is not easy to achieve. For example, if income support is to be adequate, payments may be close to net earnings in the labour market for people with low earnings potential. This discourages the acquisition of labour market experience which is essential for increasing earnings capacity. This, and other conflicts between policies, underlie the need for social policies which avoid the more perverse effects on labour market and economic incentives. The reorientation of social policies is particularly difficult when the employment market is weak, open unemployment high, and opportunities for labour market participation scarce. Nevertheless, progress in the macro-economy, in the labour market, and elsewhere, will not be complete without efficient and effective social and labour market policies working in co-ordination with economic policy. Policies in partnership rather than in conflict are necessary.

RECONCILING SOCIAL POLICY OBJECTIVES AND BUDGET LIMITATIONS

There is a need to reconcile social programme costs with overall limits on public budgets, but at the same time to ensure that economy measures are consistent with programme effectiveness and social objectives.

Resource Constraints and Social Goals

Recurrent difficulties in the economic climate in the OECD area for two decades have been constraining the availability of resources for social programmes. In the aftermath of the recessions of the 1980s and the early 1990s, the twin pressures of increasing needs for social protection and budget deficits have led to a regime in most countries of very tight budgets for social programmes.

Restrictions on social expenditures, however, could be counterproductive if the objectives of social policy are sacrificed. Jeopardising the quality of life or failing to relieve severe hardship may be the most costly route of all. But just as increased social expenditure may not always guarantee a better life for everyone, limits on expenditure need not imply a less caring society. Consistency between resource constraints and social goals can be achieved by improving the efficiency and effectiveness of social programmes and, if necessary, by other economy measures that are carefully conceived and implemented. Moreover, due attention needs to be given to the possible consequences of budgetary decisions to avoid short-term savings that generate long-term costs.

Increasing Revenue or Reducing Benefits?

Evidence from some countries suggests that taxpayers may be more willing to accept tax increases that pay for specific programmes which meet with their approval, rather than increases that support the general purposes of government. Increases which, for example, pay for old-age pensions or the costs of health care – particularly if the alternative is benefit reductions – appear to be more acceptable than income support for some groups among the non-aged. Thus, tax increases may be acceptable for some, but not all, purposes. Nevertheless, an increase in earmarked taxes may limit the ability of the tax and expenditure systems to respond quickly to needed changes. And if related to the wage bill, such taxes (or contributions) can be shifted by employers to employees by limiting increases in compensation or by limiting employment opportunities.

In many countries, the levels of taxes and contributions to systems of social protection are already high by historic standards. Tax and contribution burdens, however, are not similar in all countries. Increasing the flow of resources to social protection remains an option, but often neither attractive nor feasible. Nevertheless, taxes or contributions to systems of social protection have been raised in some countries, and some governments are considering the widening of the tax base and are searching for ways in which this might be done. Yet other governments are looking for acceptable ways in which taxpayer burdens might be reduced.

The alternative to raising taxes or contributions as a response to budgetary limitations is to reduce benefits. There are a number of ways in which benefit reductions may be accomplished; each has different revenue implications and distributional effects. For example:

Across-the-board Reductions: Income-transfer benefit levels might be reduced across all beneficiaries; in the case of health care or other services, the number of subsidised services might be reduced, or cost-sharing arrangements introduced, or existing ones modified. The "shared pain" approach affects individuals and families without regard to their needs, and therefore may have untenable consequences for some – especially if an efficient social safety net is not in place. Including benefits as taxable income escapes the above criticism, but is more appropriate for cash benefits than for those benefits where valuation problems arise.

Targeting by Income: Narrow targeting of benefits to only those with the lowest incomes also may present problems: the administrative costs of income- and asset-tested programmes can be higher than those of other programmes which do not focus on resources as an eligibility criterion. The more important problem, however, is the increased risk of error in defining the beneficiary population – some may be included or excluded, unintentionally, because of the complexities of income and asset tests.

Limiting Eligibility: An alternative way of targeting benefits is to limit other eligibility criteria, or, in the health field, to define them more appropriately. For example, increasing the age of eligibility to full retirement income benefits, often referred to as "raising the age of retirement", will lower costs by reducing the value of life-time benefits. But if retirement income is available at an earlier age through other public sources such as disability programmes, unemployment compensation, or other forms of public assistance, increases in the effective age of retirement and cost reductions may not be fully realised.

Taxing Benefits: Net benefits can be reduced selectively by subjecting some or all of the value of benefits to a progressive income tax system. Taxing cash benefits is the simplest approach administratively, and perhaps the most equitable. (Because of the difficulties in valuing non-cash benefits for tax purposes, raising contributions on the basis of ability-to-pay would accomplish a similar result with fewer complications.)

A decision between these targeting options (or any combination of options) should reflect social objectives. But economy measures that go further than improvements in administrative efficiency are invariably unpopular. If unavoidable, difficult choices should be made with fairness to beneficiaries and taxpayers, and with their understanding and support, drawing upon well-established and accepted rules for resolving conflict. Therefore, an emphasis on equity and a measure of altruism are necessary components of the new orientations in social policy.

MANAGING THE MIX OF PUBLIC AND PRIVATE RESPONSIBILITIES

The optimal balance should be sought between public and private sector responsibility in providing for the variety of needs of society, and in light of the comparative advantages of each sector.

In mixed economies, there is a partnership between the public and the private sectors. Competitive market forces are relied upon to maximise efficiency in the economy. When market failure occurs, the public role is to intervene to prevent or to compensate for such failures by implementing laws, regulations, and standards, or by supplying or subsidising those goods and services that can-

not be produced efficiently by private markets. Even efficient market outcomes may at times diverge from societal objectives, and government intervention may be required.

But public sector "failure" may also occur, not simply because policies may not achieve desired results, but also because government may inefficiently duplicate activities that the private market can perform. Hence, the public and private roles in the partnership, in principle, are based on what each can do best to achieve societal goals.

It is not always obvious, however, where comparative advantage lies. As part of the new orientations for social policy, renewed efforts are required to clarify the most efficient and effective use of public and private capacities, in light of desired results. The case of the provision of income in retirement is an appropriate example, among others, of the need to apply the principle of comparative advantage.

The Provision of Income in Retirement

The balance between public and private responsibility (including that of individuals) in the provision of retirement income has been the focus of intense interest in recent years. Short-term concerns – reduced fiscal capacity and the cost pressures arising from programme maturation – and the longer-term concern of population ageing, have moved governments to consider a greater emphasis on private collective and individual arrangements. (This option was reflected in the communiqué of the previous meeting of Ministers of Social Policy in July 1988.) At present, provisions are predominantly public, with levels of private provision that differ considerably across countries. Voluntary, employer-sponsored plans are the most frequent type. Explicit or *de facto* mandatory occupational schemes exist in but a few countries.

There is an existing public/private balance that has evolved over many years in a majority of countries. A change in the balance may well impose both costs and benefits. The relative advantages and disadvantages of public and private old-age pensions and their optimal roles were considered at an OECD conference in July 1991. Several different objectives appear to underlie the interest in moving towards greater reliance on private arrangements: *a)* the reduction of the aggregate costs to the community of supporting ageing populations; *b)* the reduction of only those costs on the public ledger; *c)* the increase of national savings and capital formation; *d)* the enhancement of retirement income.

The first objective, reducing the costs of ageing populations, cannot be met by merely changing the balance of responsibility. The real costs are appropriately measured by the current-period consumption they support, and only reducing the consumption of the elderly from all sources – public and private – reduces their cost

14

to society. The means of financing, advance-funding versus pay-as-you-go methods, does not change those costs. Increases in national savings do not alter the general conclusion, but may ease the burden of transferring consumption possibilities from the non-aged to the aged.

Confronting ageing societies is the concern that public pensions, financed on a pay-as-you-go basis, will require higher contributions from a relatively small cohort of working-age individuals if benefit levels are sustained at current levels for a relatively large cohort of elderly people. The problem is often posed as one of "intergenerational equity". But "intergenerational equity", or equivalent treatment for different generations, may refer to equivalent benefits for retirees as well as equivalent costs per worker. Therefore, the phrase "intergenerational equity" clouds the issue, rather than clarifies it. The problem, more accurately, concerns a potential tax burden on the active population that may strain their capacity or their willingness to pay. The dilemma is that reductions in tax burdens on workers do not automatically reduce the number of retirees or their needs. A partial solution may lie in providing more opportunities for potential retirees to work slightly longer.

But reducing public expenditures on old-age pensions, the second objective, entails shifting the costs, not necessarily eliminating them, particularly if private collective and individual arrangements are expected to compensate for reductions in public pension benefits. Moreover, public intervention appears to be necessary to encourage the availability of private provisions (through favoured tax treatment), and to ensure that pension promises are kept (through regulation). Hence, private employer-sponsored and individual plans are not without cost to public budgets. Of course, revenue losses that may occur on a yearly basis do not appear in public accounts, except as a hidden component of a budget deficit if one exists. If, however, favoured tax treatment is given to plan contributions and investment earnings of pension fund accumulations, but benefits are taxable when received (as occurs in many countries), revenue lost to the government may be at least partially recouped over the long term.

Can private arrangements compensate for reductions in public provisions? Private, voluntary, collective and personal plans favour higher earnings and income groups; in no country with voluntary arrangements does coverage include all or even most of those at the lower end of the earnings or income distribution. As currently constituted, voluntary employer-sponsored and personal pensions cannot substitute for public pension benefits for all retirees, but the private sector can and does play a complementary role for individuals with higher earnings, particularly those with a long career with one employer. However, if major increases in reliance on occupational schemes were to occur relatively quickly, a problem would emerge for workers during the transition period: they must continue to pay for existing obligations to the current retired generation, while also paying an added amount in support of their own retirement benefits.

The third objective, increasing national savings and economic growth, is a high priority for all countries. (Even modest increases in economic growth would substantially alleviate the problems of financing public provision of retirement income.) The evidence suggests, however, that there is a considerable gap between additions to private pension accumulations and net additions to national savings in the private sector – in part due to portfolio switching, and in part to other offsetting public and private costs. North American experience is that about 40 per cent of additions to pension funds are realised as additions to private sector savings. When the effects of favourable tax treatment of pension fund accumulations is taken into account as a revenue loss in the public sector, the net addition to national savings falls to about 20 per cent. Moreover, countries with high levels of private pension accumulations are not always the ones with high national private sector savings rates. Thus, other factors may be more important in determining savings rates than private pension funds.

The fourth goal, increasing retirement income through the enhancement of private schemes, sometimes includes concerns about public budget constraints. As such, the intent may be to shift at least some responsibility for certain groups from the public to the private domain. Which groups? Voluntary occupational schemes, on average, service higher earnings categories. The practical course is to consider confining the partial shift to private responsibility to those with high earnings, while retaining a dominant public responsibility for the provision of retirement income for the large majority without exceptional earnings or income. The alternative to voluntary private schemes, of interest in some countries, is mandatory coverage of all workers in employer-sponsored plans. In the case of government mandated plans and mandated contributions – with government tax relief, and government regulation – the distinction between private and public pension provisions virtually disappears, except that the costs do not appear on the public ledger. Nevertheless, the government may also find itself responsible for meeting pension expectations.

The foremost public interest in private pensions is in their role as a source of income in retirement, with public objectives centred on the large group who, otherwise, might not have adequate income in retirement. (Those who have resources sufficient to provide adequate income in retirement are rarely the focus of public policy.) Therefore, public goals and a shift from public to greater private responsibility for those who are relatively well off are consistent. This is not intended to suggest that private provisions should be restricted to those who are well paid, but instead, that reductions in public pension benefits that make room for private arrangements should be restricted to this group. But if individuals with greater personal resources were to rely more heavily on private pensions and less heavily on public ones, then a more equitable distribution of subsidies to private pensions across individuals should be sought: higher earnings workers receive greater tax relief in a progressive tax system – paid for across all income categories. Thus, many who subsidise private pensions through the tax system, as well as through cross-subsidies present within most occupational schemes, do not receive corresponding benefits from them.

ENCOURAGING AND FACILITATING THE DEVELOPMENT OF HUMAN POTENTIAL

High priority should be given to active measures which relate to employment, rather than to reliance on income maintenance alone; in general, the emphasis should be on the encouragement of human potential as an end in itself, as well as a contribution to market efficiency. Consistent with this objective, income transfer programmes should be structured to foster self-sufficiency through earnings, without sacrificing the goals of systems of social protection.

Reordering Policy Priorities: Moving Towards Active Measures

The provision of income for the aged over the potentially long period when they no longer can be expected to work is understood and accepted; income maintenance for the non-aged without earnings or without adequate income is provided in the belief that, for most recipients, the situation is temporary. When dependency on public income transfers persists among those who, in principle, are capable of working, then the State (unintentionally) may be facilitating a loss of human potential. (And, in this general context, social policy is often criticised as being in conflict with the objectives of competitive markets.)

The conflict does not arise simply because programme benefits are too generous, although benefit levels that are close to what one might earn if employed may be a disincentive to work. The goal of income maintenance is, however, by definition, to maintain income at some acceptable level. If benefits were reduced below that level, the goal would have been sacrificed. An alternative approach, consistent with both competitive market and social policy objectives, is to reorder policy priorities, from sole reliance on income transfers to greater emphasis on pro-active measure that are likely to move individuals into employment. This approach is also reflected in the communiqué of the Labour Ministers, who met in January 1992. The Ministers endorsed a medium- to long-term strategy for a progressive shift from passive to active labour market measures and related social policies.

The provision of income support without addressing the causes of low earnings capacity may frustrate achievement of longer-run income security through adequate earnings. There may be relatively simple remedies, such as learning job-search techniques, but more intensive (and more expensive) types of assistance may be required for some work-related deficiencies: lack of adequate job skills and work experience, no access to appropriate child-care services, or even no transportation or no affordable housing near job opportunities, are among the problems that may present serious barriers to employment. Limited success may be achieved in the shift of emphasis from passive to pro-active policies, however, if economic growth is weak and unemployment is high.

The shift in social policy priorities consists not only of an emphasis on active as opposed to passive policies for those needing income support. The ultimate guarantee of self-sufficiency through earnings is through preventive measures: educational achievement, recurrent education, training and retraining throughout active life, and the development of a work ethic and skills sufficient to meet competitive requirements in the labour market, to be acquired before difficulties occur. Housing policy and its relationship with income support is critical in facilitating self-sufficiency and labour mobility. Employers also must provide access to training for older workers, instead of pushing them into unemployment or into retirement. A significant component of this orientation is an emphasis on the encouragement of human potential as a legitimate end in itself, as well as a contribution to market efficiency – through prevention, rehabilitation, and treatment. The shift towards prevention and rehabilitation is equally important in the health field if the quality of life is to be enhanced.

Improving Efficiency and Effectiveness in Income Transfer Programmes

It is not realistic to expect everyone to work or to have adequate earnings, even if jobs are available. In addition to the elderly, who present no problem of legitimacy with respect to income support without the expectation or the requirement of job search, there also are groups among the non-aged for whom employment may not be the dominant, nor the immediate objective.

For a lone parent, the hours available for paid work may vary with the number of children, the age of the youngest, and the availability of adequate and affordable child-care services. If a child is very young, full-time employment may not be feasible – and depending on the cultural environment, desirable – even with child-care assistance. Limited hours of paid work produce limited earnings (as may full-time work); for lone mothers, public income support schemes have a role to play in providing adequate income or as an earnings supplement until their circumstances enable them to gain self-sufficiency through the labour market. Income support measures are, of course, more beneficial in this regard if they are co-ordinated with other community support measures, such as adequate child care.

Work limitations may exist for the disabled. The impairment may be sufficiently severe to prohibit any activity, but often some forms of employment are possible if there are adequate rehabilitation services, the hours are limited or the working conditions adapted to the special needs of the individual. Their needs may not be met by the active measures that are generally appropriate for the non-disabled, and the public costs involved may exceed the benefits of potential earnings. Nevertheless, the benefits of investment in the development of human potential cannot always be evaluated in labour market terms and therefore public assistance programmes which offer rehabilitation and training need not and should not always be expected to meet cost-effectiveness criteria related to job search and the eventuality of paid work.

For those who are expected to move from dependency on public income transfers into employment, the structure of income transfer programmes may not always provide appropriate signals. There are penalties embedded in public means-tested schemes which reduce benefits when income from earnings is present. If paid work results in a substantial loss of benefits, particularly if the loss equals or exceeds the value of the money earned, the benefit recipient is encouraged to ignore his or her long-run interest in acquiring work experience and enhanced earnings capacity. Counter-productive signals are not limited to benefit reductions with respect to earnings. For example, justifiable efforts to make non-custodial parents comply with financial responsibilities to children may accomplish little for the poorest families if there is an equivalent reduction in public assistance. Granted, programme expenditures may diminish or may be allocated elsewhere, but with the sacrifice of income maintenance goals – and if the benefit reduction is due to work effort and earnings, with the sacrifice of incentives for economic self-sufficiency.

At the same time, "generosity" as a priority in programme structures may itself conflict with work incentives – and with another goal, minimising public expenditures. These undesirable effects of social assistance schemes can be moderated by disregarding a portion of earnings or other income prior to the calculation of benefits or, more importantly, by orienting policies and programmes towards equipping individuals to earn a wage, such that it will always be substantially more advantageous to work than to be dependent on public support.

Social insurance, that is, social protection schemes which do not consider income and assets as an eligibility criterion (or which use such tests only to exclude high income groups or to limit their benefits), avoids some but not all conflicts. Benefit income and income from other sources may cumulate, but with eligibility extended over a larger group, either programme costs also may be larger, or benefits may be lower than otherwise to fit within a budget constraint. Hence, although social insurance approaches may moderate work-incentive concerns, the conflict between benefit adequacy and programme costs remains.

Despite these conflicts in programme design elements, systems of social protection – particularly income-transfer mechanisms – are an important part of the solution to income inadequacy, but not the whole of it. The causes of economic vulnerability also must be remedied: low earnings capacity; barriers in the labour market which limit job opportunities and the returns to working; elements of taxation systems which affect below-average earners relatively unfavourably; or lack of access to appropriate and affordable child-care services. Even without such barriers, the lack of appropriate jobs with adequate compensation may be the ultimate impediment. The areas of concern clearly go beyond the domain of social policy alone.

ACHIEVING GREATER POLICY COHERENCE

Greater policy coherence should be achieved by a renewed focus on the means by which the strands of policy, from setting goals, formulating policies, implementing them, and, thereafter, administering programmes, may be pulled together across social, labour market, education, economic policies and across levels of government.

The goal of improving societal well-being is common to all public policies. In principle, the effectiveness of public policy in moving towards this goal is the sum of the outcomes of individual policies. But even effective public policy, which does provide results in the desired direction, need not be efficient. If, for example, policies work at cross-purposes, then not only is overall effectiveness reduced, but efficiency is also lost in the sense that, for the resources expended, more might have been achieved. Hence, policy coherence in this first instance concerns the judicious setting of goals, with policies moving in tandem – efficiently and effectively.

These principles have been emphasized with respect to social, labour market and education policies, and the need, across policy domains, consistently to reinforce the opportunities for personal self-sufficiency through earnings, and to encourage an active society in which the development of human potential is stressed. The objectives are not limited to these policy spheres: economic policy must be supportive of social goals, just as social development feeds economic development. But difficulties nevertheless can and do arise when shared policy objectives are not recognised or jurisdictional barriers restrict policy coherence.

Thus, policy coherence requires the appropriate development of economic policies and widely-accepted social, labour market and education objectives – in the short run and for the longer term. In addition, policy formulation and implementation require consideration. Finally, the results of policies should be coherent from the perspective of clients. The new orientations in social policy require an increased emphasis on coherence across government portfolios and across levels of government, and between public and private actors.

Policies in Support of Children

The difficulties that may arise in structuring and implementing coherent policies is illustrated, for example, in the realm of policies towards children. The development of children's potential throughout the stages of life may be at risk under a variety of circumstances: hazardous living conditions which threaten their health and well-being; an emotional setting which leads to neglect or abuse; an inadequate learning environment at home and/or at school; the existence of economic and social deprivation in the family unit; and more generally, a lack of appropriate intervention by parents, communities, or public authorities when problems arise. Public policy, however, will best serve the interests of children and families if appropriate early intervention prevents the emergence of problems which are detrimental to the development of human potential. Clearly, the complete needs of the child as well as those of the whole family must be considered in assessing problems and in formulating solutions.

Although risks to the proper development and well-being of children can occur in many circumstances and across families at all income levels, they are frequently associated with low family income, particularly if economic disadvantage is persistent. Not only may the family be deprived of important material amenities, but the psychological effects of such deprivation may also lead to behaviour which impairs the nurturing environment, impedes the development of children, and limits aspirations below those consistent with a child's capacity. But the provision of income maintenance is not sufficient: the causes of low income must also be considered and remedied.

The majority of families who are economically vulnerable become so because of loss of earnings through unemployment, low earning capacity when at work, and, often, tenuous attachment to the labour force. For some, illness or disability may limit employment and earnings. The majority of such families, however, have a traditional structure with two parents present.

Lone-parent families experience problems which, singly or in combination, also arise for members of the larger community who are economically vulnerable. However, in contrast to other families with children, lone-parent families, predominantly headed by the mother, face difficulties which are compounded by the absence of one parent, that parent's earnings and the loss of shared responsibility in raising children. Moreover, they face a conflict in the use of their time: if, as is frequently the case, the non-custodial parent abrogates responsibility for the children, the custodial parent (typically the mother) faces the dual responsibility of meeting the financial needs of the family and the care of children. When earnings capacity and access to affordable and appropriate child-care services are limited, the paths out of economic disadvantage are also severely limited. The multiple problems of this type of family result in their disproportionate representation among the economically vulnerable.

Thus, the diverse needs of children should be addressed in the context of the family, particularly if the family is economically vulnerable and its members socially or educationally deprived. But the multiple problems cannot be addressed by a single solution such as income support. Children may need educational enrichment at home and at school, adequate nourishment and safe living arrangements, as well as a generally supportive environment; a parent or parents may need assistance in improving their earnings capacity and in finding a good job; and both may benefit from access to adequate health care, housing, and appropriate child-care services.

At the same time, a government cannot replace the natural function of the family. The role of government is to facilitate the well-being of the family and parental choice, and when situations arise in which it is incumbent upon the community and the public authorities to intervene in the interests of the child, to do so. However, there is a delicate balance to be achieved between private and public responsibilities, mindful of the potential for intrusiveness that public action may engender.

In most countries, multiple jurisdictions are called into play: Ministries of Health, Social Welfare, Housing, Education, Employment and Training, and possibly others, including different levels of government. What is meant by "prevention" in the area of family support? What approaches work best in assisting families and children at risk or in crisis? The policy implication is that there is a need for coherent planning and designation of responsibility in a manner that is not hampered by political and bureaucratic boundaries.

CONCLUSIONS

The development and implementation of effective and efficient social policies are essential for the security which facilitates economic growth and enables the whole of society to benefit from that growth. Economic constraints can no longer be seen as a reason to underestimate the importance of, or to disregard, social objectives. Nor can social policies be developed outside the reality of budgetary constraints – social policy, too, has an obligation to ensure that objectives are achieved by the most efficient means possible.

Thus, in the years ahead as populations age, particularly if countries do not attain the high growth levels of the past, improvements in welfare must be achieved by better use of the resources available to society. This entails recognising the interrelationships among policy domains and improving policy coherence; attaining a balance between public and private responsibilities that takes advantage of what each can do best; encouraging and facilitating the development of human potential, individual initiative, and self-sufficiency; improving the efficiency and effectiveness of income maintenance and health systems; and providing equal opportunities to all to enjoy the fruits of affluent societies at all stages of life.

The OECD will continue to promote a process of peer review of developments in social policy. An important facet of this will be the monitoring and evaluation of outcomes arising from different policies and changes to policy. To facilitate cross-country comparisons and mutual learning, the Organisation will develop criteria for the assessment of social policy. Of crucial importance is a strong and consistent statistical base for OECD's future work on social policy.

Chapter 2

HEALTH CARE: BALANCING QUALITY AND COST

HEALTH POLICY: OBJECTIVES AND CONSTRAINTS

The primary goal of health policy is to improve the health status of the population. This goal became part of the agenda of organised societies for ethical and welfare reasons rooted in widely held beliefs which stressed the value of each human life. The agenda has been enhanced with utilitarian objectives arising from a greater appreciation of the wider social and economic benefits to be gained from such investment in human capital.

Health policy has always had to confront and resolve choices related to the limited resources available for the pursuit of agreed objectives. An analysis of the costs and benefits of different approaches to policy implementation can help to resolve some, but not all, of these choices. The outlay of health resources may be subject to a calculation of the relative returns arising from different methods of resource allocation. The ethical questions resulting from the outcome of different approaches to service delivery for individuals must also be addressed. However, since resources are finite, decisions on the allocation of health resources will always be subject to debate about fundamental ethical principles and choice amongst social priorities. The task of the health policy-maker remains that of finding ways to improve the health status of the people while balancing the achievement of an optimal quality of care accessible to all within real expenditure constraints.

During the third quarter of the 20th century, expenditure on health services in the OECD area expanded considerably, fuelled by the availability of improved services and democratic pressures to extend the benefits of access to health care as a right of citizenship. This path was sustained by the fruits of economic growth. In the mid-1970s, disequilibria associated with the energy price upheaval, together with public resistance to further tax increases, led to a growing concern that public finances faced an impending crisis. Most countries came to terms with the need to exercise greater control over all public expenditures, including those on health care. This perspective was reinforced by a growing concern that growth in expenditure on health care did not always result in improvements in health status.

During the 1980s, a range of measures were introduced in an attempt both to contain the growth of health expenditures and to improve the return from those expenditures. These measures included:

- tighter central control of public expenditure on health services and cost-shifting away from central government;
- reforms in health system structures designed to link resources more closely to performance;
- in the face of imperfect markets, supply-side controls, such as the closure of hospital beds and re-negotiation of approaches to physician payment;
- the introduction of a range of micro-efficiency measures, such as contracting, case-mix management, and health technology assessment;
- the development of incentives for the population to adopt life styles and consumption patterns which improve health status and reduce the demand for medical intervention.

With a few exceptions, during a large part of the 1980s OECD countries, on average, managed to limit growth in health care expenditures to levels close to that of the growth of national resources (Table 2 and Chart 2). Within each decade analysed, patterns have evolved differently. Though the economies have become more sluggish in recent years, in most OECD countries, universal entitlement to medical care has been attained and consolidated. While notable problem areas persist, health status, as measured by indicators such as the decline in years of potential life lost and rising life expectancy, and the adoption of healthier lifestyles, has continued to improve (Tables 5a and 5b and Chart 5). The level of avoidable mortality has been halved in the OECD area since 1960, and life expectancy at birth continues to increase by more than one month per year. Available information suggests that, for a given level of resources, health policies have become more effective and efficient through the entire period, including the decade of expenditure restraint policies.

HEALTH POLICY IN THE 1990s

Ongoing debates about how health services should be financed, organised and delivered, and by whom, have assumed renewed urgency. A number of major national experiments are either under way or in preparation as countries embark on a restructuring of their health systems with the twin objectives of improving efficiency and effectiveness in health care provision.

The current reform process is driven by a common group of factors. Pressures from outside the health care systems include:

- *Demographic trends.* The fast growth in the number of elderly people demanding greater and different health care attention is, in part, a consequence of previous successes in reducing mortality at lower age groups. In addition, an increasing participation of women in the workforce is leading both to a substitution of family care of the elderly in the home by new arrangements and to greater demands for services directed specifically at women's needs.
- *Rising public expectations.* Once a new intervention is available, patients expect its availability on the same basis as existing procedures. The appropriate context of provision, whether in the public or private sector, acquires a new meaning in an environment which challenges the appropriateness of the present level of public spending. The balance in the public/private mix continues to be an area of concern for all health systems. At the same time, the rise of consumerism has raised the level of expectation of the quality of service delivery, both in the speed and surroundings of service response.
- *Under the twin pressures of economic globalisation and, within the European Community, deeper economic integration, there are continuing pressures to restrain public expenditures.* The expectation of slow growth in the level of public expenditure levels, together with persistent unemployment, have important implications for future policy decisions.
- *The ability of health systems to expand the range of services and outputs with limited increases in resources.* This raises expectations that additional demands can be financed out of stable resources, perhaps even out of a smaller pool of public funds.
- *Advances of medical science which generate a continuing flow of new health services and interventions.* Technological advances present a continuing challenge to existing patterns of care delivery. For example, because more diagnostic and surgical procedures can be performed on a day basis, it becomes necessary to review the balance of provision between traditional in-patient facilities and possible alternative sites of service delivery. The ethical issues raised by technological advances also generate new and difficult decisions of principle in addition to questions of the cost of extending new techniques.
- *The marginalisation of population groups.* At times, countervailing action is required to prevent inequities in access to care and to low take-up rates which lead to undesirable outcomes in health status.

Although there is still ample scope to increase the efficacy of the health systems and reasons to believe that OECD countries will harness productivity gains in ways other than increasing the scope for medical intervention, the demands placed on the various systems are vast. For the predominantly healthy and long-lived populations in OECD countries as they approach the 21st century, the major tasks on the health agenda appear to be:

- implementing and evaluating reforms in health structures designed to promote greater efficiency and effectiveness;
- targeting services on population groups which may be underserved (including those on low income, expectant mothers from groups at risk, the physically and mentally disabled and substance abusers);
- ongoing evaluation of the facilities and technology committed to the acute care sector, together with regular review of the balance of resources devoted to acute care relative to other health care programmes;
- accommodating an anticipated increase in the demand for chronic care;
- according greater priority in national policies to health promotion initiatives.

IMPLEMENTING STRUCTURAL REFORMS

In response to pressures in health systems, OECD countries have continuously reformed their approaches to delivering and financing health care. During the late 1980s and early 1990s, the initiatives taken and the reforms introduced exhibit a considerable similarity of basic options. A number of general trends can be deduced from this experience which, while not necessarily indicating total convergence in health system structures, can be considered as threads common to the policy environment in most Member countries.

First, at the aggregate level, national policy towards health care expenditure is undergoing a major change of focus. In many countries, concern about health expenditure, and subsequent policy efforts to constrain spending, have until recently been concentrated at the macro level. Many countries had relied primarily on single source financing controls, in conjunction with a variety of global budgeting procedures. Most national health policy-makers now appear to believe that financial gain in the health sector can also be achieved at the micro-service delivery level.

In the last few years, expenditure-related policy has turned towards cost containment at the micro-institutional level, and is now relying more on the application of productivity and efficiency criteria to individual service providers. This shift embodies an attempt to move away from politically-controlled allocation for national and regional expenditure, towards the imposition of output-based funding mechanisms. In traditional command-and-control planning systems, for example across Northern Europe and in New Zealand, this shift in focus is introducing specific financial incentives into what had previously been top-down bureaucracies. These moves are variously termed "internal markets", "planned markets" or "managed competition".

A second observable trend concerns not expenditure restraint as such, but rather cost shifting. Many national governments appear to be attempting to share health costs in two quite different directions. One is that of not only pushing administrative responsibility lower down the public sector onto regional, provincial or local levels, but also increasing the financing authority of those lower levels. This has been accomplished through national mandates of decentralisation without additional funding, or by ratcheting down existing sources of national health-related revenues. The second technique involves asking private insurance employers and patients, or their relatives, to bear a greater share of, in particular, ambulatory care, medicines and certain types of long-term care. This takes a wide variety of forms, from the introduction of cost-sharing mechanisms for individual patients (for example co-payments and deductibles), to dropping particular services or medicines from existing coverage, to encouraging individuals or companies to purchase private health insurance.

These shifts in financial responsibility raise questions for policy-makers. Management theories argue that closer supervision of funds occurs when responsibility for payment is tied to the user or to the local level where the services are delivered. The experience in OECD countries indicates, however, that both a high degree of public control over health care spending and single source financing have been positive factors in the effective control of health costs in the 1980s. If, in the decade ahead, national governments contribute less to the funding of health care services, their financial levers and their political legitimacy may be reduced in the framing of the wider objectives for the health care system. While a degree of separation of policy and executive responsibility is necessary for effective management of service delivery, provision must also be made for overlap in these functions. This is necessary, notably for the policy-makers to be kept informed of the effectiveness of national strategies and for the executive managers to have a systems-wide appreciation for the resource implications of service delivery decisions.

A third trend emerging from the structural reforms, observable in both tax-based and insurance-based health care systems, is the introduction or growing reliance upon contracts as a key mechanism by which to allocate funds among service providers. This is highlighted in the OECD review of health-care reforms in seven European countries (OECD, 1992) and by ongoing monitoring of policy developments in other countries. A central characteristic of contracts is that they place service providers on an objectives-based, temporary, monitorable, and not necessarily renewable form of funding. This is assumed to encourage improved efficiency, particularly in publicly operated delivery systems. By ensuring that purchasers are better informed, contracts also provide a means of redressing the imbalance between purchasers and providers. Contracts have emerged as a central mechanism by which to encourage and inform providers and achieve an increase in their productivity and, depending on the design of the contracting mechanism, increase the responsiveness of providers to the concerns of the purchasing body. Purchaser concerns may include priorities other than financial objectives. These include better quality interaction with patients, improved equity in service distribution and the strengthening of primary care rather than hospital specialties.

A fourth trend concerns the method of paying physicians. In a few countries with formerly salaried employment for general practitioners or hospital specialists, there are moves towards what might be described as a middle status which avoids the twin problems of physician-induced demand and the high costs associated with a fee-for-service approach. Much as in the case of hospitals and other provider institutions, individual physicians are increasingly being reimbursed on some type of performance basis. For general practitioners, there is considerable interest in a mix of part capitation payment with part payment for performing specified services. For hospital specialists, new mechanisms linking the volume, and to some extent the quality, of clinical activity with remuneration are being developed. In this context, some remuneration contracts specifically require the service provider to prepare practice plans and involve designated clinical audit programmes.

A further trend, which reflects the movement towards semi-autonomous provider units and health professionals, is a widespread interest in developing more uniform national information systems. While the content of these accounting and reporting systems may differ, as will the extent to which they are directly linked to financial reimbursement of services, there is an increasingly felt need for more consistent data about service delivery patterns and both clinical and financial outcomes. This is linked to a growing recognition by all parties of the importance to enhance quality of care inside provider institutions, and of the need to monitor, evaluate and publicise outcomes on a service basis.

With regard to quality of care, only a few countries have consistent and finance-related efforts to ensure that service quality is reviewed continuously inside provider institutions. With regard to monitoring and evaluation of service outcomes, the continued deregulation of administrative controls over individual providers has, in many countries, stimulated efforts towards more effective evaluation of both the clinical and financial characteristics of service outcomes. The growing interest in initiatives to improve both quality of care assessment and the evaluation and monitoring of outcomes contrasts with their still limited sophistication and irregular implementation in the OECD area. While these developments are more apparent in the field of acute care, they are no less necessary in the areas of community care and long-term care. With quality of care and outcome measurement moving higher up the national agenda, target setting for services and for health status may be expected to become more widespread. These developments signal the need for a new phase in health system reforms, and point to further developments of the OECD health systems during the 1990s.

Health care systems in the OECD area will face a growing demand for chronic care over the next few decades. While part of the response to this challenge involves a shift of some resources currently devoted to acute and psychiatric care towards the provision of a range of long-term care facilities, long-term care requires the deployment of a wide range of responses outside the medical area – further emphasizing the need for efficient and effective provision of services, accessible to the most fragile segments of the population. Even if the average health status of the elderly were constantly improving, increases in the life expectancy of elderly people imply a rise in the prevalence of disabling conditions. Thus, as the mortality rate from most infectious diseases, heart disease and accidents declines, increases in diabetic and hypertensive diseases, arteriosclerosis, arthritis and other musculo-skeletal disorders are recorded. New morbidity forms emerge and survivors of formerly fatal conditions are more likely to suffer from Alzheimer's disease and other forms of dementia, raising in the medical as well as in the social area the need for continuous adaptation, appropriate R&D funding and greater flexibility in the deployment of facilities and the training of medical care and social assistance personnel.

Societies are not powerless to affect health outcomes. Existing patterns of morbidity and mortality are also the result of human behaviour. A shift of research and development resources into investigating the causes, prevention and treatment of the conditions causing disability and dependence, principally in old age, would be a valuable investment for health systems, both in enabling the saving of scarce resources, and in greatly improving the quality of the extended life years. The scale of the increase to be devoted to chronic and some other types of medical intervention can be determined by greater integration of health and social services, and by a questioning of some of the values on which current delivery patterns rest.

FROM CURING TO PREVENTING

Improvements in the health status of populations – the ultimate measure of the success of health policy – are generated by multiple factors, in which the medical system and related institutions sometimes play a significant but not exclusive role. Much emphasis of the health systems in OECD countries is placed on treating people who are unwell. The mechanisms developed to protect against the financial consequences of needed medical intervention have strengthened that emphasis. The chief determinants of how people become unwell, in what circumstances and with what consequences, have lately received more attention. The role of individual behaviour and life styles has been enhanced by recent policy stances oriented towards improving health status, and part of the "savings" in the care and cure sub-system is being diverted into health promotion and prevention activities. Such policies have contributed to the declining incidence of many fatal diseases. During the past quarter century, the rate of death from coronary heart disease, for instance, has been halved in Australia, Japan and the United States and substantially reduced in the European Member countries. Prenatal care provides an important example of success from such policies. In this area, better services combined with the education of expectant mothers and good nutrition significantly contributes to healthier babies. The participation of patients and informed citizen action groups is considered to favour effectiveness in the attainment of health objectives.

The varying patterns of the causes of morbidity and mortality between OECD countries, and between areas and social groups within countries, also point to the overriding influence of social and environmental factors in determining health status. Japan, for example, exhibits a smaller rate of death from coronary heart disease than that found in Northern Europe and North America. Wide variations are also found in the OECD area in the incidence of certain types of cancers, diseases of the circulatory, respiratory and digestive systems, and in the rate of injury and death from domestic, work and road accidents. Because still too little information is systematised, national strategies to eradicate these diseases and their causes are often piecemeal. The emergence and spread of new diseases, chiefly the human immuno-deficiency virus (HIV) infection, and its consequence, the acquired immune deficiency syndrome (AIDS), have played havoc with societal dreams to push well back the limits of death.

These trends have led health authorities in all OECD countries to recognise the importance of a broader approach to health policy, an approach which emphasizes the promotion of healthy lifestyles and the active consideration of the health consequences of government policies across a range of policy sectors. Within this perspective, the role of the Health Minister is that of advocate and educator as much as allocator of resources and system manager. The range of issues, either in individual

OECD countries or in specific groups within countries, which have a significant impact on health, and in which Health Ministers might legitimately find themselves embroiled, is extensive: the consumption and taxation of alcohol and tobacco, the spread and use of illegal drugs, accidents in the home, workplace and on the roads, atmospheric and water pollution, standards in the food industry, the school curriculum, etc. Active involvement of government health officials in each of these areas is not the most important (or indeed viable) aim. What appears increasingly required is an overall perspective by governments whereby the health/human resource consequences in all areas are taken into consideration alongside the financial and other resource consequences when overall government strategies are shaped.

In the more affluent OECD countries, the level of education has been found to be closely related to health outcomes. Education, income and employment status are correlated. The continuing importance of the socio-economic dimension in health status, health service utilisation and health outcomes has to be explicitly recognised within an all-encompassing strategy to achieve multiple goals of rising health status, equitable access to medical and social services, quality of care and fiscal frugality.

The art of policy-making during the 1990s will be, more than in the past, one of arbitrating between apparently conflicting objectives with the reassurance that maximising the attainment of several goals has, in the 1980s, already met with sizeable achievements. The affordability criterion did not override that of equity of access and the search for greater quality. The challenge of the 1990s is that of threading a delicate balance between greater quality of care and health status for all and limited access to resources.

REFERENCES

OECD (1987), *Health Care Financing and Delivery,* Paris.

OECD (1990), *Health Care Systems in Transition: The Search for Efficiency,* Paris.

OECD (1991), *OECD HEALTH DATA* (5¼ inch high density or 3½ inch double density diskette), Paris.

OECD (1992), *The Reform of Health Care: A Comparative Analysis of Seven OECD Countries,* Paris.

OECD (1993), *OECD Health Systems: Facts and Trends 1960-1991,* Paris.

OECD (forthcoming), *Health: Quality and Choice,* Paris.

Chapter 3

THE TRANSITION FROM WORK TO RETIREMENT

INTRODUCTION

A general tendency for male lifetime working hours to decline has characterised OECD countries throughout this century. The decline has manifested itself in several ways: through delayed entry into the labour force to complete more schooling, through reduced weekly hours of work, through increases in holiday leave, and through earlier withdrawal into retirement. This fall in working hours has been made possible by steady growth in hourly labour productivity. In addition, in recent years the decreasing hours by men have been partially offset by increasing hours by women.

However, the rate of productivity growth has slowed over the last two decades, compared with the rapid rates of the previous three decades. At the same time, the tendency to retire before the "normal" retirement age (which has itself been reduced in several countries) has increased almost everywhere. The decline in labour force participation of older men (aged 55-64) over time (Table 7 and Chart 7) has reflected the falls in their employment rates across Member countries. Their employment per capita has declined in all countries over the last two decades. The long-term trend to early withdrawal from the labour force has been stronger than the cyclical changes. The decline has persisted over times of very different rates of employment growth within countries.

A particular public financing issue has heightened this concern. In many countries, early retirement has been financed either directly through public pension schemes or indirectly through other public mechanisms, such as relaxed eligibility requirements for invalidity pensions, acceptance that older long-term unemployed people need not search for a job intensively in order to qualify for income support in response to high levels of unemployment which have subsequently abated, and tax incentives for private pension provision. The question therefore arises of the extent to which the continual reductions in labour supply may be caused by these policies. If early retirement comes to be seen as an entitlement, and is encouraged by incentives in the form of social security and private transfers, the result will be a general increase in labour costs which will be accentuated when and if other sources of labour supply become

more scarce – which will be the case for young entrants into the labour market in virtually all OECD countries over the next 20 years. This would result in a permanent increase in aggregate labour costs due to a withdrawal of an important part of labour supply.

Some of the government actions were introduced in response to high unemployment. These policies were not primarily aimed at encouraging earlier retirement or otherwise influencing the process of retirement nor in most cases motivated by a concern to increase the well-being, via choice and flexibility, of older workers. They were designed as short-term crisis management. In the 1970s and early 1980s, the loss of labour supply through early retirement was accepted because it was seen as a means of reducing labour supply, at least in the short run, in the face of rising unemployment, a way of inducing a substitution of young unemployed workers for older workers, and of helping the restructuring of older industries. While many of these policy instruments have been scrapped, some still remain.

If these incentives continue into the future, when the ageing of the baby boom generation will increase the proportion of the population eligible for early retirement, and when declining flows into the labour force are projected, an increased cost burden for the working-age population is in prospect – particularly where pensions and other benefits are financed through levies on wages and salaries alone. This will compound the task of maintaining the income support of those who have already reached the normal retirement age.

THE FORCES WHICH INFLUENCE RETIREMENT

Incentives for Early Retirement

In order to understand fully how policies might influence retirement and labour force participation of older workers, it is useful to review the choice which has to be made when an early retirement pension is available on condition that the recipient leaves his or her job or (in the case of a public pension) the labour force. There are two possible alternatives: to continue in employment, receiving regular employment income until the "standard'' age of receipt of a pension, followed by a "normal'' pension, or to cease to work and spend more years not at work with an income determined by pension entitlements.

The pension system itself will provide no incentive to prefer one or the other of these alternatives if the early retirement pension is reduced in an "actuarially neutral'' manner, so that the present value of the income stream is the same, no matter at what age the pension is taken up. For example, if pensions are fully indexed, then if the real interest rate is 3 per cent (leaving aside complications due to mortality factors), the pension entitlements will need to be some 8 per cent less for each year by which retirement is anticipated (and to increase by 8 per cent for each year by which retirement is deferred after normal retirement age). In these circumstances, the "pension wealth'' of the individual is determined by the generosity of the pension benefit system, but not by age of pension receipt. Faced with such a regime, some individuals who value leisure highly will prefer to retire early, and some who greatly enjoy their work will prefer to defer their retirement – although clearly, even for those who value leisure highly, income budget constraints will limit the ability to choose earlier retirement. The burden of financing the pension, including the burden on the public finances if the pension regime is publicly financed, will be no different, whenever the pension is claimed.

However, most schemes which aim to facilitate early retirement are not "neutral'' in this way. Consider, for example, as an extreme, an early retirement which offers the same pension to early as to "normal'' retirees. In this case, any individual who works a year after becoming eligible for early retirement will lose pension wealth equal to one years' pension. His or her net earnings will therefore be earned income less the foregone pension. If the foregone pension is 60 per cent of salary, then net earnings are only 40 per cent of salary. Faced with a wage cut of 60 per cent, many will understandably choose to cease work, or will at least be more amenable to a request or a demand from their employer that they retire.

Collective Pressures to Retire Early

Choices about age of retirement are not necessarily made by individuals. Often they are being made for workers by collectivities, through trade unions or works councils which negotiate on behalf of the workforce as a whole. Even when retirement decisions are not the product of collective negotiations, it is often employers rather than employees who initiate early retirement, and early retirement benefits are often conditional on a finding of disability or a declaration of redundancy by the employer.

Labour market circumstances will be one of the most important determinants of the balance of choices facing employees (or organisations negotiating on their behalf). If employment is insecure and unemployment insurance is limited in duration, then expected income from earnings has to be discounted for the likelihood of unemployment. Thus, those offered "early retirement'' by their firm may accept it, even if the pension on offer is less than the full pension they would expect had they remained in work until "normal'' retirement age.

Income Support which Facilitates Early Retirement

Faced with the requirement to reduce their labour forces in recessions, firms have shown a tendency to target older workers disproportionately, often forcing them to rely on early retirement benefits, invalidity and unemployment benefits. In this way, firms have been able to shift some of the costs of adjusting the size and structure of their workforce to systems of social security and general tax systems.

One particular transfer payment that can finance the early departure from the labour force is invalidity benefit. In earlier decades, at a time when systems of invalidity benefit were not as developed as today, many older disabled workers had little choice except to continue working. For the recipient, invalidity benefit will often be preferred to unemployment compensation, because it can last up to the normal retirement age, while unemployment benefits are typically limited in duration and often decline after a certain period. Moreover, in some instances a recipient of invalidity benefits receives more favourable tax treatment. To some extent, invalidity pensions have been used as a route out of the labour force because firms have been keen to see less productive workers leave, especially at times when they want to cut down on their workforce.

Where there are a number of sources of income support for older workers who leave the labour force (typically lasting up to the age of "normal'' retirement, such as pensions directed at unemployed older workers in some countries), firms and trade unions can agree that the bulk of job losses will be borne by older workers. This way of managing job losses can be seen as the least contentious way of managing redundancies, and as socially acceptable. This is because long-run income support is being assured to older job-losers in a way that would not be available – either in terms of generosity or in terms of the length of time over which benefits can be received – to their younger counterparts.

Employer Policies

In some cases, pronounced incentive to retire early may not occur under public pension incentives, but can be the product of an "implicit contract'' between employee and enterprise, under which long-serving employees are paid above their own productivity later in their career (having been paid a relatively low wage or salary earlier) but with the understanding that this period of high payment will be terminated by retirement. Enterprises may well find it advantageous to offer early retirement to those at the "high earnings" end of such careers, particularly if tax-favoured pension funds can be used to finance the offer.

Occupational pension incentives, under defined-benefit schemes (with benefits being some proportion of final or recent salary), have increasingly given incentives to workers to leave "early". The proportion of covered workers in occupational pension plans that permit "early" retirement on full benefits has gone up over time. In the United Kingdom, there has been an increase in the proportion of schemes which permit early payment when retirement is at the request of the employer. Similarly, in the United States, over time, company pension plans have been reducing or even eliminating the reduction in benefit made for early retirement. In some cases, private benefits are structured so that the annual benefit for early retirees is only a little less or the same as for those who retire at the "standard" age. Where tax-favoured pension funds are available, compensation payments in the form of supplementary pensions will be less costly to the firm than compensation to younger workers. In some countries, firms have offered incentives through proposals which are open for a limited period, and restricted to a portion of the firm's workforce, especially to older workers. The number who actually retire as a result will depend, of course, on the adequacy of the pension, the preferences of the individuals and the availability of continued employment.

As in the case of public schemes, it is possible for workers to face a strong incentive to leave the workforce at a particular point. If the value of private pension wealth declines beyond a particular age, the individual who continues to work in effect suffers a wage cut.

As a result of the forms of early income support available (public and private pensions, invalidity benefits, and unemployment compensation on relaxed conditions), trade unions and employers often agree that older workers should bear most of the job losses, so that jobs can be preserved for younger workers for whom less income support is available. Finally, there is the issue of discrimination by age: some employers perceive older workers as less productive than younger ones, and as less able to adjust flexibly to technological change and innovation. While little evidence is available on the relative productivity of older workers, the relative strengths of accumulated experience and maturity are not always recognised.

In certain European countries, employment protection legislation seems to give older workers a degree of protection at the point where job losses are declared by the firm. However, in effect this protection has often been overruled. This has occurred, for instance, at local level where employers and trade unions agree that "last in, first out" rules are to be changed.

Women

With regard to women, in many countries, the trend has been that successive cohorts have shown higher retirement rates over the years. At the same time, these successive cohorts of women have had higher and higher lifetime participation rates in the labour force. In a number of countries, these two forces have more or less balanced each other out, leading to roughly constant labour force participation rates. In other countries, the impact of lifetime participation trends has been that labour force participation rates of older women have risen over time. Many of the women who leave the labour force have spent part of their working lives out of the labour market. As a result, their contribution records have been broken. Thus, many of them have much lower income from pension transfers than men of the same age.

As more women work and are also covered by pension plans, their retirement decisions are likely to be increasingly shaped by the conditions set out in occupational pension plans; however, this will be a long-term trend. Moreover, a significant number of women are not covered for occupational pension benefits; also, when means-testing occurs at the level of the household, some older women may get little return from market work.

Women in their fifties and sixties often care for elderly relatives. Women who work part-time may be able to combine caring and work roles. This raises issues about how they can be supported in this dual role.

Gradual Retirement

A number of public and private schemes give an incentive to the worker to leave the labour force entirely, in an abrupt manner. Some of the publicly-financed early retirement schemes have stipulated this; earnings tests under public pensions have acted as a disincentive to workers to earn while in receipt of pensions; severance pay and private pensions require that the recipients quit the firm. Hence, the preferences of some workers to disengage gradually from the labour force, in particular from their career employer, are not met.

Those who quit their career employer have the option of remaining in the labour force and seeking work, possibly on a part-time basis. However, except in Japan, such positions are generally difficult to obtain.

The result of these incentives is for retirement to occur at an earlier age than would be chosen if individuals were free to arrange their lifetime earnings-leisure "package" in the way which best suits their tastes and lifestyle, under the influence of a neutral set of incentives offered by public transfer payments and private pension schemes. In addition, there is a tendency for retirement to occur in an abrupt manner with a move from a full work week to zero hours of work. As a result, total labour supply is less than it otherwise would be. There are a number of problems which arise from this. In the short term, while the demand for labour is less than supply, productivity may nonetheless be lowered if highly productive and experienced workers are encouraged to withdraw. Even if they are replaced by new entrants, the overall mix of experience and skills which result may be less productive than would have been the case had the older workers not been encouraged to withdraw.

IMPORTANCE OF POLICY STANCE

Trends over Time

The trends in retirement over time can be explained by a number of underlying elements: public transfer payments, occupational pension incentives and other incentives offered by firms, changes in income and wealth and in attitudes to retirement, changes in demand and the responses of firms. These elements are now taken up in turn.

Public pensions

The value of the public pensions received by the average pensioner has increased over time, as has the spread of eligibility. These developments have meant that the total income of future retirees has increased. Even in the absence of specific provision for early retirement pensions, some people used this increased income to "consume" more leisure by retiring early – sometimes by choice, and sometimes because they have lost their jobs and can see little benefit in searching for another.

In some European countries, the age at which a public pension, without any reduction, can be obtained, has been lowered. In these cases, the present value of future public pension wealth increases and there is an incentive towards early retirement.

Some countries have offered long service pensions or pensions to those in arduous occupations (for instance Belgium, France, Germany). Many of those who have completed long service could be expected to take up these offers, on grounds of achieving their desired spread of work followed by leisure over their lives. In the case of those in arduous occupations, there are two reasons why they could be expected to accept these offers: their life expectancy tends to be lower than average, and they can derive little satisfaction from work.

In a number of European countries, conditional offers have been made – early pensions on conditions that workers leave the labour force (with the intention that young unemployed workers would replace the older workers who leave the labour force), or pensions to older workers who are long-term unemployed.

Over time, the numbers in receipt of early pensions have tended to increase. Related to this, the average age for receipt of a public pension has tended to decline (Chart 7 and Table 7).

Other transfer payments

In some countries, invalidity benefit has been made available on labour market grounds to those who otherwise would have been likely to become unemployed. In other cases, pensions have been awarded to the long-term unemployed. In a number of countries the conditions about active job search for older workers who are long-term unemployed have been relaxed as a short-term response to unemployment. This means that many of them leave the labour force, in effect, even though they are in receipt of unemployment compensation. That is, these other benefits have become extensions of public pensions.

Incentives in occupational pension schemes and severance pay

As outlined above, firms have changed the structure of their pension schemes in a way that encourages early retirement. In doing so, employers have followed a lead given by public schemes of social security. The age at which early benefits have become available has echoed that of public schemes. Supplementary payments made by firms are designed in some instances to top up unemployment compensation until public pensions are received. In some instances, top-up payments have become available under private pension plans that commence at an early retirement age and continue up to the age of full entitlement to public pensions. Thus, the incentives for early retirement have been amplified by the interactions between private and public schemes.

In a number of countries, governments have introduced early retirement schemes for their own employees, usually with the objective of reducing government expenditure.

Severance payments have been also offered by firms in order to encourage older workers to leave. These are additional to those available in many countries under statutory redundancy or severance pay, where in any case payments are highest for those with the longest period of service in the firm.

Increased household income and increased wealth

The choices which face people as they approach the conventional age of retirement have expanded over time. In earlier decades, when systems of social security were less developed and living standards were lower, people had little choice about retirement. In order to ensure sufficient income in the household, people had to continue working even though some would have wished to reduce their work effort. Now, while retirees have foregone work income, they have been supported by increases in other forms of income including the earnings of other members of the household. In recent decades, there has been a growth in multi-earner households and an increase in real income per household.

These increases in income have been amplified by increases in the wealth of households over time. Accumulated savings have yielded an increase in income.

Changes in attitudes to retirement

There are likely to have been changing attitudes to retirement over time, leading people to expect a lowering of the "normal" age of retirement. Attitudes are likely to have been influenced by signals from government about the appropriate age of retirement, leading to acceptance of a lower age from the 1970s. Despite some reversals in government policy since then, the attitudes of individuals appear to have been slower to reverse.

Changes in demand and the responses of firms

Over the past two decades, the response of firms to cyclical declines in demand has changed. Rather than use "last in, first out" rules for job losses, which formerly were a feature of industrial relations, firms have given the biggest incentives to leave the workforce to their older workers.

In some cases, the older workers have been given little choice, being selected for job cuts. Frequently they have been offered packages, either of a lump sum variety or in terms of income support for a number of years, conditional on the workers' quitting the firm. At the same time, the magnitude of future costs falling on older workers, as a result of accepting redundancy terms, may not always be clear to them.

Differences across Countries

The declines in labour force participation rates have occurred across countries which have very different arrangements for social security. In particular, they have been observed in three groups of countries:

a) Those such as Austria, Belgium, Denmark, Finland, France, Germany, Italy and Norway, where elements of social security have encouraged early withdrawal: through pensions for long service, early pensions, invalidity pensions given on labour market grounds, pensions for older workers who are long-term unemployed.

b) Those countries where social security has not contained explicit incentives for withdrawal but where collective bargaining arrangements, at the level of the firm or of the industrial sector, have been tolerated or even encouraged by government. These arrangements have encouraged voluntary withdrawal or else withdrawal by those who suffer job losses or are singled out for redundancy, with payments to the retirees being made by the firms in question or by industry-based funds; in particular, they have been observed in the Netherlands and Sweden.

c) Those countries where early pensions on favourable terms are not available under social security, but where occupational pensions – though covering only some 50 per cent of the workforce – have given incentives for workers to take up their entitlements. Particular cases where these incentives have been important, in the absence of explicit social security incentives, are Canada, the United Kingdom and the United States.

Differences across countries in the levels of labour force participation rates of older workers are in part attributable to the structure of pensions and other benefits. In some countries, such as Canada and Sweden, early pensions are available only on an actuarially neutral basis. In such countries, those who put a high value on leisure and get relatively little satisfaction from work will still choose to leave early. On average, though, in these countries the expectation is that participation rates would be relatively high – and this is observed. In other countries, such as Finland, France and the Netherlands, the high replacement rates (of net income from work) which are available through various transfer payments – including unemployment benefits, invalidity benefits as well as pensions as such – can in part explain the low labour force participation rates.

One influence on the timing and extent of exit from the labour force is the aggregate state of demand for labour. Other things equal, a low unemployment rate gives an incentive both to firms to retain older workers, and to older workers themselves to remain in the labour force. Low levels of unemployment can in part explain the relatively high labour force participation rates of older workers in Japan and in Sweden.

Other elements can partly explain the patterns in Japan. At around the age of 55, many workers are re-employed, or are employed under a changed labour contract, or are transferred to affiliated firms, all at lower earnings. There is an incentive for workers to continue in the labour force beyond the age of 60, arising from the structure of public pensions. It is possible for people to earn wage income and to receive a public pension from age 60. If they defer retirement from age 60 to age 65, they obtain an enhanced pension.

Differences in Opportunities across Individuals

Across OECD countries, it is generally true that higher-skilled and higher-earning workers tend to remain at work until a later age than low-skilled workers. The causes of this are twofold. One is the relative satisfaction obtained from leisure. Although those at the top end of the labour market often have sufficient pensions and other assets to enable them to retire early, they often enjoy their work and can "phase in" their retirement by working fewer hours. By contrast, those experiencing unpleasant working conditions and often poor health generally prefer to leave work early, and will seize the opportunity to do so, if adequate pensions or other forms of income support are available.

However, income support is often not adequate, and, as the high rates of long-term unemployment indicate, many older workers who have lost their job remain in the labour market and seek employment. Nevertheless, some give up the search and withdraw into inactivity even though their income is insufficient for their leisure to be enjoyable.

Partial Withdrawal from the Workforce

While some increase over time has occurred in the incidence of part-time work (part-time employment as a proportion of total employment) among older males, the proportions who work part-time in most countries remain relatively low (Chart 8). Most older employees cannot work part-time in their career job. By contrast, self-employed workers have more discretion over their work patterns, and can phase down from full-time to part-time work as they get older. Some former employees who remain in the labour force on a part-time basis do so by moving into self-employment. For these reasons – and also because the self-employed have reduced access to social security benefits by comparison with employees, giving them an incentive to stay longer at work – a significantly higher proportion of older workers are self-employed than is the case for all workers.

In Japan, there are a number of ways, either through re-employment on different terms, or by workers moving to firms affiliated to the larger firm, by which older workers move down to less demanding roles, often at a lower wage.

WHAT CAN POLICY MEASURES ACHIEVE?

Objectives and Possible Conflicts

One set of policy concerns for governments has centred on the adverse implications of early retirement – both for social security and its financing, and because it means a loss of resources for the labour market and the economy, in particular a loss of accumulated skills and experience. Hence, there follows an outline of policy options that could help to reverse the trend towards early retirement, and at the same time curb the loss of labour resources.

There is a need to put in perspective the losses in labour supply due to workers retiring early. If there were a neutral set of incentives – which there is not – with actuarial adjustment to pension benefits, the loss in output would be at least made up by the increased well-being of those who left the labour force "early". Output and Gross National Product would be lower, but this

would be because the national accounts do not reflect the benefits to individuals of increased leisure.

Thus, conflicts can arise when governments try to achieve all of their objectives:

– widening the degree of choice that people have about the nature of their move to retirement;
– for those who leave the workforce, ensuring at least a minimum acceptable level of income;
– seeking to control the growth of social security transfer payments and limiting the rise in the tax rates needed to fund public pensions.

Depending on the terms on which people leave the labour force early, and on who bears the cost of early exit, greater choice and flexibility to individuals will often imply some increases in government expenditure.

Possible Reversal of Retirement Trends

It is possible that projected changes in the labour market, and in particular the slowing down in labour force growth or declines in the labour force (especially of younger workers), could lead to a reversal in the trend of falling labour force participation among older workers. This could happen through a change in the incentives (e.g. to invest in training) facing firms and employees. For some countries, there is evidence that the trend towards early retirement may have stopped or even reversed in recent years. Moreover, the labour force participation rates of older workers will be higher, the lower the unemployment rate, and hence will depend in part on macro-economic conditions. The degree of reversal will depend on the extent to which younger workers and "prime-age" workers are hired if the labour market improves, in preference to the retention of older workers.

Public Pensions

Three aspects of public pensions affect the timing of their take-up: i) the age of eligibility for benefits; ii) the change in benefits that occurs when take-up is brought forward (if this is allowed) or is postponed; iii) the extent to which benefits are reduced if the recipient earns income in the labour market.

Age of entitlement

Those countries which have established a relatively low pension age have made a commitment that they will only be able to keep at the expense of other more constructive measures, such as education and training, or at the expense of more socially necessary programmes. One option is to increase the age of entitlement to a full public pension. An increase in entitlement age would mean a reduction in pension entitlements at each age lower than the current "standard" age. It would thus induce some people to postpone their voluntary retirement, although some of the impacts could be diluted by the extent to which other routes out of the labour force were available, such as by means of invalidity benefits.

Reduction and appreciation factors

The availability of an early pension only on actuarially neutral terms, combined with an actuarially neutral pension for those who defer their retirement, could help to reduce the incidence of early retirement. Those who deferred would receive a larger pension, reflecting the actuarial factor. An actuarially-neutral incentive would mean that workers' retirement decisions would depend more on a subjective comparison of costs and benefits of an extra year of work. Thus, this could also help to achieve the objective of maximising individual choice.

Earnings test

Under an earnings test, once earnings from the labour market go beyond a certain exempt amount, pension income is reduced. This acts as a restriction on the ability of older workers to phase in their retirement gradually and limits individual choice. This amounts to imposing an implicit marginal tax on work income, for those in receipt of public pensions, which can be as high as 100 per cent. Of course, if an earnings test results in the deferment of retirement and the eventual pension is actuarially adjusted to compensate, the earnings test should not affect participation.

The evidence from country studies is that there would be only a limited impact on labour supply from relaxing earnings and hours of work rules. These limitations can be explained by the following: a) by the time the earnings tests come into operation, a lot of people have left the labour force entirely; b) a relaxation of the earnings test can be expected to have little effect on two groups: those whose hourly earnings are very low, and who therefore can work many hours without reaching the exempt amount, and those whose earnings are relatively high and far beyond the income at which all current pension benefits are forfeited.

For these reasons, several countries have been reluctant to abandon earnings tests on pensions, even though they clearly inhibit some workers from contributing to the labour supply. One compromise which has been instituted in a number of instances is to "taper in" the earnings test, so that the marginal tax on earnings is reduced to 50 or 25 per cent. This ensures that work is rewarded, while still reducing or eliminating the payment of pensions to those with high earned incomes.

Invalidity Benefits

In some countries such as the Netherlands, there has been a particular problem about the relatively easy availability of invalidity benefits. This means there are distortions in the incentives in the labour market; for instance, there is a risk that invalidity benefits will be used as a route out of the labour force. As a consequence, policies of tightening eligibility and lowering rates of benefit can be necessary. However, as a general principle, this should not be overdone. A tightening in policy could mean that some workers who are genuinely disabled and unable to work or to find employment are denied income support. Moreover, these policies do not always address the root of the problem, which could be related to work conditions, or the need for investment in rehabilitation or training.

In many countries, there is little or no integration between disability benefit systems and employment and training programmes. In particular, in most countries, there has been little incentive for those in receipt of disability benefits to participate in labour market programmes. Even in Australia and Sweden, where there has been a commendable emphasis on integrating disabled persons into the workforce, the older workers on invalidity benefit have been on income support up to the public pension age. This suggests a need to shift from passive income support towards more active policies which would emphasize rehabilitation, education and training, together with assessment and counselling.

Occupational Pensions

If the current incentives for early departure are to be tackled, the main options are tax policy and regulation. One option would be to require employers to reimburse public pension funds for the value of the pension paid from the "early" retirement date up to the "normal" age of retirement. This would place the costs of adjustment back on the firm. It would remove much of the current incentive to target older workers for redundancy and would make options such as retraining and reassignment of older workers more attractive.

Training

Firms appear to be unprepared to offer training to older workers, perhaps because of the "typing" of older workers in general as being inflexible, possessing outdated skills, and incapable of adapting to new tasks and to technical change. A further reason for reluctance to invest in this training can be a perception that the time period over which firms would obtain a return on that training is too short.

Given the rate of technical change, it is likely that many workers, of all ages, require retraining if they are to continue to be productive. This implies, across all age groups, that the improvements that occur in worker productivity as a result of additional training will last for only a period. From this point of view, there is less reason to prefer younger to older workers for training or retraining.

Older workers have also tended to be only a small fraction of the participants in public training programmes. In some cases, they are not all eligible for these programmes, for instance because of the operation of age limits (either explicit or implicit). In other cases, the programmes are mainly directed at younger workers and older workers do not seem to be encouraged to enrol.

Even in countries which emphasize an "active" labour market policy, with training and continued contact with the labour market seen as being preferable to giving "passive" income support to unemployed workers, older workers have not been heavily represented in public training programmes.

With the exception of Japan, Member countries have not tended to develop particular training policies addressed specifically to the needs of older workers. There has been too little attempt (even on a limited basis by means such as pilot programmes) to fashion training and other programmes that are geared to older workers. For instance, many mainstream formal training programmes are unlikely to be suitable to older people. They are more likely than younger workers to need programmes which build on their existing skills rather than those which begin anew. Government programmes for their own employees could be used as pilot programmes.

Efforts at training and skill improvement may need to begin earlier in the work career if they are to help older workers. For instance, if people are being dismissed and excluded from the workforce because of technical change and rationalisation in the workplace, it may be necessary to help people in mid-career. Both here and in relation to older workers, there could be more public encouragement and assistance given to firms with training.

Public Employment Services

It is striking that in many countries the unemployment rate for older workers increased relative to other workers in the 1980s, and that the incidence of long-term unemployment increased – since discouragement and early retirement measures resulted in many older job-losers leaving the labour force. Long-term unemployment as a proportion of the labour force is relatively high among older workers in many Member countries (Chart 17 and Table 20). The policy response to rising unemployment in many countries has been to encourage older job-losers to leave the labour force, through social security measures. As a result, pressure has been taken off public employment services to deploy active labour market measures for the older unemployed.

In response to the rise over time in the incidence of long-term unemployment, many countries have instituted "supply side" programmes that emphasize a mixture of interviewing, counselling, support in job finding, and training. However, older workers have been a distinct minority in these programmes.

Older people who lose their jobs can experience particular difficulty in adjusting and finding a job. Coun-

selling services for the older unemployed, which emphasize ways of searching for jobs and the ways in which skills could most appropriately be updated could help here, particularly if all advice were offered under one roof.

Incentives for Employers

Employers may need to be given positive encouragement and some incentives to employ older workers. This could involve encouragement and incentives for flexibility in working conditions such as the length of the working week. As major employers, governments themselves could play a role here.

CONCLUSIONS

The trend towards earlier retirement has reflected a mixture of public and private incentives. The former have become available through adjustments to the standard public pension schemes, as well as through relaxation in other public transfer payments. The latter have taken the form of incentives through occupational pension schemes and through severance pay. There has been an interaction between the public and the private incentives. First, firms have taken a lead from changes in the public schemes. Second, they have structured their schemes to be complementary with the public ones.

At times of cyclical downturns, firms have tended to target older workers for job losses and have used the mixture of public and private incentives in order to achieve their objectives. To a degree, there has been a shift of the costs of adjustment to changes in demand from these firms to the State.

Special early retirement schemes and the other transfer payments have influenced the widely accepted age of withdrawal from the labour force. In some instances, they were introduced as a reaction to a short-term crisis, especially increased unemployment, but under these circumstances it has been difficult to contain the schemes to a once-for-all set of incentives, applicable to one particular cohort of older workers. Expectations about the appropriate age of retirement became influenced by these schemes and early retirement has, to a degree, become institutionalised. In countries where invalidity benefits have been made less attractive by means such as reduced ease of access, it has taken a number of years before the full impacts have been felt – in part, this may be because certification behaviour is slow to change. The extent to which invalidity benefits have become a means of ensuring early retirement for some, and a form of income support for the long-term unemployed, was not widely anticipated.

Some older workers choose to leave the labour market "early" – as long as transfer payments are actuarially adjusted, this need involve no burden on the economy. Problems arise when: *a)* there is no actuarial adjustment to pensions; *b)* older workers are singled out for job losses, given little or no choice about this, and often leave the labour force reluctantly as a result; *c)* those who would wish to phase down their work activity gradually are given no opportunity to do so. In these cases there are losses of output capacity or of well-being.

Actuarially-adjusted pension arrangements involve no changes in total pension wealth, but allow individuals to spend that as they choose – either on more leisure at a lower annual income or on less leisure through deferred retirement at a higher income. However, this choice is a hollow one for those whose pension wealth is too low to permit retirement below the standard age. It is particularly hollow for those who have been forced into early retirement by the loss of their job. For this reason, governments, employers and collective bargaining partners have acted to extend "full" pensions to those who retire early.

As a result, potential pension wealth has been increased – but only for those who retire early, leading to a strong and often overwhelming incentive to accept early retirement. The conditional availability of extra pension wealth then affects the arrangements that individuals and firms make, leading to a spectrum of reasons for early withdrawal. This extends from purely voluntary retirement (perhaps against the wishes of the employer) to forced retirement (where employers, sometimes with the concurrence of the relevant unions, use the pension wealth available to early retirees as a substitute for redundancy payments).

It is therefore impossible to confine a general entitlement to early retirement to those who would have lost their job involuntarily in the absence of such an entitlement. The very feature of pension entitlements that makes them attractive for this purpose – their unconditionality – brings about this result. Yet frequently, it was to ensure income adequacy to this (often initially small) group that such measures were introduced.

People who cannot sustain themselves until the standard retirement age need adequate support. This is a proper function of invalidity and unemployment benefit schemes. Expenditure on these schemes is bound to grow at times of recession when older, less fit, less skilled workers are laid off and cannot compete against younger, fitter and more skilled workers. It is not an effective or efficient policy continually to do so in large numbers. Some workers will always choose to leave the labour force early, but there is no convincing economic or social reason to facilitate this process other than for those with chronic sickness, disability or family caring responsibilities. The efficient option is to boost the level of employment opportunity and the capability of older workers to pursue these opportunities.

It is striking that over time the proportion of the older workers who are long-term unemployed has increased, at a time when, in many countries, the aggregate unemployment rate of older workers has increased more than has the rate for "prime-age" groups. This is despite the fact that the discouragement at job-finding prospects could have been expected to reduce the numbers who search for work, and the fact that older job-losers in many countries have a number of avenues open to them out of the labour force. This suggests that many older workers do seek to remain in employment, and that, therefore, active labour market policy should apply as much to older workers as to those in the prime-age groups.

Other older workers leave the labour market following the loss of a job, in some cases encouraged by public transfer payments. Some do not obtain training or retraining that could improve their chances of remaining in the workforce. Moreover, the prospects of an increasing proportion of the workforce in the older age groups raise a number of questions about whether their skill levels will be adequate to cope with the changing patterns of demand. Thus, the policy issues that arise cannot be addressed in social security terms alone. They raise questions about the operation and efficacy of labour market and employment policies, just as much as about the direction of social security policies.

Many older job-losers are in an ambiguous position, not easily fitted into the conventional labour market categories. Often they are regarded as not unemployed, for instance from the point of view of benefit administration and employment services. Yet they may not regard themselves as being retired. The policy response, observed in many countries, to encourage older job-losers to leave the labour force is under virtually all circumstances at odds with the stance of active labour market policy and would suggest a lack of coherence between social security and employment policies.

Chapter 4

THE CARE OF FRAIL ELDERLY PEOPLE: THE SOCIAL POLICY ISSUES

THE SOCIAL POLICY OBJECTIVE: AGEING IN PLACE

The OECD area has a growing population of elderly people. In particular, most countries have a growing population of the "old-old", many of whom have greater needs for social care and support. The declared intentions of policy-makers towards these frail elderly people are subject to a remarkable degree of consensus within the OECD. It is that elderly people, including those in need of care and support, should, wherever possible, be enabled to continue living in their own homes, and that, where this is not possible, they should be enabled to live in a sheltered and supported environment that is as close to their community as possible, in both the social and geographical senses. This social objective – which has been termed "Ageing in Place" – is largely shared by the relevant authorities in OECD countries, and endorsed by elderly people themselves. This chapter sets out the consequences for public policies of the pursuit of this social objective.

It examines, first, the nature of the policy challenge: the growth in the numbers of frail elderly people, the extent and nature of their need for support, and the adequacy of current care structures. It then outlines and discusses a number of factors which appear to be necessary conditions for a successful policy of Ageing in Place. A co-ordinated policy response to the growing number of frail elderly people must address each of these conditions if the social objective of Ageing in Place is to be pursued.

Finally, it is suggested that these conditions of policy success pose a number of fundamental questions for governments, and two in particular:

- Have sufficient resources been identified and committed to meet this growth in the need for the care of frail elderly people in the community?
- Has the capacity of the community to bear this additional responsibility been addressed and is it, where necessary, being strengthened?

THE NATURE OF THE CHALLENGE: NUMBERS, NEEDS AND CURRENT STRUCTURES

Ageing Populations and the Need for Care

Most OECD countries are experiencing an unprecedented change in their population structure. Between 1950 and 2050 the proportion of the population aged 65 or over will have more than doubled, from an OECD average of less than 10 per cent to an average of more than 20 per cent. The ageing of populations in advanced industrial societies poses a considerable and growing problem to those societies in sustaining the pensions and health programmes which have helped to bring it about.

Within this major shift in population balance, a second demographic change is beginning, one which is likely to have a considerable effect on the nature of the debate about the sustaining of programmes for elderly people. A secondary ageing process, sometimes termed the ageing of the aged, is under way in OECD countries and will lead to a significant increase in the numbers of people aged 80 or over. This increase in numbers ranges from up to 50 per cent in Western and Central European countries, to over 200 per cent in Australia and Canada (OECD, 1988).

The growth in the numbers of the "oldest old" poses a new policy issue in addition to that of maintaining the funding base for pensions and health care. The prevalence of disabling conditions increases sharply after age 75, and the consequent loss of independence in daily activities leads to corresponding increases in the need for care. There is a very lively scientific debate as to whether, as people live longer in old age, very elderly people will experience less illness and disability (this has been termed "the compression of morbidity" thesis), or whether, on the contrary, more elderly years will mean more years living with some dependency. Whatever the outcome of long-term trends in health in old age, however, it is clear that frail elderly people – that is, people aged 65 and over who have a chronic illness or other condition which causes some long-term loss of function – will be one of the fastest growing groups in the population of most OECD countries over the next 30 years.

The majority of frail elderly people live in private households, and in most OECD countries they are increasingly likely to live separately from younger generations. They may, however, need some care in order to be able to maintain their independence and quality of life. The nature of this care can be clarified by defining a set of related needs. The following definition of a hierarchy of needs (adapted from Willmott, 1986) helps to guide the analysis of the provision of care, by indicating the potential range of requirements and by showing where each element of support fits into the package of care. These needs are for:

a) Medical care – surgery, drugs or appliances which are administered under the supervision of a physician or nurse;

b) Other health care – such as dentistry, optical services, chiropody and physiotherapy;

c) Personal care – attending to bodily needs and comforts, including washing, bathing, dressing, feeding and toileting;

d) Domestic care – such as cooking, cleaning and laundering;

e) Domestic maintenance – such as shopping, household repairs and gardening;

f) Social support – including help in dealings with authorities, visiting and companionship;

g) Surveillance – reducing risks by keeping an eye on vulnerable people.

With the exception of the first two categories of care, by far the greatest proportion of the help given towards meeting these essential needs of everyday life comes from informal sources, primarily from the families of elderly people. Much care is given by elderly wives and husbands. A great deal is also provided by their middle-aged daughters and daughters-in-law. However, just as some demographic change is increasing the numbers of very elderly people in need of some care, other demographic and social changes may be reducing the potential of these younger generations to provide care.

The ratio of the working-age population to the over-working-age population has shrunk considerably in recent decades and will continue to do so. At the same time, the proportion of women of working age who are in paid employment has increased, thus reducing the amount of time available for family work. Those women who combine employment with care-giving face a double burden which they may be unable to sustain without help from services. Furthermore, as the contribution of women to the family income increases, the opportunity cost of reducing hours or giving up work to care for elderly relatives is increased.

All of these trends point towards a considerable increase in demand for services to provide support and care for frail elderly people, and in the public cost of such services.

A Complex Structure of Care Services

Most OECD countries have seen a growth, in the last 25 years, in the range of services provided for frail elderly people. This growth in services has, in most cases, followed a pattern of diversity and differentiation. As a consequence, in many countries, services for elderly people have grown into a very complex and overlapping set of structures, with a varied set of aims and objectives, and different sources of funding.

Diversity of services and differentiation of objectives do not of themselves necessarily constitute a problem. In part, this could be a necessary response to diverse needs. However, a number of criticisms of current systems of care have emerged which have common echoes across many OECD countries, and which together suggest that the current service mix is not always the most appropriate to achieve the objective of Ageing in Place. Indeed, for some countries and some services, there is a suggestion that the current structure may be part of the problem rather than part of the solution.

Among the most commonly expressed concerns are that:

a) The provision of long-term care in institutional settings has too often dominated the policy agenda. It would appear that an absence of sufficient and affordable alternatives has made the institutional solution the only one on offer for many families. Further, in some cases the more generous funding available for institutional care appears to have created a "perverse incentive", directing demand towards – rather than away from – hospitals and nursing homes.

b) The policy agenda has been over-medicalised. In the absence of significant medical breakthroughs in treating the main disabling conditions affecting elderly people, it is argued that policy would be best geared towards a "care solution" rather than towards a "cure solution".

c) Health and social services for elderly people have too often been the "Cinderella services" – lacking priority in policy and budgetary decisions, and not highly regarded within the relevant medical and social service professions. This does not reflect the scale of the client population or their growing importance in the social policy arena.

d) The development of professional and administrative norms has sometimes resulted in the provision of a number of standard packages of care. From this perspective, it is too often contingent on the elderly persons seeking care to accommodate themselves to service providers, rather than the reverse.

e) There is a lack of sufficient co-ordination between the different services and the professional groups providing them. This may occur at the delivery level, with a lack of communication between service personnel in contact with the elderly person, at the management level, with different agencies pursuing different efficiency and effectiveness criteria, and at the central government level, with ministries pursuing different policy objectives.

  f) The cost of providing care is growing and is likely to continue to grow. In addition, because of the structural problems outlined above, the available resources are not always related in an efficient and effective way to the most desirable outcomes.

The Framework for More Effective Care

One strong conclusion from national discussions about policies for the care of frail elderly people is that there is a need for an integrated and coherent policy framework within which individual policy issues can be addressed and successfully resolved. There are a number of separate factors which are conditions of policy success in this area, and which each need to be accommodated in this policy framework:

  – a housing environment which can support the needs of frail elderly people, including provision of communal care settings as necessary;
  – the informal care which is provided by families; and
  – an appropriate and adequate mix of home care services.

The social objective of Ageing in Place can only be pursued through a combination of these separate but related contributions to the support of elderly people. There is, in consequence, a need for new structures which are designed to manage and resource such a mixed supply of care. These new structures must both co-ordinate the provision of care in a way that takes a holistic view of the needs of the elderly person, and act as a focus for the financing of care so that the most efficient use is made of the available resources.

This chapter now considers each of these factors in turn, and outlines the main issues that have to be addressed if policy action in each respect is to contribute to the wider social policy objective of Ageing in Place.

THE PROVISION OF CARE

A Supportive Housing Environment

For most of the history of social services, the concept of creating an environment to support the needs of frail elderly people – or, indeed, for younger people with special needs – has been interpreted as involving a living environment which is separate from the community.

Large-scale institutions such as the workhouse, long-stay hospitals and nursing homes were created as separate entities, to be run by paid staff. It is arguable that these institutions were often designed more with regard to the needs of the paid staff – by minimising the work involved in the provision of care – and of other members of society – by relieving them of responsibilities to care – than to meet the needs of inmates. More recently, scientific and professional criticisms of the effects of such institutions, which have been said to result in social exclusion, loss of physical and mental faculties and denial of human rights, have led to a range of policies aimed at maintaining in the community those groups for whom these settings were designed.

Given this background, it is no surprise that in most recent policy discussions concerning the care of frail elderly people, the role of the care institution is presented in primarily negative terms. The objectives of policy are stated as the avoidance of institutionalisation and the transferral of the focus of care to the home. Many countries are introducing stricter limits on the building of such institutions, embarking on a process of reform of those that exist and developing alternative, community-based settings for care. But, at the same time, there has remained a degree of caution about the extent to which it is feasible or desirable to reduce – or perhaps even eliminate – the use of care institutions for very dependent people. What exactly should be the place of the care institution in a policy environment in which there is a strong preference for other options?

Institutional long-term care: here to stay?

In a study of institutional care in Great Britain in the early 1960s, Townsend (1962) suggested that the old-age care homes he studied were meeting three separate functions:

  a) A permanent refuge for those elderly people who cannot care for themselves in their own homes, and who cannot be supported in their homes by any practicable system of home-care services.
  b) A temporary refuge for those elderly people who are recovering from illness, to give families a period of respite or to enable other housing options (such as repairs or re-housing) to be implemented.
  c) A safety net provision for elderly people whose needs cannot be met because the conditions for independent living, for example suitable housing, adequate pensions, or a comprehensive home-care service, are not present.

This is still a useful categorisation when considering more recent policy developments. Most countries have been working to reduce the third category – those who could be sustained at home if the conditions could be met – to a minimum. While there remain a proportion of residents in institutional care who can be regarded as "inappropriately" housed, the increasing age and disability of residents in most countries suggests that this is becoming less likely. Countries are also beginning to look more imaginatively at the second function, namely, the role of institutional care as a short-term option. Short stays are now being more specifically designed as part of a package of measures whose long-term aim is to defer or avoid the need for permanent institutionalisation. Finally, many countries have been finding ways to push back the boundary of the first category, to redefine what is "practicable" as a home-care option, such that the proportion of elderly people falling into the first category is reduced.

The institutionalised care sector is thus in a condition of some change in most countries. It is becoming more specialised and more focused on the needs of the very dependent. It is often becoming less "institutional" and more "home-like", and organised in smaller units, in an attempt to avoid the negative consequences for which it has been criticised. This does not mean that this sector is necessarily shrinking in size. The data suggest that, in most OECD countries, the overall level of institutionalisation has stayed about the same in recent decades. The level of institutional living among elderly people has been estimated at between 4 and 7 per cent in most OECD countries, with some around 2 per cent and one or two around 9 or 10 per cent (Australian DCSH, 1986; Doty, 1988; Brink, 1990; Sinclair and others, 1990). However, this low overall proportion conceals a high turnover and a concentration on very elderly people, and the probability that an elderly person will spend some time in institutional care is considerably higher than this would suggest. Data from Sweden and the United States suggest that around 4 in 10 elderly people may do so (Samuelsson and Sundström, 1988; Kemper and Murtaugh, 1991).

The institutional sector may therefore be both limited in scale and residual in policy terms – for example, because it is regarded as an option to be followed only when others have been tried – but it is far from a residual event for elderly people. This emphasizes the importance of the trends referred to earlier, particularly the increasing differentiation in meeting varied needs. It also underlines the need for a more focused structure for the provision of care services, such that the choice of institutional options, and the necessary moves between care sectors, can be made in a way which maximises the effectiveness of those services in meeting the needs of frail elderly people and in supporting the overall policy goal of Ageing in Place.

Multiplying the alternatives to institutional care

If elderly people are to be enabled to live outside the more formal, institutionalised care settings, the very first issue that has to be addressed is that of the suitability of the settings in which most of them live, and in which all studies show they prefer to continue to live: their homes. It is now widely accepted that the degree to which a person with disabilities is socially handicapped is a func-tion of the interaction between those disabilities and the environment. To what extent are the domestic environments of elderly people suited to their needs? Do these environments support elderly people with disabilities, or do they, by contrast, impose constraints on the elderly person and on those providing care? To the extent that this domestic environment is not supportive of elderly people, so it will be more difficult for elderly people to help themselves – something which they would always prefer – and more difficult for families or services to help them, where this is necessary.

Frail elderly people require a housing environment that is supportive of their needs. There is, however, no single or uniform model for housing for elderly people. Elderly people have varying needs and wishes, and varying resources, both financial and social. Public policy can, however, seek to identify and progressively reduce the sources of disadvantage in the housing of elderly people, with the aim in particular of enhancing the possibilities of self-care and, therefore, limiting the degree of dependence on others. An OECD study on urban policies and ageing (OECD, 1992) suggests a number of policy options that can be considered to overcome these disadvantages:

a) Provision of a reliable advice and information service that can help elderly people and their families to identify proven adaptations and improvements to housing or domestic technology, and put them in touch with appropriate suppliers;

b) Provision of grants or subsidies to cover installation of basic amenities (such as kitchens, bathrooms and heating), to make adaptations and improvements, and to enable necessary repairs to be carried out;

c) An increase in the supply of suitable smaller homes, either by shifting the trend in building or by adapting existing dwellings;

d) Investment in larger-scale improvements to blocks of apartments or groups of dwellings, for example installation of lifts, telephone and alarm systems, security measures and laundry facilities.

This type of investment in the material infrastructure of non-specialised housing will be very necessary if it is to accommodate the needs of a growing elderly population. Some elderly people who have higher levels of disability will, however, need help with housing of a different kind. Many countries have seen the development of a range of forms of specialised housing for elderly people. These include market ventures to build and sell specialised housing to elderly people with existing savings or house values to convert, as well as development of service-supported or sheltered housing by public authorities and the voluntary sector. While these more specialised types of housing are important alternatives to traditional forms of institutional long-term care, studies in a number of countries suggest that, for many frail elderly people, suitably adapted "normal" housing, with some services provided, can be a low cost and effective care setting (Tinker, forthcoming).

If the conditions for Ageing in Place are to be met for a growing number of elderly people, public authorities are likely to have to take a pro-active response to creating a more supportive housing environment in the ways suggested above. In particular, more attention may need to be given to the potential links between the level of public support for the housing needs of elderly people, and the level of public support for long-term care in institutions. A number of countries have been seeking to reduce public outlays on housing provision, while at the same time seeing a rapid increase in expenditures on long-term care. Countries should examine these policies for potential interactions, and seek to develop mechanisms whereby long-term care funding can support community-based housing improvements.

Informal Care

The value of informal care

All but a small minority of elderly people live in private households, as part of a network of relationships with other family members. As elderly people become more frail and in need of care, it is usually the network of family members which responds first, and which is responsible for the greatest proportion of care for elderly people. The policy objective of Ageing in Place does, then, rest very largely upon the ability and willingness of family members to continue in this role. However, at the same time, there are a number of trends which seem to indicate that this capacity to care may be reducing. It is vitally important that policies which rest on an assumed pool of available care – and its continued availability – should be informed by a clear view of how that care is provided, who provides it, at what cost and under what circumstances.

Most care to frail elderly people is provided by members of their families. Attempts to estimate the value of family care, using even modest rates for bought-in care, suggest that it exceeds by a ratio of at least 3 or 4 to 1 the value of formal services, even in countries with highly-developed social services (Bouget and Tartarin, 1992; Sundström, forthcoming). This care burden is carried particularly by older members of the elderly person's family – by elderly wives and husbands, and by their children, particularly by daughters and daughters-in-law. No policy of sustaining elderly people at home could succeed without this substantial input of informal, unpaid care.

All OECD countries are experiencing social and demographic trends which seem likely to affect the potential of families to care for their elderly members. They include the shifting balance between very elderly and middle-aged people, the growing distance (social and geographical) between generations, and the increasing likelihood of women being in paid employment. There are, however, other factors to be considered; the change in potential is not, perhaps, all one way. More elderly people are married than in the past, more have a husband or wife surviving into later years, and an increasing proportion of elderly people have some children (Sundström, forthcoming). These smaller and perhaps more distant families are also on average wealthier, and widespread technology such as the telephone, motor car and washing machine adds to the capacity to keep in touch and to care. While some social and demographic changes seem likely to reduce the caring potential of families, it must be recognised that in all OECD countries the current input of family care remains very high and that not all trends point one way.

Support for informal carers

One of the conditions for a successful policy of Ageing in Place must therefore be to support the informal carers, to enable families to continue giving the care and concern for their elderly members which all current studies show is so prevalent. It is a persistent finding of such studies that, far from taking the first opportunity to place a frail elderly relative in institutional care, many families go to great lengths to avoid or postpone such an eventuality. Families frequently expand the amount of care to compensate for increasing frailty. However, an increase in the extent of some disabling conditions, particularly incontinence or mental confusion, may lead to the exhaustion of family potential – often literally, with the exhaustion of a single main care-giver – and admission to institutional care. There is scope for policy to adapt in ways that will extend supportive services to families. At the moment many services are geared very specifically towards isolated elderly people and thus directed, if unintentionally, away from families. The message to families is that services will only be supplied to the elderly person when they have given up.

The recognition of the important role of the family and the need for some formal service support is growing. A number of countries have now specifically included the needs of the family carers within their policy discussions and plans for the care of frail elderly people (Australian DCSH, 1991; Schopflin, 1991; UK Secretaries of State, 1989). The family care-giver is now more likely to be seen by service providers as a client in her own right. But as yet it does not appear that service planning in this policy area is always informed by this perspective. Although the importance of the family is frequently stated, the adaptation of policies to support family care often lags some way behind. There is also scope for the adaptation of employment and social security policies to help to maintain the careers and social entitlements of family carers.

Home Care Services to Meet Different Needs

The range of services

A wide range of services will be necessary to sustain frail elderly people in their own homes. These services can be defined in relation to their role in meeting each of the hierarchy of needs set out above. They make up a network of services meeting different but overlapping needs, comprising partly "traditional" services and partly innovative services that have been developed to meet newly defined needs.

Access to good quality health care is an absolute condition for sustaining elderly people in the community, and the organisation of those services could usefully be modified to take this objective fully into consideration. Very elderly people are likely to have a higher need for acute health care than any other age group, and it may be that a failure to meet these needs in the community is a significant cause of entry to institutional care. Physicians, nurses and other health practitioners need to be actively in touch with their elderly populations to meet these needs and thereby maintain the good health and self-care potential of elderly people.

A growing number of home-visiting services have been developed in many OECD countries to extend the provisions of care to elderly people in their own homes (Monk and Cox, 1991; Jamieson, 1991). These include:

a) Community nursing services, providing visits by nurses to monitor health status, provide advice to other carers and to administer medication or change dressings; these services may also provide help, often by nurse auxiliaries, with personal care such as feeding, dressing and bathing;

b) "Home-making" services, providing visits by domestic helpers to undertake household tasks such as cleaning, laundry, changing beds, shopping and cooking; specially trained domestic helpers may also provide the personal care elsewhere provided by nurse auxiliaries;

c) Surveillance and visiting services, sometimes carried out by professionals such as social workers or health visitors, and sometimes by volunteers, to check regularly on needs and provide social support.

By contrast with all the above services, services to support family care-givers are at a vestigial stage of development. A review of the field in the United Kingdom has provided a useful typology of such developments (Twigg et al., 1990). It is suggested that these fall into four categories:

i) Services directed at the care-giver in person. These aim to relieve the pressures of care-giving and help the carer to manage more adequately the emotional strains that arise from it. They include counselling and carer support groups, as well as the emotional encouragement and support provided by service professionals with whom the carer is in touch.

ii) Services which assist the carer with practical tasks. This partly overlaps with the work of the home-nursing and home-making services described earlier, part of whose task should be to be responsive to the care-giver's wishes and capabilities, but also includes collective services outside the home such as laundries and meals services.

iii) Services that provide some relief from caring. This can include day care and "granny-sitting" services as well as longer-term respite care, and holiday relief schemes.

iv) Services designed to enable the carer to get more from the care system and their own abilities. This includes advice services and training packages. Joint training programmes with paid care staff could prove valuable in both adding to competencies and increasing mutual understanding.

The level and quality of other services that are provided directly to the dependent elderly person is also an important source of support to the care-giver. High-quality and well-resourced help can raise the well-being and independence of the care-giver and relieve the anxieties of caring. These include, in addition to acute care services, rehabilitation services that add to the capacity of the elderly person.

There are also a growing number of schemes in OECD countries for paying cash benefits to family carers, sometimes with the intention of replacing lost earnings, and sometimes as a compensation for caring which is not pitched at an income replacement level (McLaughlin, 1991; Lingsom, 1992).

To sum up, most OECD countries have seen a growth in recent years in the scope and variety of services for elderly people and their families. There is growing realisation of the need for a closer relationship between these services and other sources of social support. The pattern is increasingly likely to be one of care that is shared between families and formal services. Family carers will remain a vital component in care delivery, but an overall growth in demand for formal care workers is to be expected. Can it be met?

The supply of labour for care services

All caring services depend on a supply of suitably trained and motivated labour. In the mid-1980s, many countries experienced shortages and high turnover in occupational groups such as nurses and social workers. A similar problem may occur with the supply of labour for semi-skilled occupations in the care services, such as nurse assistants and home helps. Employees in such occupations are overwhelmingly female, often with relatively little training or qualifications, often working part-time, and with low career prospects. There may have been an underlying assumption in organising such services that there will always be a pool of available, flexible, semi-skilled female labour. This is likely to change as the growth of the working-age population slows down, and as women benefit from greater economic opportunities. A more sustained commitment to recruitment and retention will be necessary, together with better training to develop and reinforce skills, and to improve the social standing of care workers.

A "care gap" may still exist, however, as other opportunities open up for the women who have traditionally filled these roles. One way in which the resulting "care gap" has already been filled in some countries is through the recruitment of women drawn into OECD countries from lower wage economies. Migrant workers always tend to staff the hard-to-fill jobs, but it would appear to be inequitable that improvements in personal welfare should be over-reliant on low-paid workers who do not fully share in the advantages of the welfare system. To avoid this, policies should attempt to promote the greatest degree of mutual help and social self-sufficiency.

A different way in which policy can support the provision of care is through the active promotion of the voluntary welfare sector. This could be done in a number of ways. One is by helping with the supply of material and other resources, for example by equipping volunteer centres or by organising training courses for volunteers; alternatively, training courses for paid care staff could be opened up to voluntary helpers. The active involvement of the voluntary sector in the supply of care could also be promoted by recruiting volunteers to supportive roles, perhaps involving some payment, and by entering into service contracts with voluntary organisations for some services.

The care services may also need to promote a wider understanding of the potential role of volunteers and voluntary organisations, both among their own staff and more widely in society. In Japan, for example, the growth of volunteer activities is promoted through programmes of community publicity and through the involvement of schools (Japanese MHW, 1992). Many countries may find that the growing "third age" population is itself a particularly rich source of volunteers. A greater involvement of this active older population in voluntary organisations could both help to change social attitudes towards "the elderly", as being solely a burdensome and dependent group, and would utilise a growing source of human potential.

Finally, what should perhaps be considered is to what extent the "care gap" may be filled by a change in the attitudes and behaviour of men. Women readers may already be questioning the unqualified references in this chapter to them as the care-givers, whether as unpaid domestic workers or as paid employees. This reflects the current reality: the bulk of care is provided by women. To what extent are the trends in family structures and labour participation likely to induce a significant shift in the balance of care, and a greater input from men?

Research into the division of child care and other domestic work does not encourage a belief that any significant shift will happen quickly, if at all. But some change in the balance can be predicted. Some recent surveys have indicated that the input from men is higher than previously thought (Parker, 1992). This may be related partly to the falling labour market participation of men aged 45-64, and partly to changing attitudes. Attitudes change very slowly, however, and usually between age cohorts rather than within them, in response to processes of socialisation and life experiences. This suggests it will be a long process for education and family systems to redefine the image of care work, both to help correct the imbalance in family responsibilities, and to help sustain the supply of labour to both paid caring and volunteer activities.

Evaluating the Impact of Care Provision

All statements about the desirability of new policy developments have to be subject to some qualification until their success – or lack of it – has been assessed. The desirability of community care policies has frequently been argued on the grounds not only of the socially desirable outcomes but also of being cheaper to apply. However, experience of such policies suggests that demand for services increases when community options become available – or, in other words, that demand was previously suppressed by the undesirability of what was on offer. In addition, the extent and cost of what is necessary to provide genuinely meaningful support to the most dependent people may have been under-estimated. Certainly there is a need to develop a clearer and more realistic specification of what services are trying to achieve, and better measures of what they are in fact achieving. In particular, there is a need for better measures of outcome in relation to quality of care and quality of life. In addition to their need in policy evaluation, they are essential to monitoring care delivery and managing the suppliers of care. There is also a need to take into account the considerable extent of unpaid care received by elderly people; is family care to be treated simply as a "free good", or is it to be entered into any assessment as both a cost, to the family, and a saving, to public programmes?

One of the difficulties faced when analysing the impact of the new forms of service delivery is the very diversity of pattern at the district level and variation in service mix at the individual level which are their most distinctive feature. The evaluators of traditional institutional care generally faced no such problem: the setting was closed to other influences, the service was completely standardized, and the client population certainly was not going anywhere. By contrast, the more we move away from these features, the more localised, varied, and creative is the service mix, the greater the difficulty in pinning down precisely which mix is most successful in precisely which cases. Nonetheless, there have been a number of attempts to evaluate the contribution of different mixes of community-based services towards the sustaining of elderly people at home. All of these have been linked to particular experimental projects rather than at the level of evaluating a change in system emphasis. While overall conclusions have to be subject to a degree of caution, given the wide range of social circumstances and service packages involved, a number of conclusions seem to be emerging.

At the system level, many countries are finding that the population of elderly people in nursing homes and similar forms of communal care is becoming progressively older and more disabled than in the past (Doty, 1986; Havens, 1990; Sinclair and others, 1990; Australian DCSH, 1991; Bouget and Tartarin, 1992). Two trends may be contributing to this result. On the one hand, more elderly people who might previously have entered these forms of care are doing so later, or not at all. The specific contribution of new service inputs to this development is difficult to disentangle from other potential causes, such as increases in the income of the elderly, gradual improvements in housing and new forms of pre-admission assessment. New community services are, however, one component of the package. On the other hand, reductions in long-stay hospital beds and an early discharge of elderly patients mean that many of those who might previously have been in hospitals are now (more appropriately) cared for in nursing homes.

At the programme level, it has generally been found that greater ''success'' – in the double sense of reduced institutional use and reduced cost – is achieved when the package of care is focused on a smaller number of elderly who are at high risk of entry to institutional care. Programmes such as the South Carolina Community Long Term Care project, which assessed the need for service ''at the nursing home door'' have shown that it is possible to reduce the rate of institutionalisation and reduce overall programme costs. On the other hand, most programmes have set out to supply packages of care to a wider target population of elderly people, those who are at some risk of entry to institutional care. These programmes have generally found that the overall cost of the new community services exceeds that of the pre-existing service pattern. This is because a fairly high proportion of the elderly are at some risk, and can legitimately claim to be in need of services, but only a small minority would in fact have entered institutional care in any particular period. There are also pressures to distribute the available services fairly widely (and, therefore, with budget limitations, at a less intensive level in each case). While the elderly person's quality of life has certainly been improved, the effects on entry to institutional care of this lower level of service provision have been found to be fairly small in the United Kingdom and the United States (Davies and Challis, 1986; Davies, forthcoming; Kemper et al., 1987; Weissert et al., 1988). However, the effects

of programmes in from countries with a higher level of institutional living may well be different.

THE MANAGEMENT AND DELIVERY OF CARE

The Need for New Policy Management Structures

This review of the factors that contribute to the support of frail elderly people has made it evident that adequate support in practice will usually depend on some combination of these factors. There is increasing variability in the circumstances of frail elderly people, their family situation, their housing, health status, and incomes. This is, in turn, reflected in a variable set of needs for support at the individual level. Where should the responsibility lie for mobilising the necessary resources – financial and human – and assembling the package of care in each case?

There is a strong case to be made for some public intervention before elderly people have to apply for entry to some form of institutional care, at high personal and public cost. It is not a rational response to the ageing of our societies simply to build the nursing homes and wait for very dependent elderly people to arrive on the doorstep (with or without an exhausted family care-giver). Most OECD countries have policies for the promotion of home care that accept this view. However, most OECD countries lack the systems of care co-ordination that will enable the most effective use of resources to this purpose. Such systems of co-ordination and care management are in no way incompatible with the wider policy trends of increasing consumer choice and facilitating both private actions and the use of private resources. Indeed, it can be argued that they are necessary to their achievement.

From the viewpoint of the elderly person and of their helpers within the family, they are confronted not so much with a ''system'' (let alone a single point of reference) as a set of providers, some public, some private, offering different services and with different sources and levels of funding available. Paradoxically, the most secure funding may be reserved for the outcome which all parties say they are striving to avoid: namely, the need of a destitute and totally dependent elderly person for long-term care in an institution. An absence of a suitable means of co-ordination of care will then, in some circumstances, mean that services fail to meet the needs of consumers for information and choice, fail to support private actions within families, and direct needs towards the most expensive public provision that could be made available.

Improving the Co-ordination of Care

Those OECD countries which have been first to tackle the problem of improving the co-ordination and management of care have done so through the development of case management. This involves, first, a definition of the separate steps involved in the case management process and, second, devising structures and allocating responsibilities to ensure that they are carried out. Kane (1990) sets out the separate steps:

a) Screening and case finding: the process of defining the population at risk and identifying those who are in need of support.

b) Assessment: the process of assessing the needs and resources of the individual case.

c) Care planning: the process of translating the problems and unmet needs identified in the assessment into a service package that is tailored to the individual case.

d) Implementation: the process of translating the prescribed package into practice.

e) Monitoring and reassessment: this process takes in the monitoring of changes in individual circumstances, monitoring the reliability and adequacy of services, and regular review and reassessment of cases in the programme.

While the various models of case management differ in some respects, there is agreement on the important role of care planning. This is the stage at which overall policy aims in relation to the care of frail elderly people become translated into concrete plans in the individual case. The care planning process has to balance a number of different policy considerations: the preferences of the elderly person, the capacities and needs of members of their family, the availability and cost of different services in the locality, the public and private cost of any particular care package, and the level of public and private resources that are available to meet these costs.

Towards a Coherent Care Policy

The case management process has been developed as the instrument of reform in the provision of care for elderly people. However, for the case management process to be effective in meeting wider policy goals, it is necessary for the policy itself to be well co-ordinated and clearly translated into a set of objectives and constraints within which the case manager can operate in meeting client needs. In the absence of this policy definition, there is a danger that case management might become the means of avoiding reform – a way of trying to live with a lack of coherence in and between the relevant policy areas.

A number of countries have adopted initiatives that seek to clarify the policy aims and responsibilities in this area. There seem to be three areas of policy management that have particularly required attention: a central policy focus for the care of frail elderly people; rationalisation of the levels of delivery; and a more client-centred and flexible mode of funding for care.

A central policy focus

A number of mechanisms have been adopted in an attempt to provide a clearer focus on the policy issues surrounding frail elderly people at the central government level. A particular issue for governments is how to provide appropriate linkages to enable better consideration of the wider effects of policy decisions, and to enable funds to shift when necessary between policy sectors (for example from children's services to those for elderly people), or within policy sectors (for example from acute to chronic health care). Among the more important steps that have been taken to integrate the central policy process more closely are:

a) Bringing together functions previously dealt with in separate ministries; for example, the new Department of Health, Housing and Community Services in Australia.

b) Formulating a comprehensive blueprint for policy that takes in the range of policy areas concerned; for example, the Japanese Ten-Year Strategy to Promote Health Care and Welfare Services for the Elderly (Gold Plan), the UK White Paper *Caring for People,* and the Australian Aged Care Reform Strategy. This may be preceded by a wide-ranging discussion of the options, as with, for example, the French Presidential Commission chaired by M. Schopflin.

c) Appointment of an central policy adviser on issues concerning elderly people, as in Denmark, Canada and Australia.

Rationalising the responsibility of levels of government

A further obstacle to the pursuit of coherent objectives has been identified in the attribution of accountability to different levels of government. While one task of a case-managed service is to act as a broker between different agencies, the task of the case manager can be greatly facilitated by adjustments in these responsibilities.

Many governments are, as part of this process, pursuing the decentralisation of responsibility for care to the most local level. Rationalisation of responsibility for delivery at local level seems to be considerably more feasible in those countries with decentralised governmental systems, where locally-elected authorities already have the capacity to administer a wide range of local services. Where central government agencies exist uneasily alongside sub-national elected authorities, the problems are undoubtedly greater. In many countries, the low level of confidence of central government departments in the competence of local authorities to deliver is clearly a major constraint.

The direction of funding

The third aspect of policy management that is being modified by governments in search of greater coherence is that of the source and direction of the public funding of care. Many of the departments, agencies and programmes whose policies impact on elderly people have in the past had separate budgets, separate procedures for application, and separate criteria for eligibility. There is considerable evidence that, in these circumstances, the separate agencies seek to protect their own budgets by transferring costly long-term care responsibilities to other agencies where possible. "Open-ended" programmes based on individual entitlement, whether social security schemes or health insurance schemes, then take the full impact of the growth in demand. It is the growth in expenditures on these programmes in a number of countries that has triggered the debate about the "explosion" of long-term care costs.

There are moves under way in a number of countries to modify the source and direction of funds, with a view to reinforcing the policy. These include:

a) Altering the conditions for eligibility to bring them more into line with policy objectives. For example, the introduction of pre-admission assessment for nursing home entry in Australia was an essential step in identifying people who could benefit from other uses of the funds.

b) Introducing greater flexibility in the use of funds previously earmarked for one purpose only. For example, in the United States, a large number of states are making use of legislation to permit Medicaid funding, previously largely confined to nursing homes, to be used to fund home care services.

c) Transferring funds previously administered separately to one authority with overall responsibility for care. This is being done from 1993 in the United Kingdom, when social security funds for nursing home costs will be transferred to local government authorities.

Meeting the Cost of Care

While a concern for greater coherence in the direction of funding is common to OECD countries, there remains a considerable debate about the appropriate level of public funding for care, and about how its provision should be related to the availability of private sources of funds. To what extent do private sources of funds offer a significant alternative to public responsibility for care costs? The two groups of people whose income and assets might be thought accessible for this purpose are frail elderly people themselves, and their families.

Private capacity

The growth of care services has taken place in a context, over the last 20 to 30 years, of a steady increase in the economic and social independence of elderly people. Both the real standard of living and the relative economic position of elderly people have improved considerably since the 1960s, and there are, for example, far fewer elderly people in need of public care for economic reasons alone. More elderly people also have assets, such as house values, or other savings to supplement their pension incomes. This has had a significant and welcome effect on the quality of their daily lives.

The increase in the economic position of elderly people, particularly in relation to the costs of personal care, should not, however, be overestimated. These costs may be incurred over a long period of time, and can, even in the relatively short term, be extremely high in relation to the capacity to pay of even relatively affluent elderly people (Rowland, 1989; Rivlin and Wiener, 1988; Gibbs, 1991). Pension schemes and other forms of saving for retirement have simply not been designed to cope with this level of cost of living. This is doubly the case when these care costs are incurred, not by the newly-retired "third age" who have benefited most from these changes, but very largely by the most elderly women.

A proportion of very elderly people may, through increasing home ownership, find themselves "asset rich, income poor". Should these assets be liquidated to pay for care? As a first call on these assets, they might more appropriately be turned, through housing equity schemes, into more suitable housing and adaptations to provide a more supportive home environment. This could itself be a public saving. All but the highest housing values would be consumed fairly rapidly by long-term constant care costs. If it were felt that some proportion of these assets should be recovered by public authorities as a contribution to care costs, this could be achieved through an eventual call on the estate rather than by requiring the liquidation of assets during lifetime. However, it must probably be concluded that, for the foreseeable future, only a minority of elderly people will be able to make a significant contribution to their own care costs without incurring a substantial diminution in the economic and social independence so recently gained.

The families of elderly people have similarly benefited from growth in real incomes over the last 20 to 30 years. Many families make a direct financial contribution to the cost of care for their elderly members, although only a few OECD countries impose a binding legal obligation on younger generations to support their elderly relatives in this way. In addition, families already provide a very significant share of the care of frail elderly people, at a considerable saving to potential public costs. Those families who have contributed the greatest amount of care will be likely to have borne the greatest economic sacrifice already. There is a more effective and equitable way for the families of elderly people to meet the costs of care, and that is indirectly, through the system of taxes and contributions.

The real debate about the funding of care is not, therefore, about whether the burden of care costs should be shared by other members of society, but about how and to what extent. The search is for a system of public funding which can balance the meeting of needs for care and support with an equitable distribution of costs between the current elderly and the working population, who are the children and grandchildren of the current elderly and, in their turn, the future elderly.

Public systems

The main sources of public funding for care can be grouped under three categories: block grants from central government, public health insurance (either alone or as a complement to private insurance) and social assistance-type benefits. These are frequently found operating in combination within national systems. Each of these methods of funding seeks to arrive at a balance between public underpinning of the costs of care and requiring some individual contribution. Each has some advantages and disadvantages for the provision of cost-effective care which will meet the overall criterion of sustaining Ageing in Place.

Block grants from central government can be directed to those authorities given the responsibility for care management, and there can be considerable scope for flexibility in how the grant is spent, within broad criteria. There is also an inherent incentive for the managing authorities to maximise the return on a cash-limited grant. On the other hand, there may be a lack of clear conditions for eligibility that can be readily understood by elderly people, and a tendency for control and use of funds to be overly influenced by particular professional groups in the relevant service. If the conditions of eligibility are vague, there may be a tendency for managing authorities to respond to demand by spreading the care thinly across a large population of elderly people.

Health insurance can provide a secure and effective source of funding for the individual elderly person, particularly if the terms include coverage of home nursing and other home health care. However, it directs demand towards medical facilities, which are both expensive and not necessarily the most appropriate in social care terms. Without extensive monitoring of care costs, and regulation of the amounts covered by insurance, there may be difficulties in controlling overall costs.

Social assistance provides a safety-net provision of care costs for elderly people with low incomes, while limiting the overall programme cost. Nationally-regulated schemes, such as Medicaid in the United States and Income Support in the United Kingdom, provide clear conditions for entitlement and can be directed to home care as well as institutional care. However, the rules limiting repayment to those below a certain income can be extremely unpopular, because of the necessity for the substantial proportion of elderly people on incomes just above the minimum to run down their lifetime assets before being entitled to help. As with health insurance, extensive monitoring of care costs is required to fix payment levels. More local social assistance schemes are usually of limited cover, highly discretionary and frequently avoided by elderly people as being stigmatising.

New options

Several countries are considering new options for the funding of long-term care in an attempt to distribute the risks of high costs more widely than now. Two new options in particular are being considered.

The first seeks to add to the private resources available for care costs by encouragement of private long-term care insurance. People could be encouraged, via tax concessions, or perhaps even obliged, to take out private insurance to cover the costs of care. It is argued that as people become more affluent, the boundaries of public provision should not be extended to meet new needs. Instead, people should be required to make private provisions that will enable them to make more use of their lifetime income and assets to exercise choice in the provision of care. On the other hand, it seems questionable whether the insurance industry can treat long-term care as an insurable risk at affordable terms (Rivlin and Wiener, 1988; Wittenberg, 1989). The existing coverage of private long-term care insurance is very limited – for example, in the United States, approximately 3 per cent of elderly people have a policy covering care – and for the foreseeable future it would appear that this form of insurance will remain a very expensive option for the majority of elderly people (Wiener, forthcoming).

It has also been proposed that long-term care costs should constitute a new social insurance risk. It is argued that the need for care should be considered as social risk in the same way as unemployment or disability. Within a social insurance framework, the costs could be shared among the working population and those retired people with adequate incomes, and the benefit used to meet long-term care needs, especially those of very elderly people, who have a relatively high risk of needing care (Oldiges, 1992; Evers and Olk, 1992). It has to be accepted that this represents a new call on the incomes of the working-age population, who will already have to meet the higher costs of pensions and health care which will be incurred by an ageing population. However, it can be argued that to the extent that elderly people do not have the resources to meet care costs, these costs will fall on the general population anyway, for example through the cost of means-tested public assistance, and that a social insurance model remains the most equitable and economical of the available options for sharing the risk.

The funding of care: six principles

The existing systems of health, social security and social service funding are extremely diverse, and call upon different sources of finance. These systems will continue to be governed by wider political choices, social values and economic constraints as much as by specific policy objectives. Nonetheless, it is possible to elaborate a set of principles that are applicable to all systems of funding, and which should indicate whether that system is working with the grain of the overall social objective of Ageing in Place. These can be used to evaluate the extent to which existing systems are moving in the right direction, or to evaluate new proposals. These principles are:

a) The provision of funding should be related to an assessment which takes a holistic view of the needs of the elderly person, rather than of need for a single service.

b) The funding that is provided should be accessible for expenditure on a range of care services, broadly defined, which will sustain a good quality of life in old age.

c) There should be a built-in bias towards home care solutions, while retaining a capacity for constant care in sheltered settings.

d) Notwithstanding this previous principle, access to these constant care settings should be decided on the basis of need and should not be impeded by inability to pay.

e) The conditions governing the receipt of public funding should enhance rather than reduce the degree of choice which the elderly persons have over their conditions of life.

f) Private provision of care should be encouraged and supported, but elderly people should not feel obliged – or be required – to run down their assets in the purchase of care to such an extent that their quality of life or their independence is impaired.

CONCLUSIONS

There are a number of conditions which need to be met if stated policy objectives are to be pursued with some hope of success. It is evident that the provision of care for elderly people in the community is not an easy option that will painlessly save costs as well as meet the preferences of elderly people. The breadth of the provisions that are necessary must raise the question whether governments are willing the means as well as willing the end. There are two over-riding issues for governments:

a) Have sufficient resources been identified and committed to meet the growth in the need for the care of frail elderly people in the community?

b) Has the capacity of the community to bear this additional responsibility been addressed and, where necessary, is it being strengthened?

These questions in their turn raise a number of more detailed issues to be addressed by governments. Among those raised in this chapter are:

i) Have governments given sufficient attention to redefining the role and purpose of care institutions in the new policy environment, in particular to improving the quality of care? Have sufficiently challenging standards of outcome been applied in order to bring this about?

ii) Have governments begun to tackle the improvements in housing that will be necessary if an increasing number of very elderly people are to live outside these care institutions, in domestic environments? Are the links in place that allow these housing provisions to be considered as an element in long-term care planning?

iii) Is the provision of suitable home care services lagging behind the growth in needs for such services? What forms of service mix have been found to be most cost-effective in sustaining quality of life and independence? Can benchmarks be established to guide the level and type of service provision?

iv) Are the available services reinforcing the capacity of families for mutual support? Or do services only pick up the care responsibility when family care is absent or has been exhausted?

v) Is recruitment of care workers adequate to deal with the likely increase in demand? Is there adequate and effective training for both formal and informal care workers? Is there sufficient encouragement for the voluntary care sector and a means of relating it effectively to formal services?

vi) Do countries have an appropriate means of co-ordinating the response of the mixed economy of care to individual needs? Have countries identified and addressed problems of overlapping (or absent) responsibilities at each level of government?

vii) Have suitable sources of finance for care been identified and do these flow towards the most desirable outcomes? And do care funding mechanisms accord with the six principles suggested here?

REFERENCES

AUSTRALIAN DEPARTMENT OF COMMUNITY SER-
VICES AND HEALTH (1986), *Nursing Homes and Hos-
tels Review,* Australian Government Publishing Service,
Canberra.

AUSTRALIAN DEPARTMENT OF COMMUNITY SER-
VICES AND HEALTH (1991), *The Balance of Care: A
Framework for Planning* (Mid-Term Review of Aged
Care Reform Strategy 1990/91. Discussion paper No. 7),
DCSH, Canberra.

BOUGET, D. and TARTARIN, R. (1992), *Aide informelle aux
personnes âgées dépendantes en France* (Report for
OECD), CEBS, Université de Nantes.

BRINK, S. (1990), "Living arrangements for the elderly: an
international institutional comparison", in J. Pacolet and
C. Wilderom (editors), *The Economics of Care of the
Elderly,* Avebury Publishing, Aldershot, United Kingdom.

DAVIES, B. (forthcoming), "Improving the case management
process", in *Caring for Frail Elderly People,* OECD,
Paris.

DAVIES, B. and CHALLIS, D. (1986), *Matching Resources to
Needs in Community Care,* Gower, Aldershot, United
Kingdom.

DOTY, P. (1986), "Family care of the elderly: the role of
public policy", in *The Milbank Quarterly,* Vol. 64, No. 1,
Cambridge University Press, New York.

DOTY, P. (1988), "Long-term care in international perspective", in *Health Care Financing Review,* Annual Supplement, HCFA, Baltimore.

EVERS, A. and OLK, T. (1992), "The mix of care provisions
for the frail elderly in the Federal Republic of Germany",
in A. Evers and I. Svetlik (editors), *New Welfare Mixes for
the Elderly: Vol. 3,* European Centre for Social Welfare
Policy and Research, Vienna.

GIBBS, I. (1991), "Income, capital and the cost of care in old
age", in *Ageing and Society,* Vol. 11, No. 4, Cambridge
University Press.

HAVENS, B. (1990), "Home care and day care for the elderly", in R.L. Kane, J.G. Evans and D. Macfadyen (editors), *Improving the Health of Older People: a World
View,* World Health Organisation/Oxford University Press.

JAMIESON, A. (editor)(1991), *Home Care for Older People in
Europe,* Oxford University Press.

JAPANESE MINISTRY OF HEALTH AND WELFARE
(1992), *Annual Report on Health and Welfare, 1990/91,*
Ministry of Health and Welfare, Tokyo.

KANE, R.A. (1990), "Case management and assessment of the
elderly", in R.L. Kane, J. Grimley Evans and D.
MacFadyen (editors), *Improving the Health of Older People: A World View,* Oxford University Press/World Health
Organisation.

KEMPER, P. and MURTAUGH, C.M. (1991), "Lifetime use
of nursing home care", in *The New England Journal of
Medicine,* Vol. 324, No. 9, United States.

KEMPER, P., APPLEBAUM, R. and HARRIGAN, M. (1987),
"Community care demonstrations: what have we learned?,
in *Health Care Financing Review,* Summer 1987, Vol. 8,
No. 4, HCFA, Baltimore, Maryland.

LINGSOM, S. (1992), "Paying informal caregivers", in
J. Twigg (editor), *Informal Care in Europe,* Social Policy
Research Unit, York, United Kingdom.

McLAUGHLIN, E. (1991), *Social Security and Community
Care: The case of the Invalid Care Allowance,* HMSO,
London.

MONK, A. and COX, C. (1991), *Home Care for the Elderly:
An International Perspective,* Auburn House, New York.

OECD (1988), *Ageing Populations: The Social Policy Implications,* OECD, Paris.

OECD (1992), *Urban Policies for Ageing Populations,* OECD,
Paris.

OLDIGES, F. (1992), "Need for constant nursing care: protection by the statutory social insurance or private insurance
in Germany", in *Home Care for the Elderly* (Social Security Documentation: European Series No. 18), International
Social Security Association, Geneva.

PARKER, G. (1992), "The myth of the male carer?", in *Cash
and Care,* No. 11, summer 1992, Social Policy Research
Unit, York, United Kingdom.

RIVLIN, M.A. and WIENER, J.M. (1988), *Caring for the Disabled Elderly: Who Will Pay?,* The Brookings Institution,
Washington D.C.

ROWLAND, D. (1989), *Help at Home: Long-Term Care Assistance for Impaired Elderly People,* Commonwealth Fund,
Baltimore, Md.

SAMUELSSON, G. and SUNDSTRÖM, G. (1988), "Ending
one's life in a nursing home: a note on Swedish findings",
in *International Journal of Aging and Human Development,* Vol. 27, No. 2, Baywood Publishing, United States.

SCHOPFLIN, P. (1991), *Dépendance et solidarités: mieux
aider les personnes âgées: Rapport de la Commission
présidée par M. Pierre Schopflin,* Documentation Française, Paris.

SINCLAIR, I., PARKER, R., LEAT, D. and WILLIAMS, J.
(1990), *The Kaleidoscope of Care: A Review of Research
on Welfare Provision for Elderly People,* HMSO, London.

SUNDSTRÖM, G. (forthcoming), "Care by families: an overview of trends", in *Caring for Frail Elderly People*, OECD, Paris.

TINKER, A. (forthcoming), "The role of housing policies in the care of elderly people", in *Caring for Frail Elderly People*, OECD, Paris.

TOWNSEND, P. (1962), *The Last Refuge: A Survey of Residential Institutions and Homes for the Aged in England and Wales*, Routledge and Kegan Paul, London.

TWIGG, J., ATKIN, K. and PERRING, C. (1990), *Carers and Services: A Review of Research*, HMSO, London.

UK SECRETARIES OF STATE FOR HEALTH, SOCIAL SECURITY, WALES AND SCOTLAND (1989), *Caring for People: Community Care in the Next Decade and Beyond*, HMSO, London.

WEISSERT, W.G., CREADY, C.M. and PAWELAK J.E. (1988), "The past and future of home- and community-based long-term care", in *The Milbank Quarterly*, Vol. 66, No. 2, Cambridge University Press, New York.

WIENER, J. (forthcoming), "Private sector initiatives in financing long-term care", in *Caring for Frail Elderly People*, OECD, Paris.

WILLMOTT, P. (1986), *Social Networks, Informal Care and Public Policy*, Policy Studies Institute, London.

WITTENBERG, R. (1989), *Prototype Insurance Policy for Long-Term Care*, Department of Health, London.

Chapter 5

NEW ORIENTATIONS FOR SOCIAL POLICY

THE MINISTERS' COMMUNIQUÉ

The OECD Employment, Labour and Social Affairs Committee met at Ministerial level in Paris on 8th and 9th December 1992. The meeting was chaired by Mr. Luis Martinez Noval, Minister of Labour and Social Security, Spain. The Vice-Presidents were the Honourable Neal Blewett MP, Minister for Social Security, Australia and Mr. Bengt Westerberg, Minister for Social Affairs, Sweden.

The meeting was preceded by consultations with the Business and Industry Advisory Committee and the Trade Union Advisory Committee to the OECD. Both agreed that improvements in social benefits should be sought through greater efficiency and effectiveness in programme design and execution, and not through increases in taxes and charges. The two Committees also urged that more be done to expand employment opportunities for older workers and to discourage compulsory early retirement.

Representatives from the Czech and Slovak Federal Republic, Hungary and Poland (the three OECD Partners in Transition) and from Mexico attended the meeting as observers.

THE CONTEXT

Public policy must respond to a setting that differs substantially from the initial post-war era of high growth and high expectations. The current context of slow growth, seemingly intractable labour market problems, economic insecurity and tight budgets for social programmes, has led to a search for policies and approaches that can be both more effective and more efficient in addressing economic disadvantage. In the medium term, OECD countries must also adjust the focus of social policies to take account of the process of population ageing. The central thrust of social policies will come to be more on the older age groups than is now the case. Moreover, caring for children, youth, the handicapped and the aged calls for new solutions as family structures continue to change, and as more women work in paid employment.

When they last met at the OECD in 1988, Ministers for Social Policy agreed that an active society in which all members have a constructive role was a primary goal for social policy. Since then, other concerns have extended the social policy agenda. The persistence of unemployment and the related growth in poverty have made the relief of distress a greater task, while the budgetary resources available to achieve this are themselves constrained. Young families – which are often over-represented among those with low incomes – are finding it difficult to fulfil all their aspirations for their children. In some countries, hostility to migrants and minorities is also threatening social cohesion.

After increasing markedly during the 1960s and 1970s, aggregate expenditure on social protection stabilized as a proportion of GDP in most OECD countries from the early 1980s. For a few countries, such as Italy and Greece, expenditure on old-age pensions increased markedly. Expenditure on health care, both public and private, also stabilized as a proportion of GDP during the decade in most countries other than the United States. However, the current slowing of economic growth in many economies has made it difficult to maintain this situation, and an increase in health and other social expenditures, as a proportion of GDP, may well be now under way in many OECD countries.

Unemployment in the OECD area fell from its peak of 8.6 per cent of the labour force in 1983 to 6.2 per cent in mid-1990. However, it is now increasing again, and is estimated to have reached 8 per cent in the second half of 1992. The latest OECD projections are that it could peak at around $8^1/_4$ per cent during 1993; it may only begin to fall slowly in 1994. Long-term unemployment is increasing in almost all countries. The majority of countries have experienced this general deterioration in the labour market situation, though there are exceptions, notably Japan. Expenditure on income support for the unemployed can be expected to weigh heavily on aggregate expenditure on social security in most countries for the foreseeable future.

ORIENTATIONS FOR SOCIAL POLICY

The role of social policy – encompassing as it does health, income security and service provision – is to provide a framework which enables the fullest participation possible in all aspects of society for its citizens – supporting them in their efforts to balance work, learning, care for dependants, and leisure throughout the stages of the life cycle: childhood, youth, working age, and later years of life.

To achieve this goal, social expenditures should be recognised as underpinning the quality of life of all citizens, including the enhancement of equality of opportunity. This requires partnerships between the public sector, collective actors and individuals that clarify respective roles and establish systems of mutual obligations to obtain a satisfactory balance between social and economic security, and scope for individual initiative. Furthermore, social policy cannot operate effectively in isolation: the responsibility of facilitating the full participation of citizens is shared by economic, education, training and labour market as well as social policies.

Systems of social protection must remain adequate, particularly for those who cannot achieve self-sufficiency through paid work and for whom public sources of support are, and will continue to be, dominant. In reconciling social policy objectives with budget limitations, it should be a priority to ensure that the most vulnerable members of society are properly protected.

There is a clear public role in the provision of income in retirement, both through direct provision of social insurance benefits or other public pension assistance, and through the support and regulation of employer-sponsored and personal arrangements. In public systems, financed on a pay-as-you-go basis, larger transfers will be required from the relatively fewer individuals of working age to an increasingly numerous retired generation, if current retirement ages and levels of earnings replacement are maintained. To accommodate these pressures, policies need to be put in place now to meet the needs of the growing numbers of the aged in subsequent decades. This process should give due consideration to improving the effectiveness of public schemes, including consideration of the appropriate pensionable age, in combination with an efficient and equitable mix of public and private pensions.

The integration of policies to provide a coherent framework remains a significant challenge. Many policy areas have implications for social policy, and social policy can and does affect employment, education, and other policy domains. Determined efforts are necessary to achieve a coherent approach to national policy-making, embracing a wide range of public responsibilities.

Ministers emphasize that a fundamental goal of social policy is to enable and empower people to exert greater control over the circumstances of their own lives. Policy and programme approaches should seek to avoid long-term dependency, and instead, maximise human potential, increase personal dignity and choice, thereby helping individuals to succeed in the labour market and in all aspects of life. Policies for people with disabilities can and should exemplify these goals. Ministers propose that social policy should be guided by orientations which:

a) Recognise that many types of social expenditure are an investment in society which enhance its growth potential by providing services which help underpin the efficient operation of the market economy;

b) Achieve policy coherence by a renewed focus on the means by which the strands of policy – from setting goals, to formulating policies, implementing them, and, thereafter, administering programmes – can be pulled together across social, labour market, education and training, and economic policies and across levels of government;

c) Contribute to society as well as to market efficiency by facilitating employment, rather than perpetuating reliance on public income support alone, through active labour market measures which:
- stress the development of human potential through opportunities for learning and skill upgrading;
- remove barriers in the labour market which affect women, migrants, older workers, disabled persons and marginalised groups; and
- improve the opportunities to balance work, continued training and family responsibilities;

d) Search for an appropriate balance between public, private and voluntary sector responsibility in order to respond to the variety of needs of society, and, in light of their comparative advantages, develop new partnerships and improve old ones;

e) Improve the efficiency and effectiveness of income maintenance programmes, consistent with the objective of encouraging individuals to achieve self-sufficiency through earnings, without sacrificing the goals of systems of social protection;

f) Ensure that any options for economy measures are consistent with programme effectiveness and social objectives.

g) Administer health care and other social programmes in a style that is more responsive to individual and family needs.

HEALTH CARE: BALANCING QUALITY AND COST

The health status of the population in nearly all OECD countries has continued to improve. Avoidable mortality has declined, and life expectancy and other health indicators have improved. At the same time, in virtually all OECD countries the growth of expenditure on health care has slowed over the last decade. In some countries health expenditure as a proportion of national product has been stabilized, and in others it has even declined. There has been a convergence of health system structures and a reduction in national differences in the observable health status of populations. The pursuit of non-inflationary growth in Member countries will require delicate balancing of quality and cost within health portfolios during the 1990s. Resources will be required to address systemic issues such as ageing of the population as well as for specific problems such as drug addiction and AIDS. Combating AIDS will require comprehensive programmes and international co-operation, notably through the World Health Organisation.

Most national health systems have either recently been reformed or are currently in the process of reform. These reforms, through managed competition or contractual arrangements, seek to dissociate the financing from the delivery function. According to the initial evidence, these reforms have improved the efficiency and responsiveness of health care delivery. Quality control is also an essential feature of ongoing and future reforms. New technologies promise more effective treatment, but may also involve higher costs.

Health strategies should be developed which integrate acute care, chronic care and preventive measures including screening, environmental improvements, occupational health and safety and motor vehicle safety. Such strategies would include an array of methods for health education and motivation for healthier lifestyle choices by individuals. These could help achieve the expectations of improved quality of health care and of further advances in health status which exist in all countries and may, in the long term, act to reduce costs. Although all segments of the population have benefited from past achievements, health outcomes vary by socio-economic status. The effective use of resources will in some countries require greater concentration on those most in need – although this in itself will not equalise health outcomes.

SOCIAL POLICY AND AGEING POPULATIONS

The Transition from Work to Retirement

Older workers – both men and women – have been leaving the labour force at younger ages in many OECD countries. Part of this early withdrawal from the labour force is due to health problems, manifested in premature invalidity or long-term unemployment. Encouragement of improvements in occupational health and safety and promotion of healthier lifestyles are therefore key strategies for keeping older workers active.

However, in large part, early withdrawal has been in response to measures designed to help older workers adapt to the impact of unemployment and labour market adjustment. Temporary measures intended to cope with downturns in the economy and structural change have, in many cases, become permanent encouragements to leave the labour force at a younger age, and remain in effect even if employment opportunities improve. And older workers are often singled out for redundancy when they would welcome the opportunity to remain in the labour force. Too often, the approach has been passive with support confined to the (necessary) payment of income maintenance. Even in a downturn, opportunities will emerge for older workers and positive approaches such as training and job-search services which would help reintegrate them into the labour force should be maintained.

In those countries where there are provisions encouraging early retirement on full pension, the pensions of those who retire early might be adjusted so that the total value of pension flows is independent of the age of retirement. Moreover, workers could be encouraged to remain in the labour force to maximise their income. Discrimination against older workers by firms and government organisations should be resisted by encouraging firms to offer opportunities for retraining to workers without distinction with respect to age, and by other measures to keep older workers engaged in the labour market. Until greater equality of opportunity is achieved, special support will be needed for older workers who lose their jobs, to enable them to continue to seek employment.

The Care of Frail Elderly People

The central aim of social and health policies for elderly people should be to enable them to continue to play as active a role in society as possible. To achieve this, health, social service, housing and income security policies will have to be more fully integrated. There should also be a greater focus on the elderly person's home as the focus of service provision, rather than locating most care services in institutional settings. It will be essential to ensure the most efficient use of the available resources. This will call for better needs-based assessment at the individual level, taking account of the preferences of elderly people and family carers, and for more effective case management. Better measures of service outcomes, both on cost and on quality of life, are also essential.

Because of the future growth in the elderly population, all OECD societies will have to support a substantial increase in resources devoted to care. Specific solutions to funding will vary, but both public and private sources will be called upon. In the relatively affluent OECD societies, private assets will play an important part in improving the quality of life in old age. However, the high cost of the intensive long-term care that will be needed in many cases is only likely to be met from social insurance or other public transfers. New mechanisms could permit elderly people to utilise their private resources: for example, new forms of care insurance, or schemes which enable home owners to realise their housing equity. However, both the growth in numbers and the costs of care will necessitate an increase in public expenditures if the quality of life of frail elderly people is to be maintained.

The changes needed to achieve a satisfactory quality of life for elderly people require time and skills as well as funds. As the elderly increase as a proportion of the total population, the way these resources are mobilised will have to change. While securing necessary provision of formal services, public policies will have to develop and support those resources in the community – families, neighbours, volunteers – which will, as now, be a vital source of care for elderly people. However, the changes that are under way in family structures, and the likelihood of further increases in the proportion of women who are in the paid labour force, mean that the existing pattern of family care will be subject to greater pressure in the future. It is therefore necessary to review the way that formal services interact with these informal sources of social support, to ensure that these services can best complement and support families and other informal carers. The terms of employment of those workers, men as well as women, who have both paid employment and caring responsibilities could also be made more amenable to their needs.

A PROGRAMME OF ACTION

Social protection and health delivery systems in all OECD countries face severe challenges. They cannot themselves bring about economic recovery, and yet they play an essential role in facilitating economic development and helping to maintain community cohesion. They can make a major contribution to these tasks by encouraging individuals to give full scope to their abilities throughout their lives, while ensuring that they have the basic resources they need to do this.

The new orientations for social policy set out above provide a starting point for a re-examination of all social policies. General programmes of social insurance will have to be reassessed to ensure that commitments are affordable and consistent with the goal of equitable social protection. In addition, the OECD should consider examining the suitability and adequacy of long-term care provision for all age groups and should initiate a review of the wide range of policies in support of families and children. The recent Report of the OECD Group of Experts on Women and Structural Change in the 1990s has already provided a focus for examination of many of these issues. In all such analyses, consideration of coherence between social, labour market, education, and economic policies and across levels of government is essential.

The malaise in the labour market is adversely affecting all social policy measures. The OECD Council, when it met at Ministerial level in May 1992, called on the OECD "to initiate a comprehensive research effort on the reasons for and the remedies to the disappointing progress in reducing unemployment". Ministers underline the importance of this project. Social conditions have an important influence on the quality and flexibility of labour supply. In that research effort and in developing its orientations for social policy, the OECD should address the contribution which social policy changes might make to the reduction of unemployment and thereby to the strengthening of social cohesion.

Ministers invite the OECD to continue to promote processes for the review of developments in social policy and related policies. An important facet of this should be the review and monitoring, in terms of national objectives, of outcomes arising from different policies and changes to policy. To facilitate cross-country comparison and mutual learning, they encourage the Organisation to develop a framework for the assessment of social policy. A strong and consistent data base which enables comparative trends to be tracked is an essential contribution to the policy formation process. Ministers therefore urge the OECD to intensify this work, and they undertake to assist by providing the data and information needed for this purpose.

Ministers welcome the central role OECD has played in monitoring trends in health care financing and delivery, in analysing the reform paths being adopted in Member countries, and in providing comparative health care statistics. They propose that, given the importance of health and the fundamental nature of recent and proposed reforms, the OECD should examine the possibility of convening a high-level conference to identify and publicise more widely the issues and lessons emerging from the reforms, both in relation to the reform process and the initial outcomes. The OECD should also develop and compile comparable international health outcome measures needed to monitor the pursuit of effective and efficient health policies.

With respect to care of the frail elderly, OECD governments will have to initiate informed public discussion about the costs and benefits of different funding approaches, and build public recognition of this priority need. Ministers agreed that it would be helpful if the OECD could inform this necessary public discussion through a seminar building on its ongoing work on the resourcing of such care and different approaches to funding.

Countries in transition from centrally-planned to market economies are having to reform their social policies fundamentally. The OECD should continue its contribution to this process.

This meeting has provided a useful occasion for all participants to explore the orientations for national policy. Ministers would welcome an intensification of OECD work on social policy, and look forward to a further meeting at which progress in this work can be reviewed and developments in social policy can be discussed.

Annex

TABLES AND CHARTS

Table 1a. Public expenditure on social protection as a percentage of GDP

(Historic series, 1985 data)

	1960	1961	1962	1963	1964	1965	1966	1967	1968	1969	1970	1971	1972	1973	1974	1975	1976	1977	1978	1979	1980
Australia																					
Total	7.39	7.89	7.83	7.72	7.45	7.55	7.18	7.24	7.07	7.29	7.37	7.74	8.27	8.74	10.46	12.66	13.20	13.61	13.25	12.83	12.79
Public health	2.45	2.67	2.86	2.74	2.75	2.85	2.59	2.79	2.80	2.95	3.16	3.37	3.38	3.56	4.23	5.56	5.13	4.93	4.84	4.67	4.70
Other[a]	4.94	5.22	4.98	4.99	4.70	4.70	4.59	4.45	4.27	4.34	4.21	4.37	4.89	5.18	6.24	7.09	8.07	8.68	8.41	8.16	8.09
Austria																					
Total	15.88	15.89	16.85	17.26	17.22	17.44	17.93	18.32	18.06	18.95	18.90	19.06	18.90	18.73	19.22	20.97	21.71	21.71	23.44	23.39	23.27
Public health	2.89	2.88	2.92	3.00	2.95	3.04	3.33	3.09	3.20	3.40	3.35	3.31	3.29	3.37	3.62	4.07	4.42	4.28	4.46	4.47	4.51
Other[a]	13.00	13.01	13.93	14.27	14.27	14.40	14.61	15.22	14.86	15.54	15.55	15.74	15.60	15.36	15.60	16.90	17.30	17.43	18.98	18.91	18.75
Belgium																					
Total				14.99	16.05	16.97	17.61	18.89	18.91	19.26	19.63	20.81	21.35	22.15	26.74	28.04	29.57	29.93	30.17	30.38	
Public health				2.49	2.97	2.97	3.03	3.20	3.43	3.55	3.59	3.75	3.88	3.89	4.46	4.71	4.91	5.11	5.16	5.08	
Other[a]				12.50	13.09	14.00	14.58	15.69	15.48	15.71	16.04	17.06	17.48	18.27	22.29	23.33	24.66	24.82	25.01	25.30	
Canada																					
Total	9.12	9.44	9.39	9.32	9.21	8.99	9.47	9.53	10.53	10.93	11.80	12.78	13.63	13.65	14.09	15.37	15.03	15.28	15.06	14.50	14.96
Public health	2.38	2.61	2.70	2.88	3.00	3.07	3.79	3.40	4.19	4.53	5.08	5.47	5.46	5.18	5.16	5.68	5.60	5.56	5.47	5.30	5.45
Other[a]	6.74	6.83	6.69	6.44	6.21	5.92	5.68	6.13	6.34	6.39	6.72	7.31	8.18	8.46	8.93	9.69	9.43	9.72	9.59	9.20	9.51
Denmark																					
Total											19.13	20.13	20.29	20.17	22.70	24.25	23.34	23.78	24.91	25.62	26.79
Public health											5.23	5.49	5.44	5.25	5.77	5.94	5.82	5.56	5.59	5.60	5.79
Other[a, b]											13.89	14.63	14.85	14.92	16.94	18.31	17.52	18.21	19.32	20.02	21.00
Finland																					
Total	8.81	9.10	9.62	9.80	10.27	11.12	12.58	12.38	13.62	13.39	13.56	14.44	15.14	14.76	15.09	16.70	18.44	19.96	20.27	19.29	19.19
Public health	2.27	2.28	2.28	2.46	2.66	3.14	3.87	3.37	4.04	4.05	4.10	4.19	4.51	4.38	4.40	4.94	5.29	5.35	5.21	4.99	5.05
Other[a]	6.54	6.82	7.34	7.34	7.61	7.98	8.71	9.01	9.58	9.33	9.46	10.25	10.63	10.39	10.69	11.76	13.16	14.61	15.07	14.29	14.14
France																					
Total	13.42	13.88	14.56	15.36	15.78	16.48	16.71	16.25	16.53	16.53	16.68	16.78	16.96	17.22	17.71	18.36	20.17	20.73	21.68	21.99	22.55
Public health	2.50	2.78	3.05	3.28	3.50	3.60	3.91	3.78	3.78	4.12	4.34	4.47	4.58	4.62	4.73	5.50	5.65	5.61	5.85	6.00	6.14
Other[a]	10.93	11.10	11.52	12.08	12.29	12.89	12.80	12.47	12.76	12.40	12.33	12.31	12.38	12.60	12.98	12.86	14.52	15.11	15.82	15.99	16.41
Germany																					
Total	18.10	18.06	18.10	18.65	18.08	18.95	19.33	20.72	20.57	19.95	19.53	20.40	21.17	21.55	23.52	26.23	26.78	26.59	25.95	25.42	25.66
Public health	3.14	3.23	3.30	3.37	3.28	3.44	3.88	3.77	4.03	4.00	4.24	4.68	4.94	5.37	5.95	6.36	6.42	6.33	6.33	6.31	6.53
Other[a]	14.97	14.83	14.80	15.27	14.80	15.51	15.44	16.95	16.54	15.95	15.30	15.72	16.23	16.18	17.57	19.87	20.35	20.27	19.62	19.11	19.14
Greece																					
Total		7.06	7.46	7.72	8.18	8.47	9.24	9.47	9.08	9.03	9.08	8.66	7.89	8.35	8.64	9.04	9.95	10.66	10.44	11.06	
Public health		1.90	1.92	2.09	2.22	2.22	2.30	2.13	2.14	2.14	2.27	2.28	2.17	2.36	2.44	2.72	3.03	3.13	3.18	3.52	
Other[a]		5.16	5.54	5.63	5.95	6.25	6.94	7.33	6.94	6.89	6.81	6.38	5.72	5.99	6.20	6.33	6.92	7.53	7.26	7.54	
Ireland																					
Total	8.70	8.83	8.94	9.34	9.22	9.59	10.72	10.33	10.38	10.91	11.89	12.56	12.38	13.47	15.18	17.05	16.91	16.34	16.40	16.91	19.19
Public health	3.01	2.94	3.13	3.16	3.11	3.35	3.99	3.67	3.65	3.91	4.32	4.77	5.03	5.34	5.97	6.44	6.36	6.31	6.71	7.27	8.39
Other[a]	5.69	5.88	5.82	6.18	6.11	6.25	6.73	6.66	6.73	7.00	7.57	7.79	7.36	8.13	9.21	10.61	10.55	10.04	9.69	9.63	10.80
Italy																					
Total	13.10	12.83	13.84	14.25	14.34	16.16	16.49	16.03	16.56	17.00	16.94	18.14	19.42	19.12	19.33	21.03	21.09	20.33	22.00	21.22	21.24
Public health	3.21	3.30	3.30	3.59	3.83	4.06	4.39	4.22	4.47	4.55	4.78	5.23	5.61	5.64	5.79	5.79	5.82	5.52	5.94	5.99	6.00
Other[a]	9.89	9.53	10.54	10.66	10.51	12.10	12.10	11.81	12.09	12.45	12.16	12.91	13.80	13.48	13.54	15.24	15.27	14.82	16.07	15.23	15.24
Japan																					
Total	4.05	4.58	4.89	5.10	5.15	5.51	5.66	5.59	5.56	5.55	5.72	5.98	6.47	6.68	8.09	9.32	10.04	10.43	11.22	11.44	11.94
Public health	1.33	2.04	2.21	2.35	2.46	2.70	2.83	2.75	2.82	2.77	2.95	2.98	3.14	3.11	3.69	3.98	4.17	4.15	4.51	4.50	4.64
Other[a]	2.72	2.53	2.68	2.74	2.69	2.81	2.82	2.84	2.73	2.77	2.77	3.01	3.32	3.57	4.40	5.34	5.87	6.28	6.71	6.94	7.31
Netherlands																					
Total	11.70	12.68	13.55	15.62	15.75	17.12	18.94	19.37	20.48	21.50	22.45	23.37	24.32	25.04	26.71	29.56	29.61	25.08	26.61	27.48	28.34
Public health	1.31	1.68	2.12	2.65	2.77	3.04	3.82	3.42	4.18	4.62	5.07	4.90	4.96	5.11	5.40	5.89	5.84	5.97	6.15	6.28	6.48
Other[a]	10.39	11.00	11.43	12.97	12.99	14.08	15.12	15.95	16.31	16.89	17.38	18.47	19.36	19.93	21.31	23.67	23.77	19.11	20.46	21.20	21.86
Norway																					
Total	7.85	8.36	8.83	9.25	9.54	10.15	11.30	11.83	11.51	13.44	16.13	17.40	18.66	19.08	18.65	19.50	20.23	20.73	21.76	22.04	20.99
Public health	2.77	2.83	2.91	3.10	3.20	3.19	3.68	3.57	3.49	4.11	4.59	4.81	5.65	5.79	5.84	6.45	6.67	6.98	7.12	7.00	6.53
Other[a]	5.09	5.53	5.91	6.15	6.34	6.97	7.62	8.26	8.02	9.33	11.54	12.59	13.01	13.29	12.81	13.05	13.56	13.75	14.64	15.04	14.46
New Zealand																					
Total	10.37	10.28	10.52	10.00	9.79	9.59	9.95	9.93	9.86	9.54	9.22	9.06	9.65	10.51	11.06	11.78	12.14	14.32	14.86	14.71	15.22
Public health	3.27	3.50	3.42	3.41	3.29	3.37	3.74	3.57	3.66	3.52	3.46	3.51	3.27	3.71	4.03	4.36	4.49	4.64	4.72	4.78	4.81
Other[a]	7.10	6.79	7.10	6.59	6.49	6.22	6.21	6.36	6.20	6.02	5.76	5.55	6.39	6.81	7.03	7.43	7.65	9.68	10.14	9.93	10.41
Sweden																					
Total	10.83	10.77	11.11	12.39	12.50	13.18	14.40	14.87	16.33	16.50	16.76	18.36	18.38	18.40	21.05	21.16	22.14	24.49	25.19	25.14	25.94
Public health	3.42	3.50	3.58	4.09	4.23	4.49	5.31	4.96	5.84	5.91	6.20	6.58	6.57	6.40	6.86	7.20	7.48	8.38	8.47	8.34	8.77
Other[a]	7.41	7.27	7.53	8.31	8.27	8.69	9.09	9.91	10.49	10.59	10.56	11.78	11.81	12.00	14.19	13.96	14.65	16.11	16.73	16.80	17.16

Table 1*a*. **Public expenditure on social protection as a percentage of GDP** *(cont.)*

(Historic series, 1985 data)

	1960	1961	1962	1963	1964	1965	1966	1967	1968	1969	1970	1971	1972	1973	1974	1975	1976	1977	1978	1979	1980
Switzerland																					
Total	4.92	5.12	5.90	5.69	6.61	6.83	7.19	7.28	7.48	8.78	8.49	8.77	8.82	10.90	11.53	13.57	14.38	14.51	14.53	14.52	13.86
Public health	2.50	2.40	2.45	2.30	2.39	2.62	2.99	2.87	3.14	3.23	3.23	3.42	3.55	3.80	4.16	4.83	5.10	5.16	5.25	5.42	4.90
Other[a]	2.42	2.72	3.44	3.39	4.22	4.22	4.20	4.41	4.35	5.55	5.26	5.35	5.27	7.09	7.37	8.74	9.28	9.35	9.28	9.10	8.96
United Kingdom																					
Total	10.21	10.47	10.67	11.19	11.00	11.66	12.06	12.38	13.04	13.04	13.20	13.07	13.88	13.47	14.92	15.63	16.19	16.14	16.46	16.38	16.42
Public health	3.35	3.39	3.38	3.39	3.40	3.56	3.87	3.70	3.88	3.79	3.95	4.00	4.16	4.11	4.72	5.00	4.98	4.80	4.74	4.68	5.21
Other[a]	6.86	7.08	7.28	7.79	7.60	8.09	8.19	8.69	9.17	9.24	9.25	9.07	9.72	9.37	10.19	10.62	11.22	11.34	11.72	11.70	11.21
United States																					
Total	7.26	7.93	7.81	7.95	7.85	7.86	8.57	8.20	9.10	9.32	10.38	11.22	11.39	11.62	12.75	14.50	14.32	14.05	13.62	13.84	13.36
Public health	1.31	1.41	1.46	1.53	1.56	1.57	2.38	1.80	2.54	2.65	2.81	2.95	3.00	2.99	3.31	3.65	3.69	3.68	3.71	3.80	3.60
Other[a]	5.96	6.52	6.35	6.42	6.29	6.29	6.18	6.40	6.56	6.68	7.57	8.27	8.39	8.63	9.44	10.85	10.63	10.37	9.91	10.04	9.75
Group average[c]																					
Total	10.11	10.38	10.56	10.96	11.91	11.80	12.44	12.62	13.06	13.37	14.02	14.63	15.12	15.39	16.45	18.05	18.57	18.82	19.36	19.33	19.64
Public health	2.57	2.71	2.76	2.90	3.12	3.13	3.53	3.34	3.61	3.76	4.03	4.21	4.35	4.41	4.73	5.19	5.28	5.32	5.44	5.46	5.59
Other[a]	7.54	7.67	7.79	8.07	8.80	8.67	8.91	9.28	9.45	9.61	9.99	10.42	10.77	10.98	11.72	12.87	13.29	13.50	13.92	13.87	14.05

a) Includes other expenditure on the aged and non-aged.

b) The data for 1980 are estimated.

c) Non-weighted average.

The data in this table have not been updated or modified from those published in 1985.

Source: Social Expenditure 1960-1990, OECD, Paris, 1985.

Table 1*b*. **Public expenditure on social protection as a percentage of GDP**

(OECD countries outside the EC)

	1980	1981	1982	1983	1984	1985	1986	1987	1988	1989	1990
Australia											
Total	10.98	10.98	11.43	12.70	13.65	13.52	13.39	12.61	12.23	12.18	12.96
Public health	4.58	4.66	4.69	4.96	5.49	5.53	5.64	5.47	5.30	5.34	5.59
Aged[a]	3.59	3.65	3.84	4.21	4.22	4.14	4.01	3.81	3.72	3.50	3.75
Non-aged[b]	2.80	2.67	2.90	3.53	3.94	3.85	3.75	3.34	3.21	3.34	3.62
Austria											
Total	23.43	24.22	24.13	24.35	24.44	24.77	25.09	25.42	25.31	25.07	24.54
Public health	5.42	5.71	5.44	5.35	5.28	5.41	5.62	5.63	5.57	5.61	5.56
Aged[a]	13.87	14.31	14.49	14.76	14.92	15.10	15.25	15.54	15.55	15.37	15.03
Non-aged[b]	4.14	4.20	4.21	4.24	4.24	4.26	4.23	4.24	4.19	4.08	3.95
Canada[c]											
Total	14.37	14.54	17.26	17.47	17.12	17.11	17.67	17.40	17.03	17.16	18.79
Public health	5.51	5.70	6.36	6.53	6.36	6.36	6.57	6.53	6.43	6.54	6.85
Aged[a]	3.12	3.25	3.55	3.65	3.73	3.87	4.03	4.14	4.10	4.14	4.36
Non-aged[b]	5.73	5.59	7.36	7.29	7.02	6.87	7.07	6.73	6.51	6.48	7.58
Finland											
Total	21.42	22.10	23.31	24.16	24.55	25.87	26.27	26.68	25.58	25.44	27.08
Public health	5.11	5.27	5.40	5.42	5.38	5.68	5.84	5.89	5.74	5.78	6.32
Aged[a]	5.86	6.05	6.17	6.60	7.35	6.63	7.55	7.66	7.32	7.16	7.47
Non-aged[b]	10.46	10.78	11.74	12.14	11.83	13.56	12.88	13.13	12.52	12.50	13.29
Japan											
Total	10.48	10.85	11.32	11.70	11.53	11.48	11.89	12.06	11.79	11.62	11.57
Public health	4.64	4.68	4.80	4.99	4.83	4.77	4.86	4.94	4.86	4.73	4.77
Aged[a]	3.41	3.68	3.95	4.17	4.25	4.42	4.71	4.86	4.86	4.94	4.97
Non-aged[b]	2.43	2.49	2.58	2.54	2.45	2.28	2.32	2.25	2.07	1.94	1.83
Norway											
Total	21.44	22.00	22.49	22.99	23.04	22.06	24.20	26.16	27.04	28.11	28.74
Public health	6.54	6.47	6.57	6.68	6.34	6.22	6.81	7.22	7.36	7.12	7.10
Aged[a]	6.41	6.38	6.59	6.81	7.02	6.40	6.88	7.35	7.65	7.78	7.73
Non-aged[b]	8.49	9.15	9.33	9.50	9.68	9.44	10.51	11.59	12.04	13.21	13.90
New Zealand											
Total	15.16	15.14	15.09	16.24	15.43	15.27	15.55	15.98	16.84	17.54	18.95
Public health	6.01	6.06	5.59	5.60	5.24	5.54	5.75	5.95	6.00	5.95	6.01
Aged[a]	6.03	5.78	6.22	7.15	6.58	6.22	6.24	6.07	6.16	6.21	6.67
Non-aged[b]	3.13	3.31	3.29	3.49	3.60	3.51	3.57	3.96	4.68	5.39	6.27
Sweden											
Total	32.42	33.31	33.52	33.81	32.73	32.58	33.85	33.45	34.08	33.29	33.13
Public health	8.72	8.77	8.85	8.75	8.58	7.97	7.69	7.72	7.64	7.66	6.88
Aged[a]	10.98	11.54	11.58	11.74	11.37	11.52	11.71	11.67	11.76	11.74	11.87
Non-aged[b]	12.72	12.99	13.09	13.32	12.78	13.09	14.45	14.05	14.68	13.89	14.38
United States[c]											
Total	14.10	14.30	14.95	15.30	14.29	14.31	14.41	14.42	14.36	14.49	14.58
Public health	3.88	4.01	4.27	4.35	4.24	4.35	4.50	4.63	4.68	4.87	5.22
Aged[a]	5.75	5.91	6.25	6.35	6.07	6.02	6.03	5.95	5.85	5.85	5.82
Non-aged[b]	4.47	4.37	4.43	4.60	3.98	3.95	3.88	3.84	3.83	3.77	3.54
Group average[d]											
Total	18.20	18.60	19.28	19.86	19.64	19.66	20.26	20.46	20.47	20.54	21.15
Public health	5.60	5.70	5.77	5.85	5.75	5.76	5.92	6.00	5.95	5.95	6.03
Aged[a]	6.56	6.73	6.96	7.27	7.28	7.15	7.38	7.45	7.44	7.41	7.52
Non-aged[b]	6.04	6.17	6.55	6.74	6.61	6.76	6.96	7.02	7.08	7.18	7.60

a) Includes all old-age and survivors benefits (*i.e.*, all transfers and services to the elderly and survivors). Data for Australia include veterans' pensions, data for the United States include occupational civil servants pensions. Excludes expenditure on health.

b) Includes disability pensions, disability services, employment promotion benefits, unemployment compensation, family allowances, indigenous persons benefits, housing benefits, low income benefits, sickness benefits, other miscellaneous services and benefits and administration costs. Excludes all benefits to the aged and survivors and health expenditures.

c) The data for 1990 are estimated.

d) Non-weighted average.

Sources: Health: OECD Health data bank as at July 1993.
GDP: OECD National Accounts data base as at July 1993.
Social expenditures: OECD data base on Social Expenditure (SOCX), as at July 1993.
This includes data, published and unpublished, supplied by national authorities.
These data, derived from a wide variety of sources, should be used with their limitations kept in mind.
In particular, the Australian authorities have pointed out that neither the total expenditure by programme, nor the Commonwealth Budget figures, will give a complete picture of total social welfare expenditure in Australia. This is because programmes financed by any of the six states or two territories within Australia are not included in the data. It would therefore be misleading if comparisons were made with other countries of Australia's share of GDP spent on social expenditure.

Table 1c. Public expenditure on social protection as a percentage of GDP

Provisional estimates

(OECD countries, EC members)

	1980	1981	1982	1983	1984	1985	1986	1987	1988	1989[e]	1990[e]	1991[e]
Belgium												
Total	25.44	27.42	28.06	28.42	27.86	27.45	27.17	26.61	26.29	25.23	25.21	25.39
Public health	5.54	5.84	6.35	6.22	6.16	6.08	6.02	6.37	6.84	6.75	6.78	7.00
Aged[a]	9.69	10.35	10.37	10.64	10.42	10.30	10.27	10.09	9.89	9.50	9.70	9.80
Non-aged[b]	10.22	11.23	11.35	11.56	11.28	11.07	10.88	10.15	9.56	8.98	8.72	8.58
Denmark												
Total	25.97	27.57	28.13	27.97	26.80	25.97	24.78	25.69	27.04	27.80	27.78	28.40
Public health	5.80	5.80	5.82	5.57	5.38	5.30	5.12	5.31	5.48	5.40	5.23	5.32
Aged[a]	8.69	8.85	8.87	8.72	7.97	7.84	7.59	7.70	7.92	8.22	8.12	8.17
Non-aged[b]	11.48	12.92	13.45	13.68	13.46	12.83	12.07	12.68	13.64	14.18	14.42	14.91
France												
Total	23.85	25.36	26.53	27.30	27.80	27.86	27.38	27.04	26.72	26.39	26.49	27.26
Public health	5.95	6.25	6.30	6.35	6.58	6.50	6.47	6.49	6.40	6.55	6.61	6.77
Aged[a]	10.41[e]	10.91	11.35	11.89	12.07	12.32	12.07	11.91	11.83	11.65	11.70	12.19
Non-aged[b,c]	7.48	8.20	8.88	9.05	9.16	9.03	8.84	8.64	8.50	8.20	8.17	8.30
Germany												
Total	25.40	26.34	26.64	25.82	25.41	25.15	24.74	25.04	25.11	24.11	23.47	22.94
Public health	6.32	6.53	6.39	6.23	6.33	6.39	6.34	6.37	6.53	6.00	5.96	6.10
Aged[a]	11.08	11.12	11.28	10.96	10.77	10.61	10.35	10.44	10.44	10.22	9.90	9.66
Non-aged[b]	8.00	8.69	8.97	8.64	8.32	8.14	8.05	8.23	8.13	7.89	7.61	7.18
Greece												
Total	13.36	14.86	17.86	18.40	19.14	20.09	20.58	20.84	20.36	20.86		
Public health	3.56	3.78	4.03	4.06	3.98	3.94	4.32	4.14	4.15	4.01		
Aged[a]	7.34	8.10	10.30	10.38	11.23	11.88	11.98	12.40	12.24	12.84		
Non-aged[b]	2.46	2.97	3.53	3.96	3.94	4.28	4.27	4.30	3.97	4.01		
Ireland												
Total	20.56	21.08	22.54	23.47	23.01	23.10	23.30	22.45	21.23	19.56	19.72	20.77
Public health	7.54	7.28	6.87	6.77	6.41	6.32	6.17	5.72	5.32	5.01	5.20	5.56
Aged[a]	6.18	6.39	6.82	6.94	6.80	6.66	6.70	6.58	6.33	5.88	5.85	6.05
Non-aged[b]	6.83	7.41	8.85	9.76	9.80	10.13	10.43	10.15	9.59	8.67	8.67	9.17
Italy												
Total	19.75	20.80	21.54	22.98	22.19	22.68	22.54	23.20	23.34	23.67	24.53	24.96
Public health	5.57	5.32	5.43	5.53	5.33	5.42	5.27	5.71	5.89	5.87	6.28	6.46
Aged[a]	10.79	11.65	12.42	13.62	13.08	13.53	13.71	14.08	14.13	14.34	14.85	15.29
Non-aged[b]	3.39	3.83	3.69	3.84	3.78	3.73	3.56	3.42	3.32	3.46	3.40	3.22
Luxembourg												
Total	25.99	27.16	26.40	26.00	24.98	25.00	24.41	25.86	25.32	26.57	27.32	29.33
Public health	6.34	6.59	6.43	6.04	5.91	6.05	5.99	6.72	6.59	6.19	6.39	6.65
Aged[a]	12.07	12.71	12.29	12.11	11.42	11.33	11.08	11.59	11.36	13.23	13.55	15.23
Non-aged[b]	7.58	7.85	7.68	7.85	7.65	7.63	7.34	7.56	7.37	7.15	7.37	7.45
Netherlands												
Total	27.16	28.37	30.23	30.81	29.66	28.78	28.42	28.97	28.57	27.92	28.78	28.98
Public health	5.87	6.03	6.23	6.19	5.99	5.87	5.76	5.97	5.85	5.72	5.73	6.00
Aged[a]	8.69	8.77	9.21	9.24	8.88	8.90	9.06	9.28	9.30	9.22	9.92	9.90
Non-aged[b]	12.60	13.56	14.79	15.38	14.80	14.01	13.61	13.71	13.41	12.97	13.14	13.08
Portugal												
Total	13.61	15.19	14.12	13.57	13.55	13.78	14.25	14.86	15.94	14.89	15.30	15.44
Public health	4.25	4.54	3.94	3.47	3.44	3.93	3.81	3.91	4.11	4.15	4.10	4.14
Aged[a]	5.19	5.58	5.29	5.86	5.68	5.62	5.97	6.40	6.50	6.28	6.73	5.47
Non-aged[b]	4.16	5.08	4.89	4.25	4.43	4.23	4.47	4.55	5.33	4.47	4.47	5.84
Spain												
Total	16.76	17.92	17.97	18.71	18.52	18.95	18.37	18.22	18.58	18.76	19.34	19.95
Public health	4.53	4.58	4.70	5.07	4.71	4.59	4.44	4.47	4.93	5.07	5.30	5.48
Aged[a]	6.61	7.20	7.33	7.61	7.76	7.98	7.89	7.79	7.72	7.74	7.93	7.91
Non-aged[b]	5.62	6.15	5.94	6.03	6.05	6.38	6.04	5.97	5.93	5.95	6.11	6.56
United Kingdom												
Total	21.30	23.31	23.56	23.95	23.97	24.12	23.88	22.92	21.92	21.27	22.34	24.03
Public health	5.17	5.40	5.20	5.38	5.29	5.15	5.12	5.08	5.44	5.02	5.18	5.53
Aged[a]	9.17	9.73	10.01	10.01	10.04	9.96	10.04	9.85	9.23	9.28	9.72	10.36
Non-aged[b]	6.96	8.18	8.36	8.56	8.63	9.01	8.72	7.99	7.25	6.97	7.43	8.13

Table 1c. **Public expenditure on social protection as a percentage of GDP** *(cont.)*

Provisional estimates

(OECD countries, EC members)

	1980	1981	1982	1983	1984	1985	1986	1987	1988	1989[e]	1990[e]	1991[e]
EC average[d]												
Total	21.60	22.95	23.63	23.95	23.58	23.58	23.32	23.47	23.37	23.09	21.69	22.29
Public health	5.54	5.66	5.64	5.57	5.46	5.46	5.40	5.52	5.63	5.48	5.23	5.42
Aged[a]	8.83	9.28	9.63	9.83	9.68	9.74	9.73	9.84	9.74	9.87	9.00	9.17
Non-aged[b]	7.23	8.01	8.36	8.55	8.44	8.37	8.19	8.11	8.00	7.74	7.46	7.70

The following procedure has been used in view of the fact that revised ESSPROS data are available to date only for the Old Age, Invalidity, Survivors and Family functions.

For each country in the European Community, provisional estimates from 1980 onward have been derived as follows: (Each number refers to a source below).

Public health expenditure: Total public expenditure from (1).

a) Social protection for the aged: Total Old Age government benefits from (3); LESS Redundancy and Early Retirement benefits from (3); LESS Voluntary pensions from (3); PLUS Survivor's benefits from (5). Includes all old age and survivors' benefits (*i.e.*, all transfers and services to the elderly and survivors), and all compulsory supplementary, occupational and civil servant pensions. Excludes all voluntary supplementary pensions and voluntary occupational pensions.

b) Social protection for the non-aged: Total government benefits from (7); PLUS Redundancy and Early Retirement benefits from (3); PLUS Invalidity benefits from (4); LESS Medical Care from (4); LESS Old Age, Survivors, Invalidity, Family and Sickness benefits from (7); LESS all voluntary supplementary pensions from (4) and (5); PLUS Family benefits from (6). Includes invalidity/disability, occupational accidents and diseases, maternity, family placement, vocational guidance, resettlement, unemployment, housing and miscellaneous. Excludes all benefits to the aged and survivors, and health expenditures.

c) The data for 1980 Invalidity is estimated.

d) Unweighted average.

e) Secretariat estimates.

Sources: 1) Health: OECD Health data bank as at July 1993.

2) GDP: OECD National Accounts data base as at July 1993.

3) Eurostat, *Digest of Statistics on Social Protection in Europe, Vol. 1: Old Age*, Luxembourg, 1992.

4) Eurostat, *Digest of Statistics on Social Protection in Europe, Vol. 2: Invalidity/Disability*, Luxembourg, 1992.

5) Eurostat, *Digest of Statistics on Social Protection in Europe, Vol. 3: Survivors*, Luxembourg, 1993.

6) Eurostat, *Digest of Statistics on Social Protection in Europe, Vol. 4: Family*, Luxembourg, 1993.

7) *Social Protection Expenditure and Receipts 1980-1991*, Eurostat, Luxembourg, 1993.

Chart 1. **Public expenditure on social protection as a percentage of GDP**
Provisional estimates

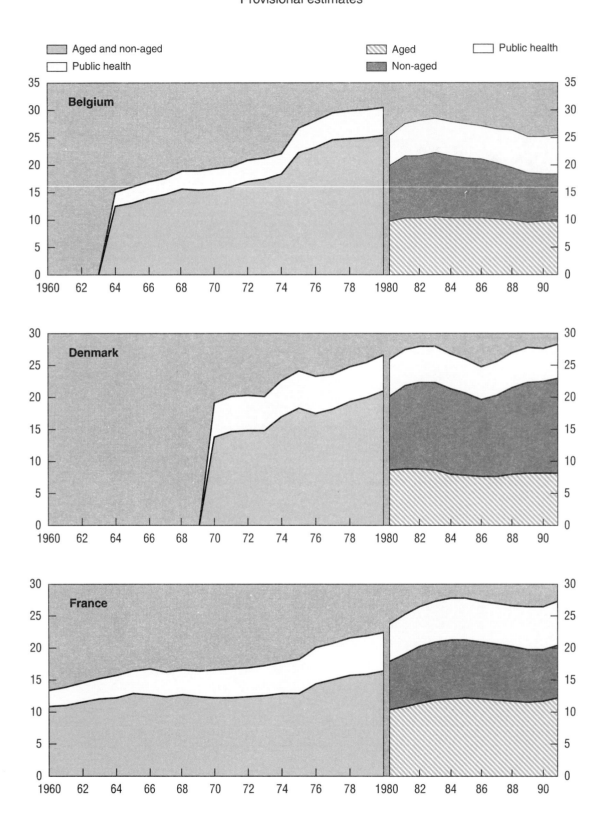

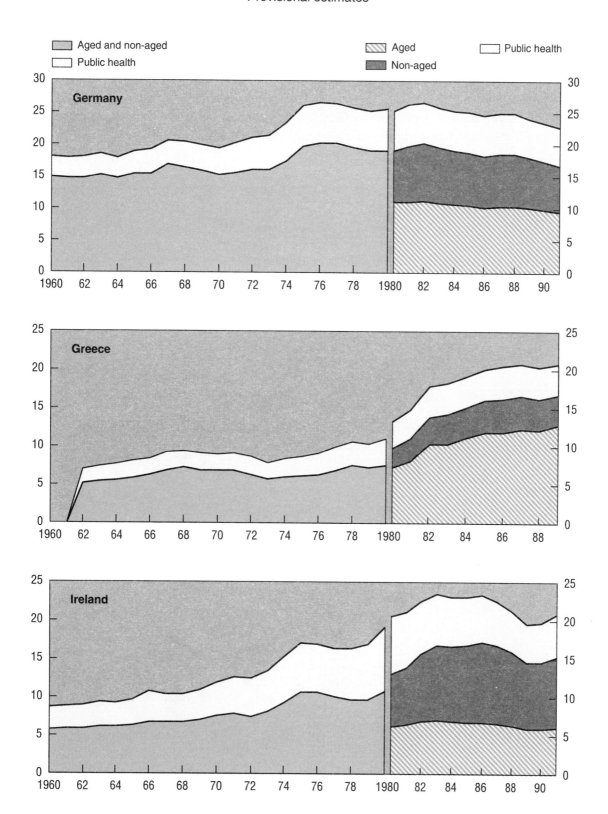

Chart 1 *(cont.)*. **Public expenditure on social protection as a percentage of GDP**
Provisional estimates

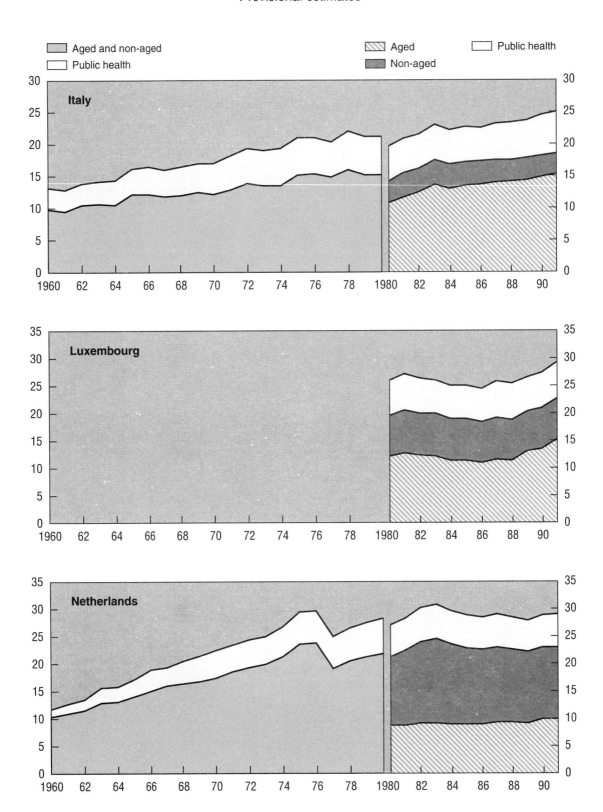

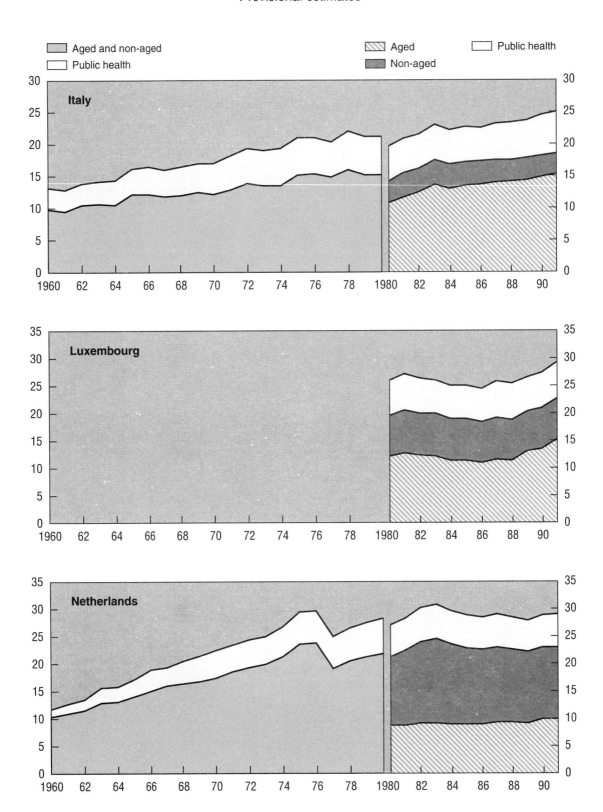

Source: See Tables 1a and 1c.

Chart 1 *(cont.)*. **Public expenditure on social protection as a percentage of GDP**
Provisional estimates

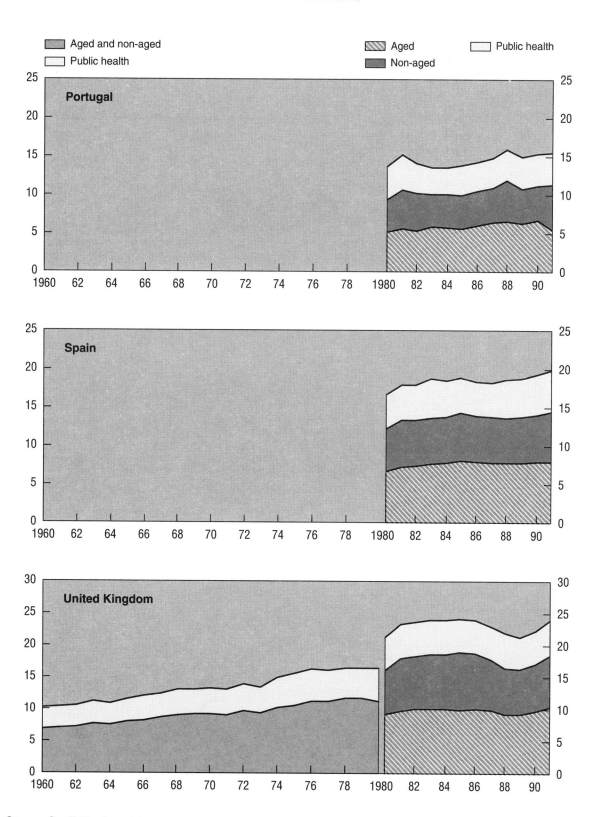

Chart 1 *(cont.).* **Public expenditure on social protection as a percentage of GDP**
Provisional estimates

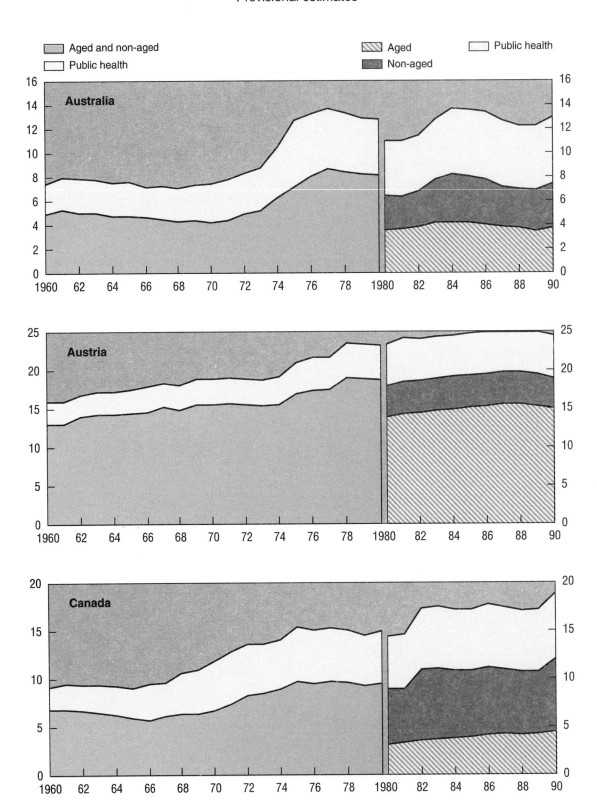

Source: See Tables 1*a* and 1*c*.

Chart 1 *(cont.).* **Public expenditure on social protection as a percentage of GDP**
Provisional estimates

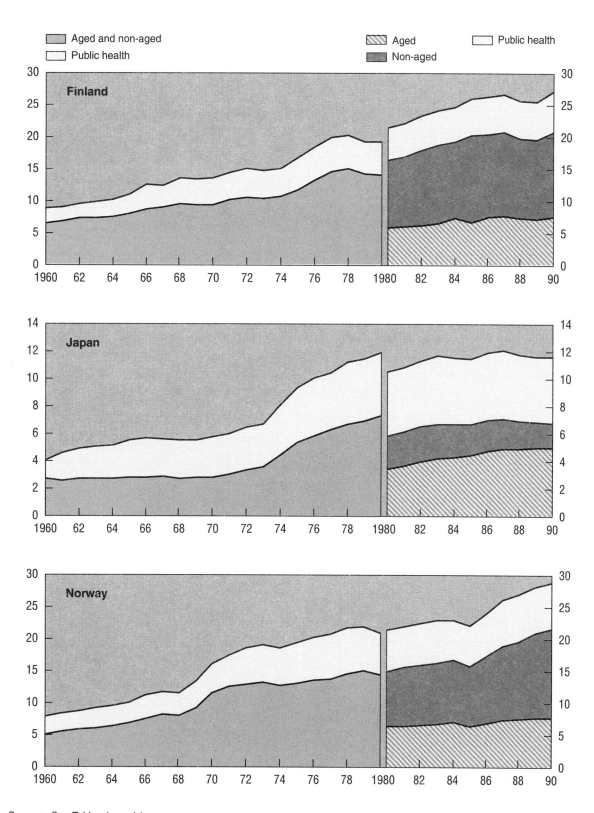

Aged and non-aged
Public health
Aged
Non-aged
Public health

Finland

Japan

Norway

Source: See Tables 1*a* and 1*c*.

Chart 1 *(cont.).* **Public expenditure on social protection as a percentage of GDP**
Provisional estimates

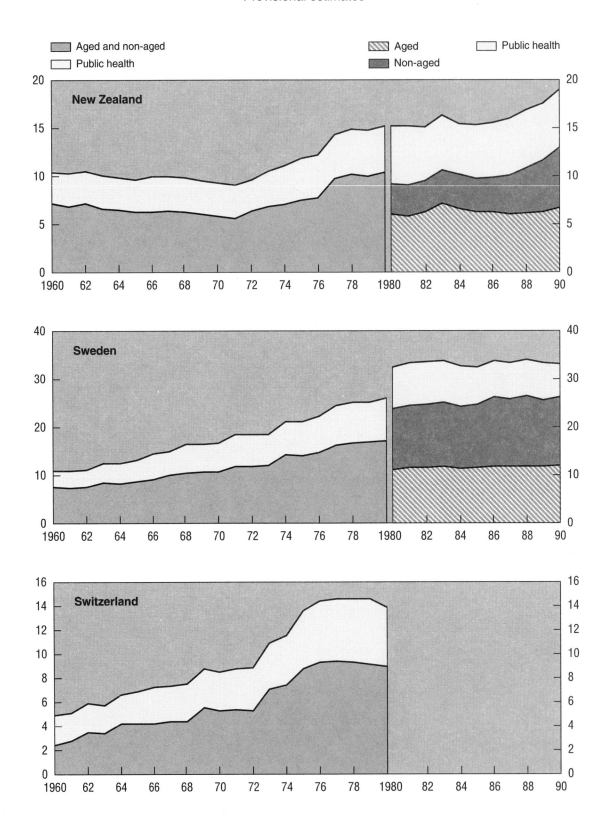

Chart 1 *(cont.).* **Public expenditure on social protection as a percentage of GDP**
Provisional estimates

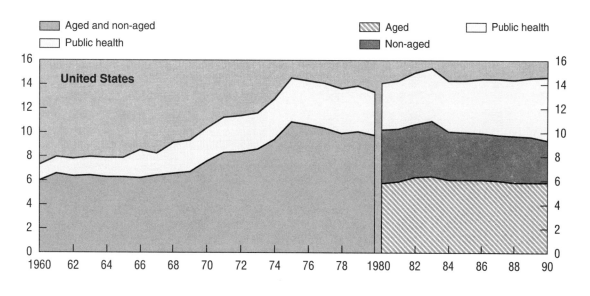

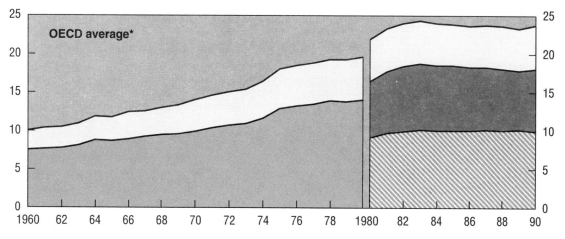

Notes: 1960-1980, aged and non-aged, Table 1*a*. Excludes: Iceland, Luxembourg, Portugal, Spain and Turkey.
1980-1988, aged and non-aged, Tables 1*b* and 1*c*. Excludes: Iceland, Switzerland and Turkey.
* Unweighted average.
Source: See Tables 1*a*, 1*b* and 1*c*.

Table 2. Health expenditure in the OE

	1960	1961	1962	1963	1964	1965	1966	1967	1968	1969	1970	1971	1972	1973	1974
Australia															
Total	4.94	5.29	5.01	4.86	4.89	5.06	4.72	5.18	5.14	5.24	5.67	5.88	5.85	5.87	6.54
Public	2.35	2.57	2.74	2.63	2.64	2.73	2.68	2.48	2.69	2.83	3.22	3.42	3.42	3.56	4.18
Non public	2.59	2.72	2.26	2.23	2.25	2.33	2.05	2.70	2.45	2.41	2.46	2.46	2.43	2.31	2.36
Austria															
Total	4.42	4.65	4.71	4.83	4.76	4.71	5.03	5.36	5.44	5.46	5.45	5.43	5.38	5.55	5.69
Public	3.07	3.10	3.15	3.24	3.18	3.31	3.35	3.61	3.49	3.70	3.43	3.47	3.41	3.54	3.71
Non public	1.35	1.55	1.56	1.59	1.59	1.40	1.68	1.75	1.96	1.76	2.01	1.97	1.97	2.01	1.98
Belgium															
Total	3.44	3.37	3.40	3.50	3.61	3.94	3.92	3.98	4.04	3.94	4.08	4.17	4.34	4.64	4.71
Public	2.12	2.15	2.18	2.33	2.41	2.97	3.03	2.97	3.20	3.43	3.55	3.59	3.75	3.88	3.89
Non public	1.32	1.22	1.22	1.17	1.20	0.97	0.90	1.01	0.83	0.51	0.53	0.58	0.59	0.77	0.83
Canada															
Total	5.47	5.85	5.80	5.92	5.90	5.98	6.00	6.30	6.56	6.68	7.07	7.37	7.23	6.88	6.77
Public	2.33	2.68	2.86	3.03	3.10	3.11	3.60	4.12	4.47	4.69	4.96	5.40	5.37	5.09	5.07
Non public	3.13	3.17	2.95	2.89	2.80	2.86	2.40	2.19	2.09	1.99	2.11	1.97	1.86	1.79	1.70
Denmark															
Total	3.65	4.23	4.43	4.62	4.54	4.85	5.39	5.81	6.07	6.23	6.07	6.42	6.31	6.46	7.10
Public	3.23	3.64	3.80	3.97	3.90	4.16	4.55	4.97	5.25	5.43	5.23	5.49	5.44	5.25	5.77
Non public	0.41	0.58	0.64	0.65	0.64	0.69	0.84	0.84	0.83	0.79	0.83	0.92	0.87	1.21	1.33
Finland															
Total	3.93	3.92	4.11	4.27	4.51	4.91	5.14	5.60	5.85	5.79	5.70	5.87	5.98	5.85	5.79
Public	2.12	2.15	2.34	2.51	2.74	3.24	3.47	4.02	4.19	4.27	4.21	4.27	4.40	4.45	4.48
Non public	1.80	1.78	1.76	1.76	1.78	1.67	1.68	1.58	1.66	1.52	1.50	1.60	1.58	1.40	1.31
France															
Total	4.24	4.50	4.63	4.82	5.04	5.22	5.45	5.59	5.50	5.82	5.82	6.04	6.17	6.21	6.29
Public	2.45	2.74	3.01	3.24	3.46	3.55	3.73	3.85	3.72	4.07	4.35	4.51	4.66	4.68	4.77
Non public	1.79	1.76	1.62	1.57	1.59	1.66	1.71	1.74	1.77	1.75	1.47	1.52	1.51	1.54	1.51
Germany															
Total	4.80	4.82	4.98	4.87	4.89	5.12	5.50	5.67	5.81	5.79	5.88	6.26	6.50	6.84	7.40
Public	3.17	3.26	3.36	3.42	3.41	3.63	3.99	4.14	4.32	4.31	4.09	4.51	4.73	5.14	5.69
Non public	1.63	1.57	1.62	1.45	1.48	1.49	1.51	1.53	1.50	1.48	1.79	1.75	1.77	1.70	1.72
Greece															
Total	2.89	3.04	3.21	3.24	3.36	3.14	3.56	3.63	3.77	3.92	4.04	4.04	3.92	3.75	3.95
Public	1.85	1.77	1.89	1.89	2.10	2.23	2.30	2.24	2.16	2.16	2.16	2.29	2.29	2.18	2.38
Non public	1.03	1.27	1.32	1.35	1.26	0.91	1.26	1.39	1.61	1.77	1.88	1.74	1.63	1.58	1.57
Iceland															
Total	3.52	3.38	3.76	3.73	4.21	4.19	4.31	4.95	5.83	5.48	5.24	5.41	5.69	5.31	5.77
Public	2.70	2.77	2.99	3.01	3.43	3.40	3.53	4.07	4.77	4.54	4.29	4.42	4.71	4.44	5.08
Non public	0.82	0.61	0.77	0.72	0.79	0.79	0.78	0.88	1.07	0.94	0.96	0.99	0.97	0.87	0.70
Ireland															
Total	3.96	3.83	4.08	4.17	4.11	4.38	4.85	5.26	4.98	5.21	5.55	6.58	6.66	6.81	7.36
Public	3.01	2.94	2.99	3.16	3.33	3.34	3.66	3.99	3.69	3.89	4.54	4.77	5.03	5.40	5.89
Non public	0.95	0.88	1.09	1.01	0.78	1.04	1.19	1.27	1.28	1.32	1.02	1.81	1.63	1.41	1.48
Italy															
Total	3.61	3.58	3.50	3.71	4.04	4.33	4.53	4.67	4.76	4.91	5.18	5.52	5.95	5.91	5.96
Public	3.00	3.09	3.09	3.36	3.58	3.80	3.95	4.11	4.19	4.26	4.47	4.91	5.29	5.23	5.25
Non public	0.61	0.50	0.41	0.36	0.46	0.53	0.58	0.56	0.57	0.65	0.71	0.61	0.66	0.68	0.72
Japan															
Total	3.00	3.44	3.63	3.90	3.54	4.46	4.56	4.67	4.69	4.65	4.55	4.67	4.78	4.65	5.11
Public	1.81	2.07	2.19	2.35	2.47	2.74	2.74	2.82	2.82	2.77	3.18	3.07	3.23	3.20	3.79
Non public	1.19	1.37	1.44	1.55	1.07	1.72	1.82	1.85	1.87	1.88	1.37	1.60	1.55	1.45	1.32
Luxembourg															
Total															
Public															
Non public															
Netherlands															
Total	3.80	3.98	4.09	4.17	4.12	4.28	4.56	4.83	5.06	5.18	5.85	6.25	6.54	6.67	6.93
Public	1.27	1.63	2.05	2.57	2.68	2.94	3.31	3.70	4.04	4.47	4.93	4.78	4.61	4.74	4.97
Non public	2.54	2.36	2.04	1.60	1.44	1.34	1.25	1.13	1.02	0.71	0.92	1.47	1.94	1.93	1.96
New Zealand															
Total	4.34	4.72	4.78	4.80	4.75	4.71	4.86	4.99	5.01	5.17	5.24	5.19	5.25	5.46	6.14
Public	3.50	3.68	3.68	3.60	3.61	3.70	3.90	3.90	3.93	3.94	4.21	4.39	4.57	4.54	5.11
Non public	0.84	1.04	1.10	1.20	1.14	1.01	0.96	1.09	1.08	1.23	1.03	0.80	0.69	0.92	1.04

1975	1976	1977	1978	1979	1980	1981	1982	1983	1984	1985	1986	1987	1988	1989	1990	1991
7.46	7.53	7.84	7.60	7.38	7.29	7.46	7.71	7.69	7.65	7.73	7.99	7.82	7.70	7.75	8.22	8.62
5.44	5.04	4.85	4.75	4.55	4.58	4.66	4.69	4.96	5.49	5.53	5.64	5.47	5.30	5.34	5.59	5.84
2.03	2.50	2.99	2.85	2.83	2.71	2.80	3.02	2.73	2.17	2.20	2.35	2.35	2.40	2.42	2.63	2.78
7.33	7.53	7.49	7.87	7.86	7.88	8.22	8.03	8.02	7.95	8.10	8.29	8.39	8.37	8.41	8.29	8.40
5.11	5.24	5.22	5.50	5.37	5.42	5.71	5.44	5.35	5.28	5.41	5.62	5.63	5.57	5.61	5.56	5.64
2.23	2.29	2.26	2.38	2.49	2.46	2.51	2.59	2.67	2.67	2.69	2.67	2.76	2.80	2.80	2.73	2.76
5.90	6.13	6.64	6.85	6.84	6.64	7.17	7.38	7.56	7.42	7.44	7.58	7.66	7.67	7.59	7.63	7.88
4.70	4.93	5.55	5.69	5.69	5.54	5.84	6.35	6.22	6.16	6.08	6.02	6.37	6.84	6.75	6.78	7.00
1.20	1.20	1.09	1.15	1.15	1.11	1.32	1.04	1.34	1.26	1.35	1.56	1.29	0.83	0.84	0.85	0.87
7.21	7.19	7.17	7.20	7.08	7.38	7.54	8.38	8.58	8.45	8.52	8.83	8.91	8.81	8.97	9.48	10.01
5.51	5.54	5.51	5.48	5.36	5.51	5.70	6.36	6.53	6.36	6.36	6.57	6.53	6.43	6.54	6.85	7.23
1.70	1.65	1.66	1.72	1.72	1.86	1.84	2.02	2.05	2.09	2.16	2.26	2.38	2.38	2.43	2.64	2.78
6.46	6.82	6.57	6.60	6.57	6.80	6.83	6.82	6.57	6.36	6.27	5.99	6.30	6.55	6.50	6.32	6.53
5.94	5.82	5.56	5.59	5.60	5.80	5.80	5.82	5.57	5.38	5.30	5.12	5.31	5.48	5.40	5.23	5.32
0.52	0.99	1.00	1.00	0.97	1.01	1.02	1.00	1.00	0.99	0.98	0.87	0.99	1.07	1.09	1.09	1.21
6.34	6.68	6.87	6.78	6.54	6.46	6.61	6.75	6.85	6.85	7.22	7.36	7.40	7.23	7.23	7.81	8.91
4.99	5.23	5.41	5.28	5.12	5.11	5.27	5.40	5.42	5.38	5.68	5.84	5.89	5.74	5.78	6.32	7.21
1.36	1.45	1.46	1.50	1.42	1.36	1.34	1.35	1.43	1.47	1.54	1.53	1.51	1.49	1.45	1.49	1.70
6.95	7.00	7.02	7.28	7.41	7.56	7.87	7.97	8.15	8.50	8.45	8.48	8.50	8.57	8.70	8.89	9.09
5.37	5.31	5.40	5.65	5.79	5.95	6.25	6.30	6.35	6.58	6.50	6.47	6.49	6.40	6.55	6.61	6.77
1.58	1.69	1.62	1.63	1.62	1.60	1.61	1.67	1.80	1.92	1.95	2.01	2.01	2.17	2.16	2.28	2.32
8.14	8.07	8.08	8.09	8.14	8.42	8.70	8.56	8.50	8.66	8.69	8.56	8.65	8.84	8.31	8.32	8.50
6.28	6.17	6.11	6.11	6.09	6.32	6.53	6.39	6.23	6.33	6.39	6.34	6.37	6.53	6.00	5.96	6.10
1.86	1.89	1.97	1.98	2.05	2.10	2.17	2.17	2.27	2.34	2.30	2.22	2.28	2.31	2.31	2.36	2.40
4.07	4.05	4.13	4.13	4.36	4.34	4.49	4.42	4.62	4.54	4.86	5.36	5.21	5.02	5.35	5.38	5.19
2.45	2.73	3.04	3.14	3.19	3.56	3.78	4.03	4.06	3.98	3.94	4.32	4.14	4.15	4.01	4.14	4.09
1.62	1.32	1.09	0.99	1.17	0.77	0.70	0.38	0.56	0.56	0.92	1.03	1.06	0.88	1.34	1.24	1.10
6.20	5.92	5.95	6.29	6.51	6.43	6.64	6.93	7.56	7.01	7.06	7.85	8.00	8.57	8.56	8.33	8.39
5.41	5.18	5.24	5.67	5.81	5.67	5.90	6.18	6.77	6.09	6.40	6.79	6.99	7.47	7.40	7.24	7.30
0.79	0.74	0.71	0.62	0.69	0.76	0.74	0.76	0.79	0.93	0.66	1.06	1.01	1.11	1.15	1.09	1.09
8.04	7.95	7.57	8.05	8.22	9.18	8.79	8.39	8.48	8.22	8.17	8.08	7.67	7.32	6.86	6.95	7.34
6.36	6.26	6.02	6.34	6.81	7.54	7.28	6.87	6.77	6.41	6.32	6.17	5.72	5.32	5.01	5.20	5.56
1.69	1.69	1.55	1.71	1.41	1.63	1.51	1.52	1.72	1.80	1.85	1.91	1.94	2.00	1.85	1.75	1.78
6.08	6.01	5.60	5.82	5.92	6.87	6.71	6.91	7.02	6.83	7.03	6.94	7.35	7.55	7.65	8.09	8.33
5.24	5.21	4.89	5.20	5.22	5.57	5.32	5.43	5.53	5.33	5.42	5.27	5.71	5.89	5.87	6.28	6.46
0.85	0.80	0.71	0.61	0.70	1.30	1.38	1.48	1.49	1.49	1.61	1.68	1.65	1.66	1.77	1.81	1.87
5.65	5.65	5.79	5.99	6.11	6.56	6.64	6.82	6.90	6.67	6.57	6.64	6.80	6.71	6.75	6.81	6.86
4.07	4.24	4.21	4.55	4.54	4.64	4.68	4.80	4.99	4.83	4.77	4.86	4.94	4.86	4.73	4.77	4.81
1.58	1.41	1.58	1.43	1.57	1.92	1.96	2.02	1.90	1.84	1.80	1.78	1.86	1.85	2.02	2.03	2.05
5.65	5.72	6.21	6.57	6.61	6.83	7.10	6.91	6.77	6.64	6.78	6.69	7.33	7.19	6.79	6.99	6.99
5.19	5.25	5.68	6.05	6.13	6.34	6.59	6.43	6.04	5.91	6.05	5.99	6.72	6.59	6.19	6.39	6.39
0.46	0.47	0.53	0.52	0.48	0.49	0.50	0.49	0.73	0.73	0.73	0.71	0.61	0.60	0.60	0.60	0.60
7.40	7.32	7.39	7.53	7.42	7.85	8.02	8.20	8.22	7.92	7.80	7.95	8.11	8.06	7.93	8.04	8.22
5.43	5.37	5.47	5.62	5.72	5.87	6.03	6.23	6.19	5.99	5.87	5.76	5.97	5.85	5.72	5.73	6.00
1.97	1.95	1.92	1.91	1.70	1.98	1.99	1.96	2.03	1.94	1.93	2.19	2.14	2.21	2.20	2.31	2.21
6.70	6.26	6.61	7.07	7.00	7.19	6.87	6.63	6.50	6.09	6.51	6.66	7.02	7.08	7.19	7.30	7.58
5.62	5.39	5.70	6.09	6.14	6.01	6.06	5.59	5.60	5.24	5.54	5.75	5.95	6.00	5.95	6.01	5.98
1.08	0.87	0.91	0.98	0.86	1.18	0.81	1.04	0.90	0.85	0.96	0.91	1.07	1.08	1.25	1.30	1.60

Table 2. **Health expenditure in the OEC**

	1960	1961	1962	1963	1964	1965	1966	1967	1968	1969	1970	1971	1972	1973	1974
Norway															
Total	3.31	3.48	3.73	3.91	3.99	3.94	4.17	4.21	4.40	4.65	5.01	5.36	5.93	6.12	6.16
Public	2.57	2.72	2.91	3.10	3.20	3.19	3.57	3.68	3.82	4.11	4.59	4.81	5.65	5.79	5.84
Non public	0.74	0.76	0.81	0.81	0.79	0.75	0.60	0.54	0.58	0.53	0.42	0.55	0.28	0.33	0.32
Portugal															
Total											3.15	3.55	4.23	4.46	4.68
Public											1.86	1.95	2.46	2.69	2.93
Non public											1.29	1.61	1.77	1.77	1.74
Spain															
Total	1.55	1.63	1.82	1.94	2.31	2.61	2.79	3.02	3.09	3.38	3.71	4.19	4.41	4.29	4.65
Public	0.91	0.87	0.99	0.97	1.13	1.33	1.47	1.86	1.92	2.14	2.43	2.70	2.99	3.27	3.37
Non public	0.64	0.75	0.84	0.97	1.18	1.28	1.33	1.17	1.17	1.24	1.29	1.48	1.42	1.02	1.28
Sweden															
Total	4.68	4.73	4.81	5.25	5.33	5.56	6.05	6.42	6.89	6.94	7.17	7.54	7.54	7.39	7.59
Public	3.40	3.48	3.56	4.03	4.17	4.43	4.89	5.23	5.76	5.83	6.17	6.54	6.53	6.36	6.82
Non public	1.28	1.26	1.25	1.22	1.15	1.14	1.16	1.19	1.14	1.11	1.00	1.00	1.01	1.03	0.77
Switzerland															
Total	3.27	3.21	3.54	3.65	3.68	3.78	4.59	4.90	5.13	5.22	5.18	5.56	5.53	5.78	6.21
Public	2.01	2.09	2.17	2.22	2.23	2.30	2.91	3.06	3.19	3.26	3.31	3.55	3.66	3.83	4.11
Non public	1.27	1.12	1.37	1.42	1.44	1.48	1.68	1.85	1.93	1.97	1.87	2.01	1.87	1.95	2.10
Turkey															
Total															
Public															
Non public															
United Kingdom															
Total	3.91	3.99	3.98	4.09	4.10	4.13	4.24	4.43	4.46	4.36	4.50	4.58	4.68	4.65	5.25
Public	3.33	3.39	3.37	3.39	3.38	3.54	3.68	3.87	3.88	3.77	3.91	3.99	4.11	4.07	4.71
Non public	0.58	0.59	0.61	0.70	0.71	0.59	0.57	0.57	0.58	0.60	0.59	0.59	0.57	0.58	0.54
United States															
Total	5.27	5.45	5.51	5.69	5.86	5.91	5.95	6.34	6.57	6.84	7.35	7.50	7.64	7.59	7.95
Public	1.29	1.37	1.39	1.44	1.44	1.46	1.76	2.35	2.45	2.56	2.74	2.85	2.91	2.91	3.19
Non public	3.98	4.08	4.12	4.25	4.42	4.45	4.19	3.99	4.12	4.28	4.62	4.65	4.74	4.68	4.75
OECD average[a]															
Total	3.90	4.18	4.17	4.28	4.36	4.53	4.77	5.04	5.19	5.28	5.34	5.61	5.75	5.78	6.09
Public	2.45	2.71	2.70	2.83	2.93	3.10	3.34	3.57	3.71	3.83	3.90	4.08	4.24	4.28	4.59
Non public	1.45	1.47	1.47	1.45	1.43	1.43	1.43	1.47	1.48	1.45	1.44	1.53	1.51	1.50	1.50

a) Non-weighted average.
− Non public health expenditure:
  Canada − extrapolated figures: 1961-1964 and 1966-1969.
  New Zealand − extrapolated figures: 1961-1967, 1969 and 1971-1972.
  Portugal − extrapolated figures: 1971-1973.
  Turkey − extrapolated figures: 1981-1983.
− Public health expenditure:
  Canada − extrapolated figures: 1961-1964 and 1966-1969.
  Turkey − extrapolated figures: 1976 and 1981-1983.
Sources: Health: OECD Health data bank as at July 1993.
  GDP: OECD National Accounts data base as at July 1993.

1975	1976	1977	1978	1979	1980	1981	1982	1983	1984	1985	1986	1987	1988	1989	1990	1991
6.70	6.85	7.10	7.68	7.19	6.64	6.58	6.76	6.82	6.52	6.44	7.07	7.40	7.68	7.44	7.46	7.72
6.44	6.67	6.98	7.12	7.00	6.54	6.47	6.57	6.68	6.34	6.22	6.81	7.22	7.36	7.12	7.10	7.46
0.25	0.18	0.12	0.56	0.19	0.11	0.10	0.19	0.14	0.17	0.23	0.26	0.18	0.32	0.33	0.35	0.26
6.42	6.19	5.61	5.84	5.68	5.88	6.37	6.33	6.17	6.26	6.97	6.60	6.76	7.11	7.18	6.65	6.82
3.78	4.08	3.93	3.92	3.93	4.25	4.54	3.94	3.47	3.44	3.93	3.81	3.91	4.11	4.15	4.10	4.14
2.64	2.10	1.69	1.92	1.75	1.62	1.83	2.38	2.70	2.82	3.05	2.79	2.86	3.00	3.03	2.55	2.68
4.89	5.34	5.60	5.59	5.52	5.66	5.82	5.92	6.00	5.77	5.68	5.62	5.71	6.00	6.27	6.58	6.66
3.78	3.94	4.23	4.39	4.37	4.53	4.58	4.70	5.07	4.71	4.59	4.44	4.47	4.93	5.07	5.30	5.48
1.11	1.40	1.36	1.20	1.15	1.14	1.24	1.22	0.93	1.06	1.08	1.18	1.24	1.08	1.20	1.28	1.19
7.93	8.25	9.13	9.20	9.05	9.42	9.55	9.66	9.57	9.37	8.84	8.55	8.61	8.55	8.59	8.62	8.63
7.16	7.44	8.33	8.41	8.29	8.72	8.77	8.85	8.75	8.58	7.97	7.69	7.72	7.64	7.66	6.88	6.73
0.78	0.81	0.79	0.78	0.75	0.70	0.78	0.81	0.81	0.79	0.87	0.86	0.89	0.91	0.93	1.75	1.89
7.00	7.21	7.25	7.19	7.20	7.26	7.30	7.46	7.80	7.76	7.64	7.60	7.65	7.78	7.52	7.81	7.88
4.83	4.92	4.92	4.83	4.85	4.90	4.99	5.11	5.34	5.29	5.24	5.22	5.13	5.30	5.13	5.33	5.38
2.17	2.29	2.33	2.36	2.34	2.36	2.31	2.35	2.46	2.47	2.40	2.38	2.52	2.47	2.39	2.48	2.49
3.46	3.36	3.95	4.30	4.27	4.03	4.44	3.57	3.64	3.54	2.80	3.51	3.60	3.75	3.91	3.97	4.07
1.69	1.28	0.95	0.80	0.99	1.10	1.60	1.83	1.84	1.47	1.41	1.47	1.43	1.43	1.43	1.41	1.49
1.77	2.08	3.00	3.50	3.28	2.93	2.84	1.74	1.80	2.07	1.40	2.04	2.18	2.32	2.48	2.56	2.58
5.48	5.48	5.34	5.31	5.26	5.77	6.06	5.92	6.14	6.09	5.97	6.03	6.03	6.01	6.01	6.20	6.64
4.99	4.99	4.80	4.78	4.71	5.17	5.40	5.20	5.38	5.29	5.15	5.12	5.08	5.44	5.02	5.18	5.53
0.49	0.49	0.53	0.53	0.55	0.60	0.66	0.72	0.77	0.79	0.82	0.91	0.95	0.58	0.99	1.02	1.11
8.37	8.60	8.71	8.69	8.74	9.24	9.56	10.34	10.56	10.35	10.52	10.75	10.99	11.25	11.61	12.35	13.40
3.47	3.52	3.55	3.58	3.63	3.88	4.01	4.27	4.35	4.24	4.35	4.50	4.63	4.68	4.87	5.22	5.88
4.90	5.07	5.16	5.11	5.10	5.35	5.55	6.07	6.22	6.11	6.17	6.25	6.36	6.57	6.74	7.14	7.52
6.49	6.55	6.65	6.81	6.79	6.98	7.14	7.20	7.28	7.14	7.17	7.29	7.41	7.47	7.46	7.60	7.86
4.97	4.99	5.07	5.19	5.21	5.36	5.49	5.53	5.56	5.42	5.43	5.48	5.57	5.64	5.55	5.63	5.83
1.53	1.56	1.58	1.62	1.58	1.63	1.65	1.67	1.72	1.72	1.73	1.81	1.84	1.84	1.91	1.97	2.04

Chart 2. Health expenditure in OECD countries as a percentage of GDP
(1960-1990)

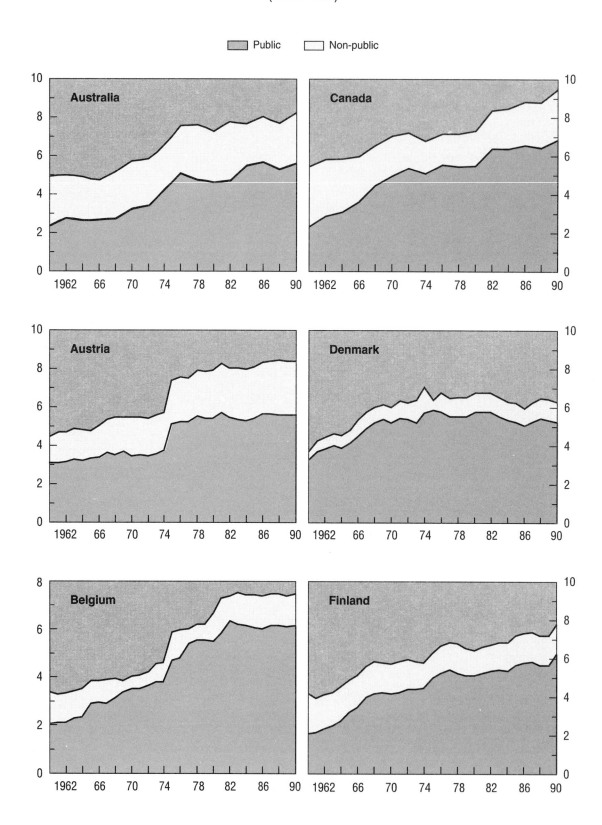

Chart 2 (*cont.*). **Health expenditure in OECD countries as a percentage of GDP**
(1960-1990)

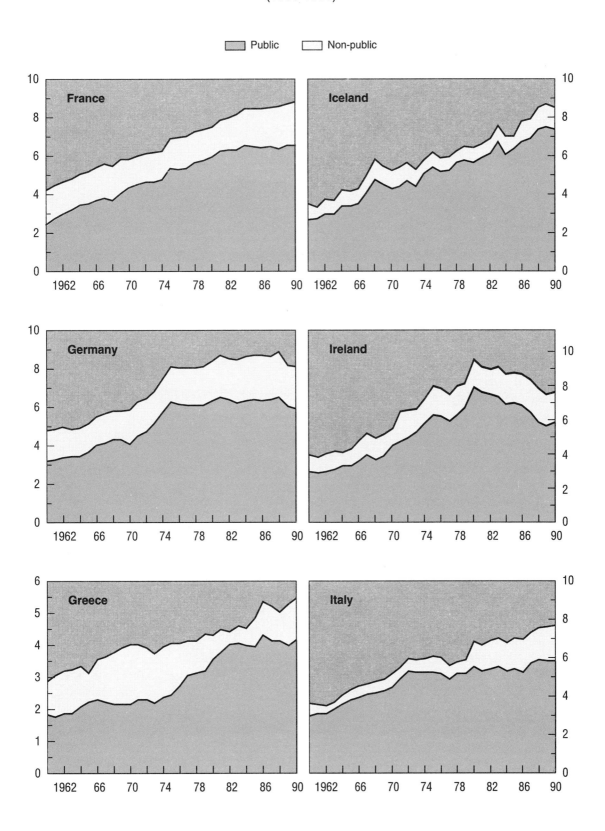

Chart 2 (*cont.*). Health expenditure in OECD countries as a percentage of GDP
(1960-1990)

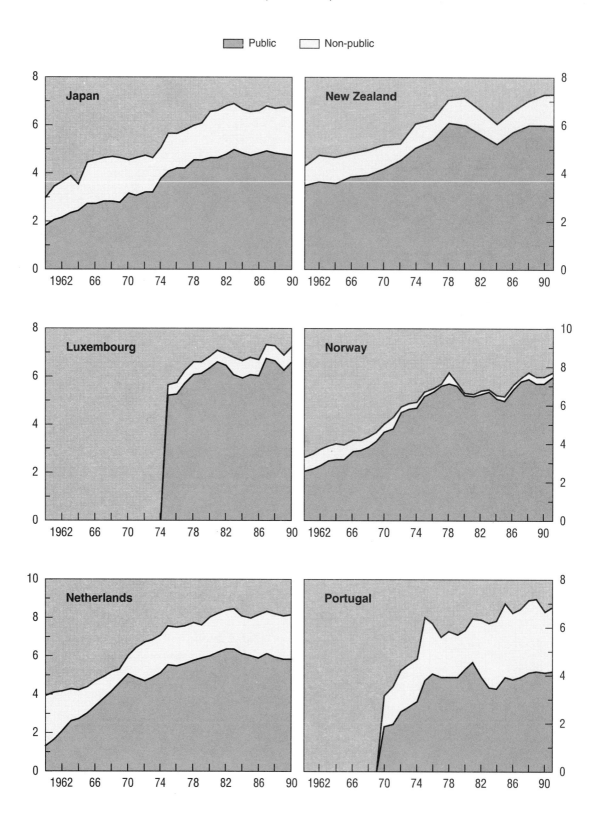

Chart 2 (*cont.*). Health expenditure in OECD countries as a percentage of GDP
(1960-1990)

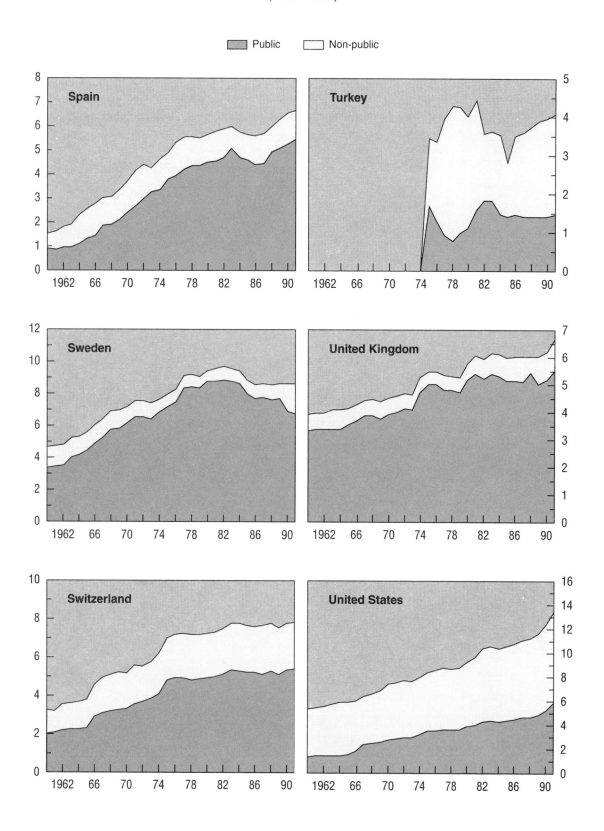

Chart 2 (*cont.*). **Health expenditure as a percentage of GDP**
(OECD average*)

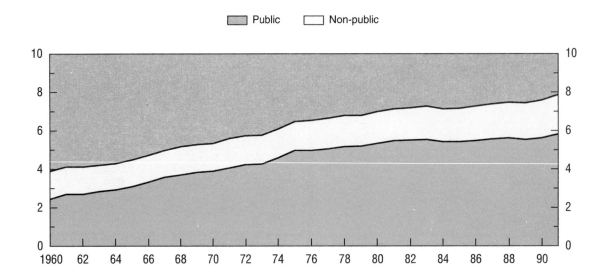

* Unweighted average.
Source : See Table 2.

Table 3. **Distribution of health spending, 1990**

	Share of total health expenditure in total domestic expenditure	Health expenditure per capita in PPPs United States = 100
United States	12.2	100.0
Canada	9.1	67.4
France	8.9	60.1
Sweden	8.8	57.6
Iceland	8.7	52.8
Germany	8.6	57.9
Netherlands	8.5	49.3
Austria	8.5	54.3
Ireland	8.2	31.2
Norway	7.9	45.6
Italy	7.7	48.1
Switzerland	7.7	63.7
Australia	7.7	47.8
Belgium	7.7	47.8
Finland	7.6	49.0
New Zealand	7.3	38.0
Luxembourg	7.2	54.3
Japan	6.7	45.6
Denmark	6.6	41.1
Spain	6.4	30.3
Portugal	6.1	21.7
United Kingdom	6.1	38.0
Greece	4.8	15.7
Turkey	3.8	5.1

Source: OECD Health Systems: Facts and Trends 1960-1991, Paris, 1993.

Table 4. **Personal health care: total medical consumption**

(Per cent)

	In-patient care	Ambulatory medical services	Pharmaceutical goods	Therapeutic appliances
Australia	59.0	28.7	10.0	2.3
Austria	45.5	32.9	17.4	4.3
Belgium	35.9	44.1	18.4	1.6
Canada	57.5	26.4	13.4	2.7
Finland	48.7	37.7	10.2	3.4
France	48.1	31.1	18.2	2.5
Germany	41.3	30.5	22.6	5.6
Italy	48.9	28.8	19.3	2.8
Japan	36.1	38.1	20.7	5.0
Netherlands	59.0	27.1	11.0	2.7
Spain	58.3	14.6	23.2	3.9
United States	52.8	33.8	9.3	2.1

Source: OECD Health Systems: Facts and Trends 1960-1991, Paris, 1993.

Chart 3. Distribution of health spending, 1990

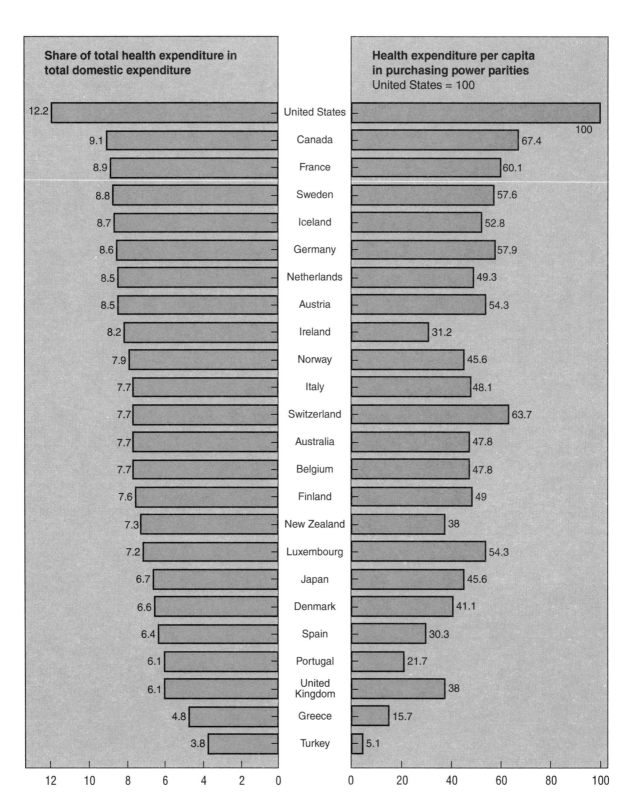

Share of total health expenditure in total domestic expenditure | Country | **Health expenditure per capita in purchasing power parities** United States = 100

Share	Country	Per capita
12.2	United States	100
9.1	Canada	67.4
8.9	France	60.1
8.8	Sweden	57.6
8.7	Iceland	52.8
8.6	Germany	57.9
8.5	Netherlands	49.3
8.5	Austria	54.3
8.2	Ireland	31.2
7.9	Norway	45.6
7.7	Italy	48.1
7.7	Switzerland	63.7
7.7	Australia	47.8
7.7	Belgium	47.8
7.6	Finland	49
7.3	New Zealand	38
7.2	Luxembourg	54.3
6.7	Japan	45.6
6.6	Denmark	41.1
6.4	Spain	30.3
6.1	Portugal	21.7
6.1	United Kingdom	38
4.8	Greece	15.7
3.8	Turkey	5.1

Source: OECD Health Data. See Table 3.

80

Chart 4. **Personal health care: total medical consumption (%)**

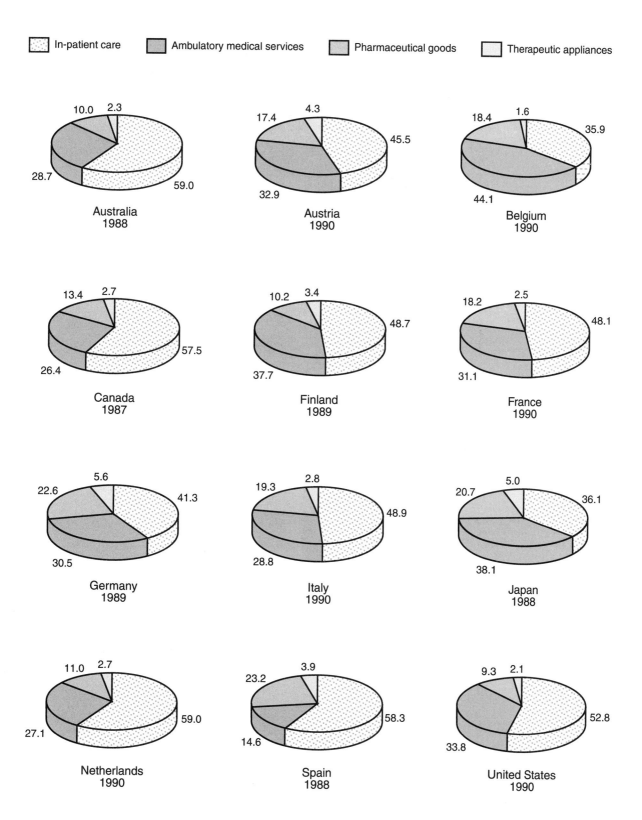

Source: See Table 4.

Males

	1960	1961	1962	1963	1964	1965	1966	1967	1968	1969	1970	1971	1972	1973
Australia														
Diseases of circulatory system	2 161.6	2 162.7	2 218.0	2 209.0	2 275.7	2 239.4	2 197.5	2 235.4	2 236.8	2 211.5	2 147.5	2 110.1	2 067.0	2 037.2
Ischaemic heart diseases	1 442.5	1 467.5	1 534.4	1 577.3	1 616.1	1 604.4	1 587.2	1 620.9	1 561.0	1 567.4	1 514.4	1 509.3	1 492.4	1 454.8
Cerebrovascular diseases	370.5	358.2	347.3	311.8	326.4	334.1	320.7	323.3	350.9	342.3	316.8	295.6	306.1	307.9
Malignant neoplasms	979.7	951.7	992.5	1 016.4	1 010.8	1 017.6	1 041.2	1 016.3	1 031.9	1 075.8	1 076.2	1 069.4	1 073.0	1 046.7
Lung neoplasms	174.3	183.3	193.0	203.1	204.5	201.4	210.1	214.7	217.7	235.8	223.2	239.5	232.4	234.0
Liver cirrhosis	65.6	62.8	78.9	71.8	71.5	70.5	82.8	92.2	109.1	102.0	91.3	113.4	120.0	133.9
Japan														
Diseases of circulatory system	1 584.3	1 555.0	1 562.6	1 501.4	1 440.4	1 442.8	1 387.2	1 351.0	1 372.7	1 330.2	1 331.1	1 278.3	1 206.9	1 198.9
Ischaemic heart diseases	414.7	394.1	405.0	383.4	376.0	382.8	366.3	384.0	217.5	209.6	213.1	201.9	192.2	186.0
Cerebrovascular diseases	905.6	914.5	917.1	897.6	854.9	857.3	830.8	786.2	789.0	761.2	745.0	713.6	669.4	651.9
Malignant neoplasms	1 077.0	1 068.7	1 071.9	1 089.5	1 093.1	1 075.0	1 058.5	1 067.9	1 059.0	1 048.2	1 049.5	1 019.6	1 017.5	1 001.3
Lung neoplasms	59.9	63.9	68.1	68.4	71.6	71.4	73.8	75.0	76.0	77.7	78.1	80.1	80.4	80.0
Liver cirrhosis	135.9	135.4	144.2	150.6	150.8	152.5	156.3	175.4	182.3	192.0	202.1	211.5	217.3	229.1
United States														
Diseases of circulatory system	2 626.5	2 558.9	2 573.0	2 592.4	2 552.0	2 536.1	2 540.3	2 482.2	2 516.4	2 445.6	2 391.8	2 343.1	2 312.1	2 248.9
Ischaemic heart diseases	1 777.0	1 751.0	1 772.4	1 796.7	1 781.6	1 777.2	1 784.9	1 758.5	1 770.6	1 724.3	1 673.9	1 643.5	1 605.6	1 569.0
Cerebrovascular diseases	320.2	306.4	304.9	309.8	304.9	300.6	298.4	287.3	307.1	293.1	291.7	285.1	278.4	260.2
Malignant neoplasms	1 147.9	1 135.1	1 136.1	1 152.7	1 160.2	1 157.7	1 169.9	1 167.7	1 177.7	1 173.2	1 173.0	1 159.8	1 145.8	1 144.0
Lung neoplasms	245.5	251.6	262.9	267.0	277.4	284.9	293.1	299.5	317.3	323.1	331.9	328.5	338.3	338.7
Liver cirrhosis	192.3	195.4	204.2	203.5	211.4	227.4	250.7	260.6	273.7	282.7	292.7	294.7	304.6	301.3
France														
Diseases of circulatory system	1 143.2	1 134.7	1 172.4	1 179.2	1 087.0	1 119.9	1 089.9	1 064.0	1 147.6	1 114.1	1 063.4	1 083.6	1 066.1	1 051.3
Ischaemic heart diseases	350.7	354.7	379.0	391.4	370.4	391.9	390.0	387.3	386.3	363.8	366.4	376.0	380.7	378.5
Cerebrovascular diseases	304.3	305.2	307.8	303.4	276.5	276.7	270.5	262.7	311.5	311.5	280.7	293.6	281.3	279.5
Malignant neoplasms	1 163.1	1 157.6	1 192.3	1 170.3	1 200.2	1 198.9	1 228.1	1 222.2	1 253.5	1 251.4	1 253.3	1 273.6	1 336.8	1 323.6
Lung neoplasms	165.3	169.9	171.9	182.9	183.5	190.9	195.6	192.2	195.3	201.0	197.7	205.8	221.8	226.0
Liver cirrhosis	326.4	330.7	348.9	382.7	363.8	395.2	406.6	414.6	401.9	407.0	388.1	408.9	406.9	421.9
Italy														
Diseases of circulatory system	1 391.3	1 390.3	1 476.2	1 523.5	1 451.5	1 444.7	1 359.1	1 350.0	1 380.7	1 388.0	1 256.0	1 215.9	1 182.2	1 200.0
Ischaemic heart diseases	651.6	657.6	704.5	741.9	742.6	735.8	690.7	696.4	602.2	605.8	575.0	568.6	552.3	581.7
Cerebrovascular diseases	282.9	279.3	290.3	299.8	277.4	281.5	273.4	273.7	273.6	266.0	268.8	256.0	254.6	253.1
Malignant neoplasms	1 182.4	1 173.9	1 189.7	1 210.6	1 219.4	1 234.2	1 225.2	1 225.3	1 268.0	1 267.6	1 260.8	1 285.4	1 291.0	1 275.2
Lung neoplasms	203.4	207.3	213.7	220.1	228.5	236.3	235.2	251.7	261.6	269.7	271.4	290.2	294.3	299.4
Liver cirrhosis	189.8	208.5	227.8	243.1	241.2	277.8	269.7	287.3	313.8	330.4	339.9	354.8	369.4	371.6
Sweden														
Diseases of circulatory system	1 066.2	1 065.9	1 088.7	1 085.5	1 075.5	1 088.8	1 078.3	1 080.8	1 106.7	1 078.1	1 080.9	1 155.8	1 119.7	1 074.1
Ischaemic heart diseases	600.0	629.0	650.0	680.3	669.6	687.6	678.5	681.5	698.6	629.5	684.2	752.5	737.4	744.3
Cerebrovascular diseases	207.8	206.5	193.9	193.8	180.7	191.3	180.3	198.3	188.8	188.0	176.8	208.3	188.6	170.5
Malignant neoplasms	895.7	890.9	885.3	853.3	857.9	846.3	833.0	835.7	834.6	829.1	812.7	912.5	876.6	911.5
Lung neoplasms	93.1	96.5	92.8	90.1	91.6	94.8	87.7	95.8	84.0	103.6	99.4	97.2	105.2	111.0
Liver cirrhosis	35.4	54.0	48.9	55.8	56.5	59.8	71.1	80.7	82.7	112.9	111.2	105.2	137.8	141.3

Source: OECD Health data base, 1992.

82

Males

1974	1975	1976	1977	1978	1979	1980	1981	1982	1983	1984	1985	1986	1987	1988	1989
1 993.1	1 887.7	1 816.2	1 751.4	1 590.3	1 578.9	1 489.8	1 405.8	1 341.3	1 256.5	1 182.9	1 153.7	1 079.6	990.5	957.8	957.8
1 417.8	1 358.6	1 301.0	1 259.5	1 148.3	1 082.7	1 010.2	960.9	935.7	880.0	827.5	782.8	746.1	687.3	660.9	660.9
288.4	289.4	256.8	236.3	219.4	231.1	207.6	196.1	172.2	162.9	148.8	154.3	138.1	121.0	106.5	106.5
1 086.3	1 045.7	1 035.3	992.9	1 037.9	987.3	1 034.0	1 044.4	1 021.9	990.7	988.9	1 004.7	936.6	906.8	924.3	924.3
254.5	249.8	246.1	223.4	238.2	226.1	242.8	243.9	225.4	234.1	223.3	225.3	197.6	199.7	197.3	197.3
149.8	154.7	156.7	172.8	158.0	152.9	148.2	150.5	142.7	132.1	127.0	114.5	115.9	115.0	109.0	109.0
1 169.8	1 112.2	1 085.7	1 043.1	999.2	992.9	1 002.9	943.2	899.6	874.3	851.3	821.5	793.7	752.1	756.4	719.2
187.1	169.6	168.6	165.3	159.5	156.0	160.0	151.0	143.1	142.4	133.9	127.5	117.3	111.0	109.3	104.8
621.4	580.7	558.8	532.1	500.4	459.4	449.5	418.9	387.2	368.3	338.7	320.1	301.9	269.9	274.7	251.2
995.5	993.5	1 000.3	994.1	981.9	986.9	985.6	973.2	953.3	960.4	951.3	940.7	927.2	920.6	886.9	887.7
83.9	86.6	88.4	91.4	90.0	94.8	98.0	97.6	98.4	100.2	103.4	102.1	102.0	102.5	101.5	106.2
231.6	231.8	235.1	223.9	229.5	231.0	220.1	210.5	200.8	201.1	189.4	184.5	171.7	156.2	152.5	144.4
2 125.9	2 015.1	1 964.4	1 886.5	1 831.8	1 738.1	1 706.2	1 658.9	1 597.8	1 565.4	1 513.8	1 481.5	1 428.4	1 378.4	1 323.4	1 249.8
1 480.8	1 411.9	1 360.8	1 305.1	1 253.7	1 079.2	1 044.1	1 010.2	969.1	917.5	870.8	838.6	781.4	736.1	685.6	654.0
246.5	223.7	214.8	200.2	189.4	176.4	167.9	162.3	154.6	150.4	149.0	143.0	137.7	137.5	137.2	127.7
1 138.6	1 109.2	1 105.2	1 108.2	1 095.7	1 083.1	1 089.1	1 067.0	1 064.1	1 048.0	1 042.0	1 036.2	1 021.9	999.4	988.5	974.2
345.2	341.1	343.2	343.9	346.2	341.8	343.1	342.7	335.4	326.6	326.6	321.4	314.6	312.6	305.2	297.9
297.0	277.0	273.4	259.5	243.5	239.0	237.1	216.8	201.3	192.3	187.3	181.2	173.1	174.9	173.5	169.8
1 077.4	1 069.4	1 032.6	977.9	971.8	993.9	944.3	888.2	871.9	855.0	847.6	843.7	827.0	778.2	721.0	682.6
401.7	410.3	411.7	397.7	396.3	385.1	369.8	353.5	350.8	338.8	348.3	345.5	347.1	314.1	301.4	273.1
276.5	263.3	245.3	233.9	226.0	226.4	221.6	200.3	191.0	194.4	189.1	181.9	175.0	165.6	141.7	143.7
1 388.0	1 369.7	1 408.7	1 417.9	1 443.1	1 409.1	1 438.1	1 429.0	1 423.9	1 406.5	1 409.1	1 422.5	1 412.3	1 374.2	1 353.2	1 343.9
242.2	242.8	260.4	260.1	278.5	280.2	288.1	290.7	285.5	294.6	292.9	300.6	312.8	310.2	315.8	311.0
399.1	413.5	414.4	398.9	378.9	359.7	336.0	324.0	324.7	306.9	297.2	275.0	256.6	238.3	233.7	221.0
1 254.8	1 279.7	1 267.1	1 234.3	1 251.0	1 198.5	1 141.7	1 113.4	1 069.0	1 074.3	1 020.1	976.1	911.2	888.5	809.5	784.9
621.7	641.6	659.1	646.2	669.2	626.4	569.3	560.3	535.9	532.4	495.2	473.6	451.7	439.9	402.9	391.7
258.7	266.1	256.2	253.7	264.0	240.4	238.8	231.3	221.5	217.6	215.3	202.8	192.2	188.6	163.3	157.2
1 290.1	1 293.3	1 295.3	1 328.1	1 323.7	1 327.3	1 334.5	1 300.1	1 287.4	1 304.2	1 260.9	1 237.2	1 229.3	1 220.3	1 179.9	1 122.9
316.7	317.1	334.2	342.6	358.1	365.0	375.9	362.5	363.2	377.1	358.9	351.9	343.3	344.8	330.5	315.1
366.2	377.8	390.9	379.4	381.0	381.9	365.9	343.5	332.2	334.9	317.4	294.9	273.5	240.1	235.1	225.3
1 120.5	1 090.8	1 137.0	1 128.0	1 171.5	1 127.5	1 131.9	1 123.8	1 074.7	1 012.9	964.4	1 009.5	953.1	940.0	903.2	801.8
755.6	730.4	766.9	789.6	783.9	795.0	768.2	797.6	741.8	688.1	656.2	676.3	642.3	610.5	569.7	513.5
199.3	184.8	191.1	167.5	177.8	150.5	155.9	159.4	134.4	130.6	114.0	135.8	111.2	116.5	121.2	106.2
864.3	859.2	850.4	828.5	847.0	810.6	804.3	790.3	759.8	735.9	739.7	731.6	682.3	698.1	699.9	683.3
120.2	119.0	115.2	125.9	129.7	127.7	117.2	114.5	124.3	122.6	126.5	125.4	108.2	113.7	117.6	112.1
149.0	169.5	186.2	174.2	178.0	196.7	157.5	133.4	116.8	88.7	100.5	82.7	97.1	77.8	71.8	84.6

Females

	1960	1961	1962	1963	1964	1965	1966	1967	1968	1969	1970	1971	1972	1973
Australia														
Diseases of circulatory system	1 082.0	980.9	1 000.3	987.8	1 053.4	1 032.1	1 018.7	996.3	995.1	929.8	988.6	959.9	907.5	858.8
Ischaemic heart diseases	408.8	377.2	415.2	406.4	448.3	435.4	436.6	442.7	415.9	391.1	410.1	420.3	393.7	374.7
Cerebrovascular diseases	366.0	346.8	339.2	319.4	354.0	340.4	337.4	314.5	322.0	292.0	333.3	314.2	299.3	291.5
Malignant neoplasms	983.7	957.7	952.4	1 046.0	982.1	951.0	976.9	947.2	993.6	960.9	996.0	994.2	981.3	962.5
Lung neoplasms	32.4	29.6	29.2	32.2	38.8	34.3	44.5	46.4	44.3	41.7	52.7	58.6	54.7	58.5
Breast cancer	202.7	222.9	206.2	229.7	217.6	204.6	207.3	212.6	218.0	215.6	219.9	236.7	220.1	221.8
Japan														
Diseases of circulatory system	1 193.2	1 134.0	1 086.2	1 019.2	956.5	933.8	862.8	835.8	825.6	789.2	763.9	702.4	661.1	652.4
Ischaemic heart diseases	339.3	316.6	301.1	272.0	259.8	262.0	231.4	233.8	81.5	80.8	80.5	70.6	68.4	66.5
Cerebrovascular diseases	588.5	572.1	551.6	543.6	497.2	477.5	458.7	434.8	414.6	407.5	383.1	357.9	340.0	326.0
Malignant neoplasms	1 039.8	1 033.9	1 020.5	1 022.3	1 004.9	991.4	990.4	970.4	954.5	938.8	924.2	913.3	899.5	886.1
Lung neoplasms	30.4	35.4	35.1	33.6	35.0	37.0	37.6	40.1	37.9	38.7	37.1	37.1	38.2	37.4
Breast cancer	55.4	56.3	56.0	59.4	57.6	60.2	62.5	60.5	62.2	60.6	65.7	71.8	70.2	73.1
United States														
Diseases of circulatory system	1 167.6	1 123.5	1 134.1	1 136.1	1 116.0	1 098.1	1 082.5	1 060.5	1 080.1	1 026.2	1 004.1	992.1	963.8	949.8
Ischaemic heart diseases	447.0	436.5	450.3	461.5	452.4	448.7	449.5	442.8	481.1	456.0	451.1	444.1	426.1	421.5
Cerebrovascular diseases	285.7	274.6	282.1	272.6	272.7	265.9	257.5	261.8	270.3	257.8	250.8	248.3	237.6	238.0
Malignant neoplasms	1 149.0	1 142.9	1 132.5	1 131.5	1 129.6	1 125.5	1 116.2	1 109.3	1 110.3	1 090.0	1 089.0	1 073.8	1 063.7	1 054.3
Lung neoplasms	46.1	49.3	52.5	58.6	59.7	65.9	69.4	75.3	84.0	90.7	97.7	104.2	112.0	112.6
Breast cancer	261.7	259.0	259.6	260.3	269.0	267.1	266.9	268.6	273.0	264.6	270.5	262.0	265.5	263.7
France														
Diseases of circulatory system	609.0	588.1	611.8	592.0	533.7	531.3	490.8	491.2	496.7	490.3	477.8	468.1	455.9	424.4
Ischaemic heart diseases	79.4	78.8	85.3	80.3	77.7	82.9	74.6	80.6	69.2	69.3	70.4	68.5	69.9	61.9
Cerebrovascular diseases	209.0	201.9	201.3	195.8	175.1	175.2	159.5	160.2	173.6	172.4	166.9	169.9	160.5	153.3
Malignant neoplasms	982.6	933.6	936.4	932.4	923.3	920.2	930.4	885.5	910.2	885.8	863.1	867.7	887.9	868.3
Lung neoplasms	29.7	28.8	28.8	30.9	29.3	28.0	30.6	31.4	28.2	24.4	24.7	24.7	25.2	23.2
Breast cancer	177.0	158.2	166.8	176.9	173.1	182.9	189.4	187.0	192.6	186.9	191.7	191.9	204.0	201.6
Italy														
Diseases of circulatory system	937.8	909.1	947.4	922.8	829.3	844.2	783.5	790.4	788.2	755.3	670.1	624.6	601.4	603.6
Ischaemic heart diseases	255.4	249.8	250.8	261.2	219.5	225.9	211.3	213.2	135.4	135.6	124.0	120.2	116.8	121.5
Cerebrovascular diseases	215.7	214.5	213.9	213.6	202.4	204.9	191.2	192.2	194.4	185.1	183.8	175.0	176.4	175.2
Malignant neoplasms	1 034.0	1 010.9	1 034.6	1 046.3	1 033.0	1 026.6	1 013.2	1 009.3	1 007.1	1 030.2	1 003.2	982.8	1 011.3	991.3
Lung neoplasms	37.7	38.1	38.5	38.7	41.2	38.1	42.1	39.9	39.6	39.0	39.8	37.6	40.9	44.8
Breast cancer	182.7	189.6	189.4	190.5	193.1	201.8	198.9	209.3	204.0	219.0	220.3	223.2	228.4	227.5
Sweden														
Diseases of circulatory system	560.7	576.5	551.0	545.9	512.0	526.6	470.2	465.4	487.4	448.0	398.8	446.5	392.9	401.3
Ischaemic heart diseases	165.6	153.0	161.9	162.7	158.8	180.3	165.7	157.3	159.7	133.8	141.4	153.2	142.1	138.4
Cerebrovascular diseases	179.7	200.5	179.9	172.6	168.5	159.0	143.6	153.2	163.8	150.6	145.0	175.2	147.8	160.9
Malignant neoplasms	1 124.0	1 023.7	989.3	1 006.1	1 037.2	974.9	993.3	953.4	970.9	994.3	965.1	986.9	997.0	937.7
Lung neoplasms	25.7	33.0	25.1	28.9	18.8	31.6	26.1	31.6	33.7	37.5	38.3	38.8	32.9	38.4
Breast cancer	210.9	197.0	194.1	186.5	201.4	179.8	198.8	189.6	191.4	195.7	179.9	194.0	203.2	208.7

Source: OECD Health data base, 1992.

Females

1974	1975	1976	1977	1978	1979	1980	1981	1982	1983	1984	1985	1986	1987	1988	1989
899.0	836.7	744.7	729.2	676.5	615.8	560.4	528.7	512.6	484.4	431.8	442.3	410.9	356.0	345.9	345.9
412.2	383.0	342.4	326.5	305.9	271.7	252.9	251.0	241.9	234.5	194.8	196.1	187.9	171.8	149.5	149.5
285.5	268.7	236.5	236.2	217.3	192.2	174.6	149.9	142.8	142.9	123.4	133.3	103.2	91.9	92.8	92.8
932.4	933.8	918.9	943.9	898.9	859.0	896.4	860.3	893.0	885.2	876.2	918.5	887.2	862.6	838.7	838.7
53.6	56.1	62.3	69.6	63.0	65.7	72.5	66.1	69.8	75.0	77.6	76.5	83.1	73.9	78.0	78.0
214.0	215.6	225.8	234.4	223.4	201.8	206.9	218.2	228.8	215.0	219.6	238.8	227.8	229.9	221.0	221.0
625.9	589.4	558.9	525.3	498.3	492.8	480.8	456.0	438.9	427.8	412.0	394.8	378.0	364.5	347.6	330.8
63.8	57.1	49.9	51.4	44.6	44.2	44.7	42.5	40.9	39.2	37.6	34.1	32.0	30.8	29.3	27.5
313.6	297.0	282.1	265.4	249.4	239.5	229.0	214.1	206.4	198.5	186.8	173.2	165.4	155.6	146.4	135.2
861.9	854.4	834.4	816.0	807.6	785.8	771.3	762.4	731.1	723.5	718.6	697.5	680.3	665.9	668.9	659.3
37.2	39.4	38.4	39.5	40.0	39.5	40.1	41.8	41.5	41.3	43.9	40.8	43.5	43.4	44.0	44.2
75.3	77.7	76.4	78.3	79.5	81.0	83.9	85.5	81.0	83.0	89.2	88.1	91.5	88.6	96.1	96.7
883.0	825.2	791.4	765.9	746.9	691.7	695.5	681.1	647.1	644.4	630.6	616.3	606.7	591.0	575.1	537.6
391.4	367.6	351.4	341.4	328.1	272.0	267.9	263.6	255.6	246.0	236.6	227.8	215.0	209.6	200.0	186.7
214.6	199.2	189.6	173.4	164.6	150.6	147.0	143.5	133.1	129.2	127.1	120.9	117.7	115.8	112.7	107.6
1 045.2	1 016.1	1 006.4	995.3	986.4	966.3	968.8	954.7	956.0	944.1	943.0	934.2	924.2	910.4	900.9	890.9
117.6	123.5	128.8	136.0	140.6	141.5	146.3	148.0	152.7	156.5	155.6	157.5	156.2	158.2	159.5	157.5
261.5	253.9	250.8	255.4	250.1	245.9	247.3	244.8	245.0	239.5	246.1	244.1	242.5	239.2	239.8	236.5
430.9	412.1	396.9	372.1	351.9	348.1	343.3	315.5	304.4	310.0	287.1	279.3	275.8	263.3	252.4	237.8
63.1	63.3	62.1	58.6	56.7	55.9	54.8	51.0	50.8	49.8	48.3	50.3	49.2	47.4	45.5	42.1
158.0	148.6	138.5	138.1	126.9	119.5	121.6	109.7	106.2	112.4	103.7	95.1	90.3	90.6	80.7	78.4
874.7	843.0	849.1	822.3	827.7	814.5	821.9	795.6	781.3	790.9	791.8	761.6	754.0	762.2	741.2	743.9
26.0	25.3	27.3	27.3	27.7	28.3	28.7	28.4	28.8	28.9	28.8	30.2	30.9	36.8	38.2	37.3
205.9	205.2	203.5	194.6	195.7	202.1	200.3	204.5	213.8	205.9	209.5	199.9	211.7	204.5	207.7	206.6
583.0	571.2	560.5	532.2	510.1	483.5	455.8	440.4	422.4	423.6	399.7	377.3	357.9	343.2	316.4	298.2
121.3	121.5	123.4	122.7	125.0	113.0	101.7	97.5	93.7	92.9	83.0	80.8	77.4	75.6	75.9	69.3
175.5	173.9	173.5	175.3	166.6	158.3	141.9	147.1	143.6	142.3	143.9	127.6	125.5	114.0	109.0	103.1
979.9	957.2	943.1	939.2	915.2	931.0	906.7	895.8	882.5	889.3	866.3	843.7	862.9	851.8	839.7	823.6
44.1	41.8	44.1	45.9	42.4	46.0	44.1	43.7	44.2	44.8	46.2	45.9	48.6	48.0	47.6	49.7
226.8	220.4	222.9	218.6	229.0	222.8	220.2	226.9	225.2	231.6	231.7	222.3	223.3	233.1	231.7	235.1
377.2	411.3	393.1	396.2	352.2	360.8	349.0	327.6	352.0	309.2	315.6	293.3	281.5	300.4	308.1	272.1
142.1	166.0	144.6	143.1	136.8	147.6	138.9	130.2	123.2	128.6	118.9	119.7	101.6	111.3	113.9	107.0
145.0	156.5	157.1	148.3	112.9	117.1	122.4	115.1	123.9	88.2	106.1	86.3	90.6	85.6	86.6	74.2
960.1	941.8	898.5	928.6	902.5	875.4	878.9	821.8	863.7	849.1	802.7	823.3	825.0	804.4	799.6	777.1
40.5	42.2	45.9	49.8	46.5	46.5	58.4	63.3	60.5	63.0	63.1	66.8	76.0	80.9	77.6	68.5
206.4	195.5	177.3	201.5	164.2	178.1	196.9	178.2	189.1	195.7	189.8	187.9	182.2	179.0	202.5	191.6

Chart 5. **Declining trends in avoidable premature death, 1950-1990**
(per 100 000 years of life, males and females aged 0-64)

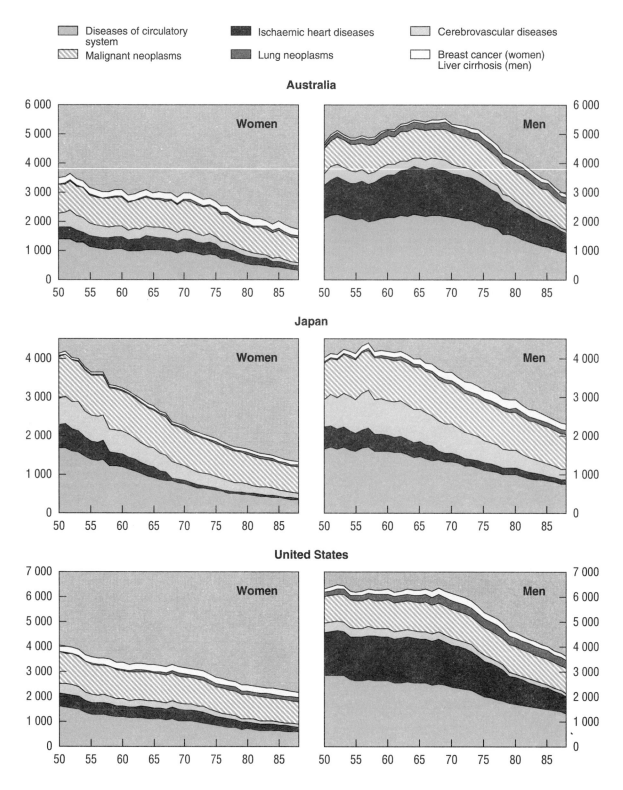

Note: The number of years under the age of 65 lost by premature death associated with disease considered avoidable by the widespread use of medical knowledge and its social application.

Chart 5 (*cont.*). **Declining trends in avoidable premature death, 1950-1990**
(per 100 000 years of life, males and females aged 0-64)

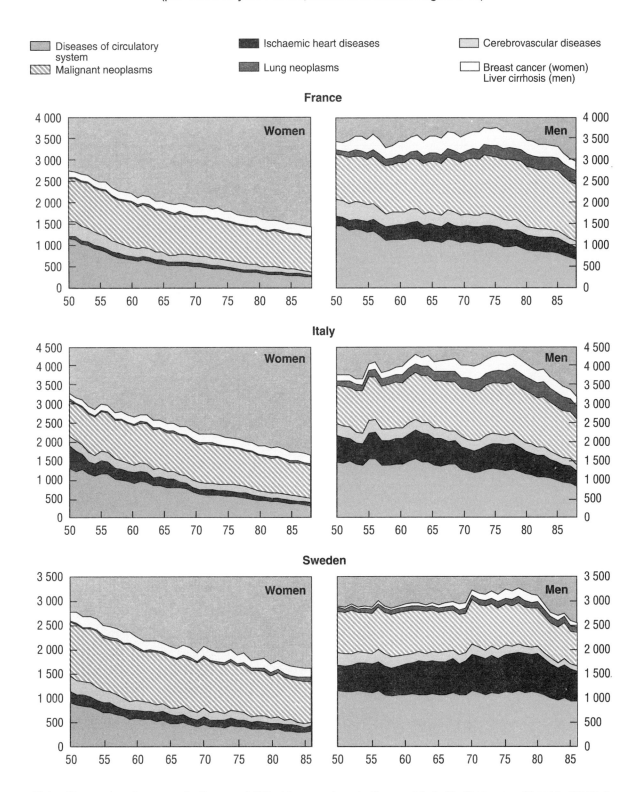

Note: The number of years under the age of 65 lost by premature death associated with disease considered avoidable by the widespread use of medical knowledge and its social application.
Source: See Table 5.

Table 6. **Smoking habits, 1970-1990**

(% of relevant population aged 15 and over)

	Females		Males	
	1970	1990	1970	1990
Canada	30.0	26.9	49.0	29.5
Denmark	46.5	40.3	68.3	47.1
Finland	16.0	21.0	44.0	36.0
Japan	15.6	14.3	77.5	60.5
Netherlands	42.0	31.0	75.0	39.0
United Kingdom[a]	41.0	29.0	52.0	31.0
United States	31.1	22.8	43.5	28.4

a) United Kingdom data = 1972.

Source: OECD Health data base, 1992.

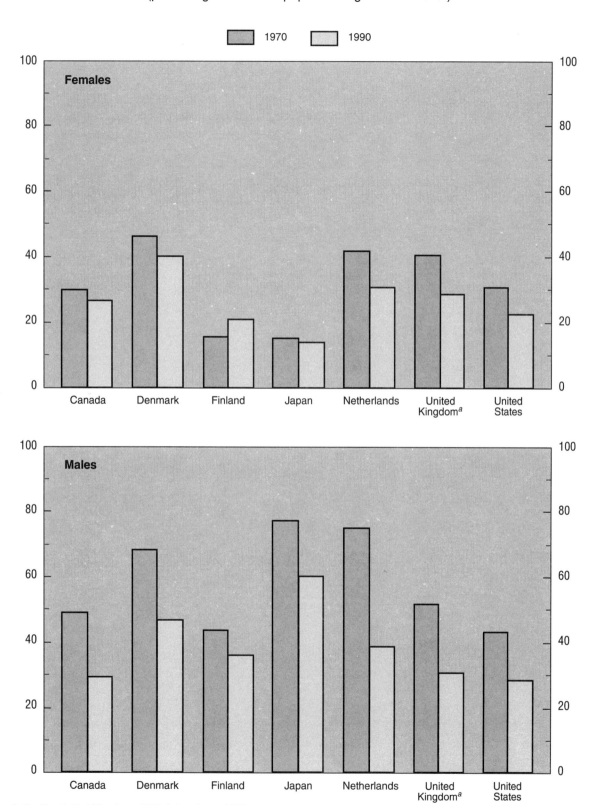

Chart 6. **Smoking habits, 1970-1990**
(percentage of relevant population aged 15 and over)

a) For the United Kingdom, 1970 data refer to 1972.
Source: See Table 6.

89

Table 7. **Average retirement age in public old-age schemes in OECD countries, 1960-1990**

		1960	1970	1975	1980	1983/84	1987	1990
ʊria								
Employees and	males	–	64.2	64.3	62.5	62.1[a]	61.7	62.0
self-employed	females	–	61.5	61.5	59.5	59.5[a]	59.4	59.6
Belgium								
Employees	males	–	–	–	63.2	63.3	–	–
	females	–	–	–	60.1	60.7	–	–
Canada								
Canadian Pension Plan	males	–	66.7	66.2	65.2	65.1	63.3	63.3
	females	–	66.7	66.0	65.2	65.1	63.0	63.1
Finland[d]								
	males	–	65.2	65.0	63.2	62.0[a]	64.9	61.9
	females	–	65.1	64.9	64.0	62.8[a]	64.5	62.5
Germany								
Blue-collar workers	males	65.2	65.2	64.0	62.6	62.6[a]	62.7	62.7
	females	64.0	63.4	63.2	63.2	63.6[a]	64.2	63.8
White-collar workers	males	65.2	65.1	64.3	62.7	62.9[a]	62.9	63.0
	females	62.8	63.0	62.7	61.7	62.5[a]	62.9	63.1
France								
Employees	workers	–	64.0	63.6	63.4	62.4[b]	62.4	62.0
(general scheme)	survivors	–	68.4	65.2	64.9	64.6[b]	64.5	64.8
Japan								
Employees	males	–	–	–	62.2	61.6[a]	62.1	62.1
	females	–	–	–	60.0	59.4[a]	60.4	61.0
Self-employed	males	–	–	–	63.1	62.7[a]	63.4	64.1
	females	–	–	–	62.6	62.5[a]	63.0	63.7
Luxembourg								
Employees	males	63.4	63.3	63.9	62.5	60.6	–	–
	females	66.0	64.9	70.4	64.3	63.0	–	–
Portugal								
Employees	males	–	–	69.1	66.5	67.0[b]	66.9	65.8
(general scheme)	females	–	–	70.5	64.6	63.4[b]	63.9	63.6
United Kingdom								
Category A pensions	males	–	–	65.7	65.6	65.5[a]	65.4	65.5[c]
	females	–	–	61.0	60.4	61.5[a]	61.0	61.0[c]
United States								
Employees	males	66.8	64.4	64.0	63.9	63.6	63.6	63.7
	females	65.2	63.9	63.7	63.5	63.3	63.3	63.5

a) 1985.
b) 1984.
c) 1988.
d) Data up to 1984 cover the basic old-age pension. Data for 1987 and 1990 are weighted averages for the basic pension and early old-age pension.
Sources: OECD, *Reforming Public Pensions*, Paris, 1998, Table 7.1; CNAV, *Recueil Statistique 1986-1997*, Paris; submissions by national authorities.

Chart 7. Average age of receipt of public pensions, 1975-1989/90

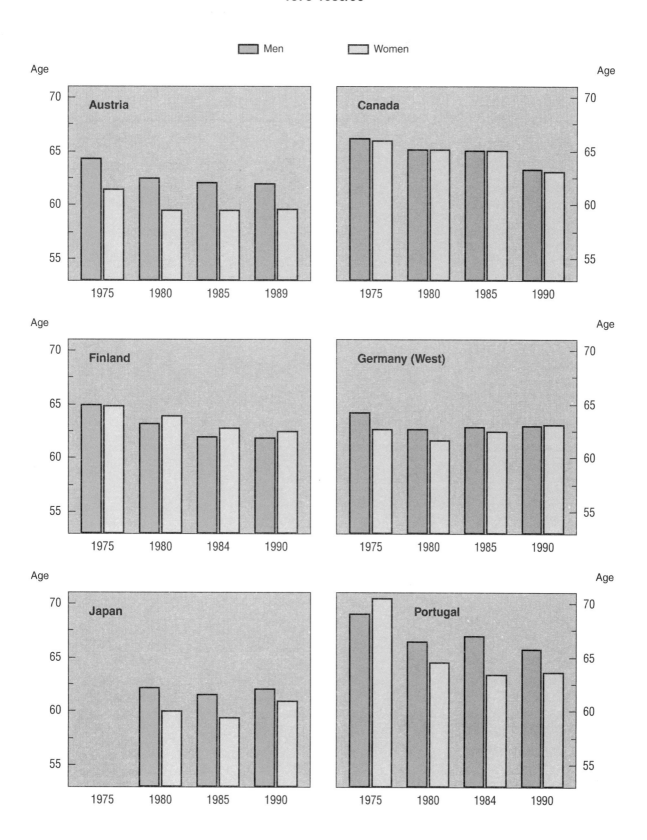

Chart 7 (*cont.*). **Average age of receipt of public pensions,
1975-1989/90**

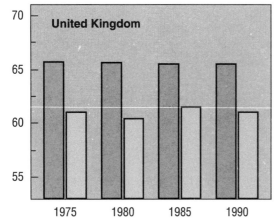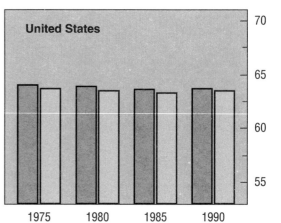

Schemes covered:
Austria: Old-age pensions (employed and self-employed).
Canada: Canada Pension Plan, old-age pensions.
Finland: National pension insurance, all categories.
Germany (West): Old-age pensions (white-collar workers).
Japan: Old-age pensions, employees.
Portugal: Old-age pensions (general scheme).
United Kingdom: Old-age pensions, category A pensions.
United States: Old-age pensions, out of OASDHI.
Source: National sources.

Table 8. **Part-time employment as a percentage of total employment, 1989-1990**

	Males					
	Early 1980s			1989-1990		
	55-59	60-64	All ages	55-59	60-64	All ages
Australia	5.0	9.6	5.4	9.0	14.3	7.8
Belgium	2.3	4.3	2.0	1.7	2.8	2.0
Canada	— 2.8 —		6.6	3.9	7.6	2.0
Denmark	5.0	7.7	6.6	2.9	17.7	10.4
Finland	5.3	16.7	4.5	7.0	16.1	4.6
France	3.0	8.4	2.5	5.5	14.8	3.3
Germany	1.3	5.1	1.7	1.8	6.5	2.6
Greece	3.1	5.2	3.7	2.0	3.4	2.2
Ireland	2.6	3.1	2.7	3.2	3.9	3.4
Italy	3.3	7.3	2.4	2.7	4.6	2.4
Japan	8.9	16.7	7.2	7.8	18.7	7.9
Netherlands	7.5	12.4	6.9	14.8	27.6	15.0
Norway	11.8	15.1	12.5	6.6	9.7	8.2
Sweden	4.2	25.8	7.0	6.2	30.5	7.3
United Kingdom	2.0	5.4	3.3	4.7	12.4	5.2
United States	3.1	7.0	8.0	6.0	14.4	10.0

	Females					
	Early 1980s			1989-1990		
	55-59	60-64	All ages	55-59	60-64	All ages
Australia	40.8	48.7	34.4	45.3	58.8	56.6
Belgium	21.7	26.6	19.7	24.1	30.2	25.8
Canada	— 25.5 —		24.8	26.7	33.9	27.2
Denmark	54.8	60.1	44.7	44.5	60.3	38.4
Finland	15.2	24.4	12.5	13.7	24.1	10.3
France	26.9	30.9	20.1	30.3	34.6	23.6
Germany	34.1	37.9	30.0	42.5	47.1	33.8
Greece	13.6	15.2	12.1	8.1	10.1	10.8
Ireland	26.8	23.0	15.6	27.2	25.3	17.6
Italy	14.2	17.4	9.4	10.5	10.3	9.6
Japan	31.7	41.0	29.0	33.8	43.1	31.7
Netherlands	65.9	67.0	50.3	76.5	80.1	59.2
Norway	63.1	61.4	57.4	59.3	56.8	48.2
Sweden	50.3	65.3	46.4	45.8	61.2	40.5
United Kingdom	48.9	65.9	42.1	54.0	71.2	42.6
United States	19.3	25.8	23.5	24.9	33.6	25.5

Sources: National sources; Eurostat.

Chart 8. **Proportion of employment that is part-time in 1989/90**

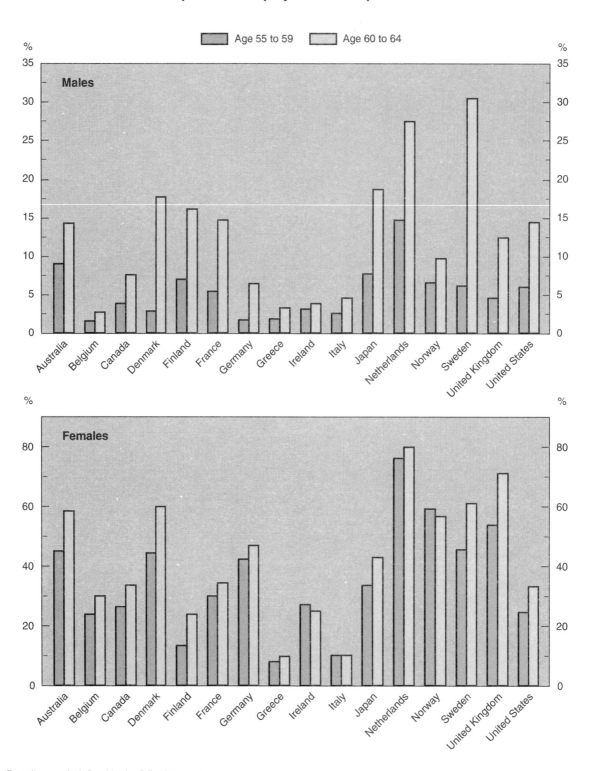

Part-time work defined in the following way:
– less than 37 hours per week: Norway;
– less than 35 hours per week: Australia, Japan, Sweden;
– less than 30 hours per week: Canada, Finland;
– based on self-description: remaining countries (EC countries).
Source: National sources, Eurostat.

Table 9. **Age-specific employment rates by cohort**[a]

Finland

A. Employment/population ratios at ages

Born in:	Men					Women				
	40-44	45-49	50-54	55-59	60-64	40-44	45-49	50-54	55-59	60-64
1901-05					72.4					47.4
1906-10				85.8	65.0				60.4	31.3
1911-15				79.3	55.1				56.8	27.8
1916-20			69.8	74.2	41.4			63.4	56.7	26.2
1921-25		82.2	71.1	65.2	35.6		70.7	66.7	53.8	29.7
1926-30		92.0	80.0	59.4	28.2		74.1	71.5	55.3	19.7
1931-35		82.1	73.2	59.3			80.7	80.5	57.7	
1936-40		77.6	73.9				87.2	81.6		
1941-45		59.6					88.6			
1946-50										

B. Per cent leaving employment over previous five years

Born in:	Men					Women				
	40-44	45-49	50-54	55-59	60-64	40-44	45-49	50-54	55-59	60-64
1901-05										
1906-10					–24.3					–48.2
1911-15					–30.5					–51.1
1916-20				6.4	–44.3				–10.5	–53.7
1921-25			–13.5	–8.3	–45.4			–5.7	–19.2	–44.8
1926-30			–13.1	–25.8	–52.5			–3.5	–22.7	–64.4
1931-35			–10.8	–19.0				–0.4	–28.3	
1936-40			–4.9					–6.5		
1941-45										
1946-50										

France

A. Employment/population ratios at ages

Born in:	Men					Women				
	40-44	45-49	50-54	55-59	60-64	40-44	45-49	50-54	55-59	60-64
1901-05										
1906-10					66.6					33.2
1911-15				81.5	55.1				44.8	28.9
1916-20			92.4	81.3	44.9			49.2	41.9	25.7
1921-25		95.5	91.8	77.4	29.4		49.6	50.5	44.4	17.6
1926-30	96.5	94.1	90.4	62.6	22.0	48.6	52.9	51.7	39.4	16.2
1931-35	95.7	94.1	86.1	62.9		52.7	55.6	53.6	41.6	
1936-40	95.2	91.3	85.3			58.7	62.3	57.1		
1941-45	92.2	92.0				64.6	63.7			
1946-50	92.3					68.4				

B. Per cent leaving employment over previous five years

Born in:	Men					Women				
	40-44	45-49	50-54	55-59	60-64	40-44	45-49	50-54	55-59	60-64
1901-05										
1906-10										
1911-15					–32.4					–35.4
1916-20				–12.0	–44.7				–14.7	–38.7
1921-25			–3.8	–15.7	–62.0			1.8	–12.1	–60.3
1926-30		–2.5	–3.9	–30.7	–64.8	8.8	–2.3		–23.8	–58.9
1931-35		–1.7	–8.5	–26.9		5.5	–3.7		–22.4	
1936-40		–4.2	–6.6			6.2	–8.4			
1941-45		–0.2				–1.4				
1946-50										

a) See notes at the end of the table.
Source: OECD, *Labour Force Statistics 1970-1991*, Paris, 1992, Part III.

Table 9. **Age-specific employment rates by cohort**[a] *(cont.)*

West Germany

A. Employment/population ratios at ages

	Men					Women				
	40-44	45-49	50-54	55-59	60-64	40-44	45-49	50-54	55-59	60-64
Born in:										
1901-05										
1906-10					70.1					20.2
1911-15				87.5	55.2				36.1	15.2
1916-20			94.2	82.7	41.4			43.4	37.2	11.8
1921-25		96.4	90.2	78.3	31.7		48.4	47.3	37.5	9.8
1926-30	98.3	93.8	90.5	70.7	31.8	48.5	50.9	47.1	33.7	9.5
1931-35	94.8	94.5	87.9	69.1		49.9	52.4	46.2	34.3	
1936-40	96.0	92.6	85.8			54.6	53.4	49.3		
1941-45	93.8	90.1				57.1	58.1			
1946-50	90.8					60.2				

B. Per cent leaving employment over previous five years

	Men					Women				
	40-44	45-49	50-54	55-59	60-64	40-44	45-49	50-54	55-59	60-64
Born in:										
1901-05										
1906-10										
1911-15					-37.0					-57.8
1916-20				-12.2	-49.9				-14.2	-68.4
1921-25			-6.4	-13.1	-59.6			-2.2	-20.6	-73.9
1926-30		-4.5	-3.6	-21.8	-55.0		5.1	-7.4	-28.5	-71.7
1931-35		-0.4	-6.9	-21.4			4.9	-11.9	-25.7	
1936-40		-3.6	-7.3				-2.2	-7.7		
1941-45		-4.0					1.8			
1946-50										

Japan

A. Employment/population ratios at ages

	Men					Women				
	40-44	45-49	50-54	55-59	60-64	40-44	45-49	50-54	55-59	60-64
Born in:										
1901-05										
1906-10					79.8					39.1
1911-15				89.2	76.8				48.7	37.6
1916-20			94.9	89.3	74.2			58.5	48.1	38.4
1921-25		96.2	94.6	88.4	67.4		62.7	57.1	49.8	37.9
1926-30	96.7	95.3	94.6	86.8	69.2	62.6	60.7	58.5	49.9	39.0
1931-35	96.1	95.3	93.6	89.9		59.2	63.5	60.0	53.2	
1936-40	96.6	95.4	95.3			63.2	66.9	64.5		
1941-45	95.6	96.2				66.6	70.6			
1946-50	96.4					68.4				

B. Per cent leaving employment over previous five years

	Men					Women				
	40-44	45-49	50-54	55-59	60-64	40-44	45-49	50-54	55-59	60-64
Born in:										
1901-05										
1906-10										
1911-15					-13.9					-22.8
1916-20				-5.9	-16.9				-17.8	-20.1
1921-25			-1.7	-6.6	-23.8			-8.8	-12.8	-24.0
1926-30		-1.5	-0.7	-8.3	-20.3		-3.0	-3.6	-14.8	-21.8
1931-35		-0.8	-1.8	-3.9			7.2	-5.4	-11.4	
1936-40		-1.3	-0.1				5.9	-3.5		
1941-45		0.6					6.0			
1946-50										

a) See notes at the end of the table.
Source: OECD, *Labour Force Statistics 1970-1991*, Paris, 1992, Part III.

Table 9. **Age-specific employment rates by cohort**[a] *(cont.)*

Netherlands

A. Employment/population ratios at ages

Born in:	Men 40-44	45-49	50-54	55-59	60-64	Women 40-44	45-49	50-54	55-59	60-64
1901-05										
1906-10										
1911-15					74.2					27.6
1916-20				82.4	65.9				36.9	29.0
1921-25			90.5	82.1	58.7			38.7	34.5	25.8
1926-30		96.9	87.7	73.2	57.1		46.1	42.4	37.4	24.7
1931-35	96.4	93.0	85.9	75.2		42.7	44.5	47.2	39.8	
1936-40	96.7	93.9	86.9			51.2	54.1	50.5		
1941-45	96.7	93.6				61.3	61.7			
1946-50	96.2					67.8				

B. Per cent leaving employment over previous five years

Born in:	Men 40-44	45-49	50-54	55-59	60-64	Women 40-44	45-49	50-54	55-59	60-64
1901-05										
1906-10										
1911-15										
1916-20					−20.0					−21.2
1921-25				−9.2	−28.6				−11.0	−25.0
1926-30			−9.5	−16.5	−22.1			−8.0	−11.8	−33.9
1931-35		−3.6	−7.6	−12.4			4.2	6.1	−15.6	
1936-40		−2.8	−7.5				5.7	−6.6		
1941-45		−3.3					0.5			
1946-50										

Norway

A. Employment/population ratios at ages

Born in:	Men 40-44	45-49	50-54	55-59	60-64	Women 40-44	45-49	50-54	55-59	60-64
1901-05										
1906-10					79.4					38.2
1911-15				87.8	76.9				46.2	40.0
1916-20			90.5	86.6	73.4			53.1	49.6	40.2
1921-25		92.6	89.8	85.0	71.3		53.8	55.5	59.0	45.7
1926-30	93.5	91.2	91.7	89.1	64.2	55.2	57.7	72.0	61.5	46.5
1931-35	92.2	93.0	91.5	82.0		60.6	76.0	73.4	62.0	
1936-40	98.1	98.0	89.2			73.0	81.0	74.5		
1941-45	97.7	93.9				78.6	83.5			
1946-50	94.0					81.9				

B. Per cent leaving employment over previous five years

Born in:	Men 40-44	45-49	50-54	55-59	60-64	Women 40-44	45-49	50-54	55-59	60-64
1901-05										
1906-10										
1911-15					−12.5					−13.5
1916-20				−4.3	−15.2				−6.6	−19.0
1921-25			−3.0	−5.4	−16.1			3.1	6.4	−22.6
1926-30		−2.4	0.6	−2.9	−27.9		4.4	24.8	−14.5	−24.4
1931-35		0.8	−1.6	−10.3			25.5	−3.5	−15.6	
1936-40		−0.0	−9.0				11.0	−8.0		
1941-45		−3.9					6.2			
1946-50										

a) See notes at the end of the table.
Source: OECD, *Labour Force Statistics 1970-1991*, Paris, 1992, Part III.

Table 9. **Age-specific employment rates by cohort**[a] *(cont.)*

Portugal

A. Employment/population ratios at ages

Born in:	Men					Women				
	40-44	45-49	50-54	55-59	60-64	40-44	45-49	50-54	55-59	60-64
1901-05										
1906-10										
1911-15					73.7					27.2
1916-20				80.4	65.3				36.4	28.6
1921-25			88.9	82.1	57.6			38.4	34.1	25.7
1926-30		95.3	86.8	71.3	56.2		44.7	41.7	36.6	24.5
1931-35	93.2	91.9	83.7	73.3		41.7	42.5	46.3	38.9	
1936-40	96.2	90.7	85.5			48.5	51.4	49.0		
1941-45	93.6	92.2				57.9	59.5			
1946-50	94.4					64.6				

B. Per cent leaving employment over previous five years

Born in:	Men					Women				
	40-44	45-49	50-54	55-59	60-64	40-44	45-49	50-54	55-59	60-64
1901-05										
1906-10										
1911-15										
1916-20					-18.7					-21.6
1921-25				-7.6	-29.9				-11.1	-24.6
1926-30			-8.9	-17.8	-21.2			-6.9	-12.1	-33.1
1931-35		-1.4	-8.9	-12.5			2.1	8.8	-15.9	
1936-40		-5.7	-5.8				6.0	-4.6		
1941-45		-1.5					2.7			
1946-50										

Spain

A. Employment/population ratios at ages

Born in:	Men					Women				
	40-44	45-49	50-54	55-59	60-64	40-44	45-49	50-54	55-59	60-64
1901-05										
1906-10					76.4					19.0
1911-15				88.8	68.6				24.7	19.5
1916-20			93.1	84.4	60.2			25.5	26.0	17.1
1921-25		95.5	90.8	79.4	48.0		25.2	26.6	24.0	15.6
1926-30	95.5	93.5	85.5	68.9	43.6	24.2	27.1	26.1	21.6	14.9
1931-35	94.8	88.7	78.3	69.6		26.4	26.9	23.0	21.1	
1936-40	90.4	82.1	82.3			27.3	24.6	25.9		
1941-45	84.7	88.2				28.1	29.8			
1946-50	89.3					34.9				

B. Per cent leaving employment over previous five years

Born in:	Men					Women				
	40-44	45-49	50-54	55-59	60-64	40-44	45-49	50-54	55-59	60-64
1901-05										
1906-10										
1911-15					-22.8					-20.9
1916-20				-9.3	-28.6				2.0	-34.2
1921-25			-5.0	-12.5	-39.6			5.6	-9.6	-35.1
1926-30		-2.1	-8.5	-19.5	-36.7		11.7	-3.5	-17.1	-31.3
1931-35		-6.4	-11.8	-11.0			1.9	-14.5	-8.1	
1936-40		-9.2	0.3				-9.9	5.3		
1941-45		4.0					6.1			
1946-50										

a) See notes at the end of the table.
Source: OECD, *Labour Force Statistics 1970-1991*, Paris, 1992, Part III.

Table 9. **Age-specific employment rates by cohort**[a] *(cont.)*

United States

A. Employment/population ratios at ages

	Men					Women				
	40-44	45-49	50-54	55-59	60-64	40-44	45-49	50-54	55-59	60-64
Born in:										
1901-05				84.4	76.6				40.4	33.6
1906-10			90.1	83.0	69.9			47.5	43.6	33.9
1911-15		92.0	92.2	85.7	61.6		49.4	48.9	47.4	31.3
1916-20	91.8	93.2	89.1	79.8	57.7	43.6	50.0	51.6	45.2	31.9
1921-25	93.6	92.7	84.7	78.3	52.7	46.2	52.9	50.0	46.5	32.0
1926-30	92.8	88.9	85.3	75.5	53.0	50.1	52.3	55.0	47.7	34.4
1931-35	90.4	89.3	84.0	76.0		53.2	59.0	57.8	53.4	
1936-40	90.9	88.3	85.3			62.8	64.2	64.5		
1941-45	89.7	88.0				68.0	71.9			
1946-50	89.8					74.4				

B. Per cent leaving employment over previous five years

	Men					Women				
	40-44	45-49	50-54	55-59	60-64	40-44	45-49	50-54	55-59	60-64
Born in:										
1901-05					–9.3					–16.7
1906-10				–7.9	–15.8				–8.2	–22.1
1911-15			0.1	–7.0	–28.1			–1.0	–3.1	–33.9
1916-20		1.6	–4.4	–10.4	–27.7		14.5	3.2	–12.4	–29.4
1921-25		–0.9	–8.6	–7.6	–32.7		14.6	–5.6	–7.0	–31.2
1926-30		–4.2	–4.1	–11.5	–29.8		4.3	5.2	–13.3	–28.0
1931-35		–1.1	–6.0	–9.5			10.8	–2.0	–7.6	
1936-40		–2.9	–3.4				2.3	0.5		
1941-45		–1.9					5.7			
1946-50										

Note: Table 9 shows how five-year cohorts have moved into retirement over time in a a number of OECD countries, for men and women separately. Panels A show age-specific employment/population ratios for a period of 25 years, arranged in birth cohorts. Thus, for example, the table for France shows that 62.6 per cent of men born in 1926-30 were in employment when this birth cohort was in the age range 55-59 – that is, in the year 1985. By the time this cohort reached the age 60-64 – that is, in 1990 – 22.0 per cent of them were in employment.

Panels B show the percentage of each cohort which moved out of employment over a period of five years. Thus, it shows that between 1985 and 1990, employment of French men born in 1926-30 fell by 64.8 per cent. Arithmetically, the percentages are calculated using the formula:

[Employment/Population Ratio (t) – Employment/Population Ratio (t – 5)*100/Employment/Population Ratio (t – 5)].

Movements out of employment are shown as negative figures. Where (as in the case of women aged 45-49) there is a net increase in employment by a cohort over the previous five years, a positive percentage is shown.

This method of calculation implicitly assumes that the population of men in France aged 60-64 is directly comparable in terms of labour market behaviour to those aged 55-59 in 1985: that is, departures through deaths and emigration and new arrivals through immigration are assumed to have no effect on employment/population ratios, allowing the ratios to be compared directly.

The purpose of presenting the data in this way is to allow cohort effects to be seen distinctly. Over time, the participation rates of successive cohorts of women has been increasing in most OECD countries, while those for men (being close to 100 per cent for the age group 25-44) have been static or falling.

This means that the employment/population ratios of women aged 50 to 59 have either increased or remained static over time, while those for men have fallen. However, as the table shows, the rate of withdrawal from employment of each successive cohort of women has been as great or greater than that of men.

Source: OECD, *Labour Force Statistics 1970-1991*, Paris, 1992, Part III.

Table 10*a*. **Working-age population per elderly person in selected OECD countries**

(15-64 years/65 years +)

	1960	1980	1990	2000	2020	2040
Australia	7.2 (1961)	6.6 (1981)	6.0	5.5 (2001)	3.7 (2021)	2.9 (2031)
Austria	5.4	4.2	4.5	4.3	3.3	2.1
Belgium	5.2 (1961)	4.6 (1981)	4.5	3.9	3.1	2.2
Canada	7.7 (1961)	7.0 (1981)	5.9 [b]	4.9 (2001)	3.1 (2021)	2.3 (2036)
Denmark	6.0	4.5	4.3	4.4	3.3	..
Finland	8.5	5.6	5.0	4.6	2.9	2.7
France	..	4.6	4.7	..	..	..
Greece	..	5.0	4.9 (1988)	..	..	..
Japan	11.2	7.4	5.8	4.0	2.4	2.1
New Zealand	9.0 (1961)	6.4 (1981)	5.8 (1991)	5.6 (2001)	4.1 (2021)	2.7 (2031)
Norway	5.7	4.3	4.0	4.3	3.6	2.8
Portugal	7.9	5.5 (1981)	5.0 [b]	4.6	3.1 (2025)	2.6 (2035)
Spain	7.6	5.6	5.0	4.2	3.7	2.1
Sweden	5.5	3.9	3.6	3.7	3.0	..
Switzerland	6.2	4.7	4.5	4.2	3.2	2.6
Turkey	15.1	11.3	13.8	11.3	11.0 (2005)	..
United Kingdom [a]	5.5	4.3	4.2	4.1	3.5	2.8
United States	6.5	5.9	5.3	5.4	3.6	2.7
Group average [c]	7.5	5.6	5.4	5.0	3.8	2.5

a) United Kingdom elderly = women 60+ and men 65+.
b) Canada and Portugal, 1990 estimated.
c) Non-weighted averages.
Source: Replies to OECD questionnaire on the care of the frail elderly, 1992.

Table 10*b*. **Working-age population per dependent person in selected OECD countries**

15-64 years/[(0-14) + (65 years +)]

	1960	1980	1990	2000	2020	2040
Australia	1.6 (1961)	1.9 (1981)	2.0	2.1 (2001)	1.9 (2021)	1.7
Austria	1.9	1.8	2.1	..	..	..
Belgium	1.8 (1961)	1.9 (1981)	2.0	2.0	1.8	1.4
Canada	1.4 (1961)	2.1 (1981)	2.1 [b]	2.1 (2001)	1.8 (2021)	1.5
Denmark	1.8	1.8	2.1	2.0	1.8	..
Finland	1.7	2.1	2.1	2.1	1.7	1.6
France	..	1.8	1.9	..	..	..
Greece	..	2.8	..	..	..	..
Japan	1.8	2.1	2.3	2.1	1.5	1.3
New Zealand	1.4 (1961)	1.7 (1981)	1.9 (1991)	1.9 (2001)	1.9 (2021)	1.1
Norway	1.7	1.7	1.8	..	..	..
Portugal	..	1.7 (1981)	1.9 [b]	2.0	1.8 (2025)	1.6
Spain	1.8	1.7	2.0	2.1	2.2	1.5
Sweden	1.9	1.8	1.8	1.6	1.6	..
Switzerland	1.8	1.9	2.0	2.0	1.8	1.6
Turkey	1.1	1.2	1.4	..	..	..
United Kingdom [a]	1.9	1.8	1.9	1.8	1.8	1.5
United States	1.5	1.9	1.9	2.3	1.8	1.6
Group average [c]	1.7	1.9	2.0	2.0	1.8	1.5

a) United Kingdom elderly = women 60+ and men 65+.
b) Canada and Portugal, 1990 estimated.
c) Non-weighted averages.
Source: Replies to OECD questionnaire on the care of the frail elderly, 1992.

Chart 9. **Working-age population per elderly person**
(15-64/65+)

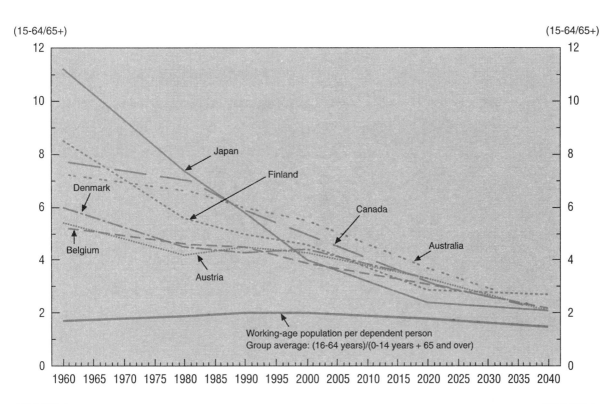

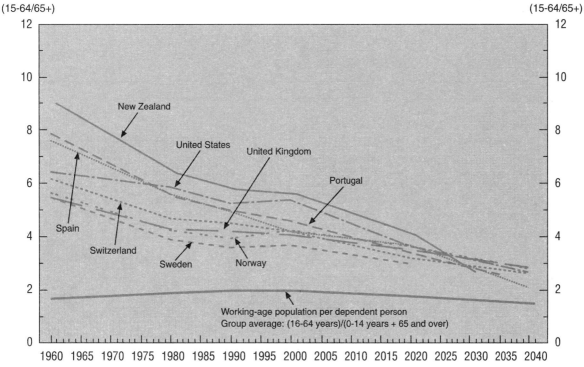

Notes: See Tables 10*a* and 10*b*.
Source: Replies to OECD questionnaire on care of the frail elderly, 1992.

Chart 10. **Growth in the number of people aged 80 and over**
(1960 = 100)

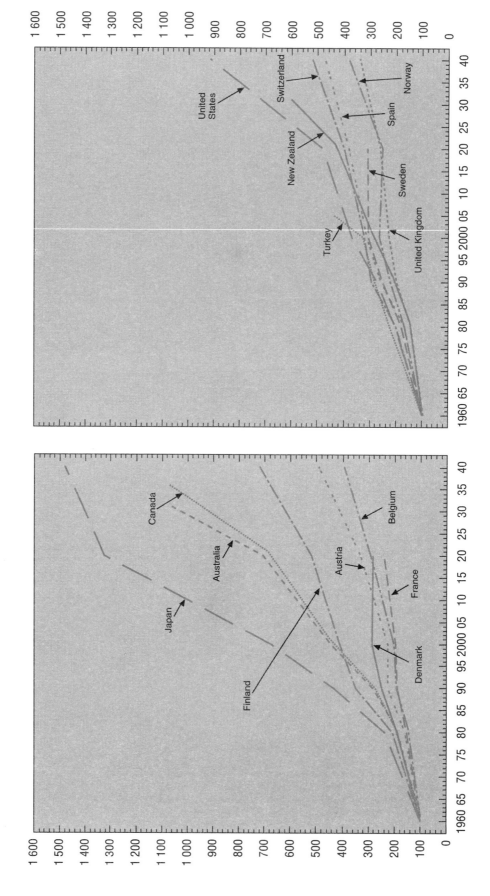

New Zealand: 1961 = 100.
Turkey: age group is 75+.
Notes: See Table 11.

Australia, Belgium and Canada: 1961 = 100.
France: age group is 75+.
Source: Replies to the OECD questionnaire on the care of the frail elderly, 1992.

102

Table 11. **Growth in the number of people aged 80 and over in selected OECD countries, 1980-2040**

(1960 = 100)

	1980	1990	2000	2020	2040
Australia[a]	194 (1981)	286	445 (2001)	705 (2021)	1 062 (2031)
Austria	162	228	226	334	494
Belgium[a]	150 (1981)	193	202	293	396
Canada[a]	198 (1981)	277 [c]	446 (2001)	690 (2021)	1 075 (2036)
Denmark	190	252	286	285	..
Finland	210	349	410	521	723
France[b]	156	192	197	242	..
Japan	239	435	673	1 327	1 480
Luxembourg[b]	164 (1981)	190 (1987)	199	268	313 (2030)
New Zealand[a]	148 (1981)	212 (1991)	292 (2001)	434 (2021)	605 (2031)
Norway	170	225	268	255	385
Spain	170	260	314	384	474
Sweden	181	255	309	312	..
Switzerland	203	296	324	403	522
Turkey[b]	227	285	331	442 (2005)	..
United Kingdom	151	209	239	274	357
United States	206	276	373	483	918
Group average[d]	184	260	326	454	694

a) 1961 = 100.
b) Age group is 75+.
c) The figure for 1990 is estimated.
d) Non-weighted average.
Source: Replies to OECD questionnaire on the care of the frail elderly, 1992.

Table 12. **Percentage of people aged 65 and over living alone, 1945-2000**

Australia	*1976* 19	*1986* 21	..	..	..
Austria	*1961* 24	*1980* 32	*1990* 35	*2000* 34	*2020* 33
Belgium	*1961* 22	*1981* 30	*1986* 24	*2001* 34	..
Canada	*1971* 18	*1976* 22	*1981* 24	*1986* 25	*2001* 34
Denmark	*1962* 35	*1977* 48	*1988* 53	..	..
Finland	*1950* 18	*1980* 32	*1987* 38	..	..
France	*1954* 16	*1962* 22	*1975* 25	*1982* 28	
Germany (West)	*1975* 36	*1982* 39	*1985* 41	..	..
Hungary	*1980* 20	..	..	..	..
Iceland	*1988* 32	..	..	..	..
Ireland	*1961* 11	*1979* 18	*1981* 20	*1986* 23	..
Italy	*1981* 24	*1990* 31	..	..	..
Japan	*1975* 7	*1980* 8	*1985* 9	*1988* 10	*1990* 11
Netherlands	*1981* 27	*1986* 31	..	..	..
New Zealand	*1954* 17	*1971* 22	*1981* 27	*1986* 28	*1991* 28
Norway	*1990* 35.1	..	..	..	..
Poland	*1978* 21	*1988* 20	..	..	..
Portugal	*1981* 18	..	..	..	..
Spain	*1970* 10	*1981* 14	*1989* 19	..	..
Sweden	*1954* 27	*1980* 38	*1990* 39	*2000* 42	..
Switzerland	*1980* 19	35	..	..	..
Turkey	*1988* 16				
United Kingdom	*1945* 12	*1962* 22	*1981* 34	*1985* 36	*2001* 40
United States	*1952* 20	*1962* 22	*1968* 22	*1981* 29	*1984* 32

Sources: Replies to OECD questionnaire on the care of the frail elderly, 1992; *Caring for Frail Elderly People*, OECD (forthcoming).

Table 13. **Percentage of people aged 65 and over living with their children, 1950-1990**

Austria	*1979* 24	*1987* 25	..	..	..
Denmark	*1962* 20	*1977* 10	*1988* 4		..
Finland	*1950* 55	*1987* 14	..	..	..
France	*1975* 24	*1982* 20	..	..	..
Germany (West)	*1987* 14	..	..	..	..
Iceland	*1987* 23	..	..	..	..
Italy	*1981* 35	*1990* 39	..	..	..
Japan	*1953* 80	*1960* 82	*1974* 75	*1985* 65	..
Netherlands	*1979* 12	*1983* 11	*1987* 8	..	..
Norway	*1953* 44	*1967* 29	*1973* 15	*1988* 11	..
Poland	*1968* 65	*1985* 35	*1988* 28	..	..
Spain	*1970* 58	*1985* 37	..	..	..
Sweden	*1954* 27	*1975* 9	*1986* 5	..	..
Switzerland	*1980* 16	..	..	..	..
United Kingdom	*1962* 42	*1980* 16	..	..	..
United States	*1952* 33	*1962* 28	*1968* 21	*1984* 19	*1987* 15

Source: *Caring for Frail Elderly People*, OECD (forthcoming).

Chart 11. **Percentage of elderly (65+) living alone**

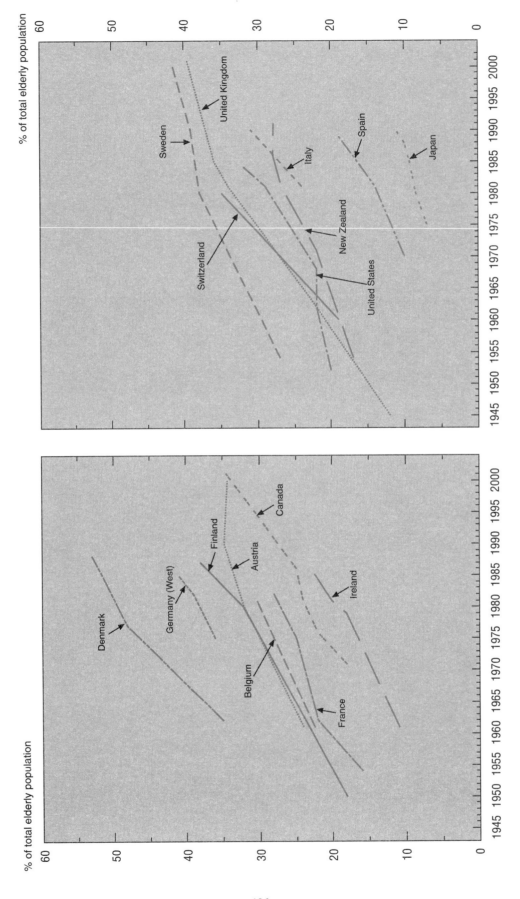

See Table 12.
Source: Caring for Frail Elderly People, OECD (forthcoming).

Chart 12. **Percentage of elderly (65+) living with their children**
1950-1990

% of total elderly population

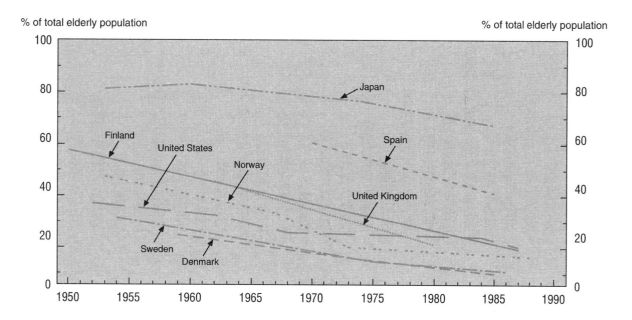

See Table 13.
Source: *Caring for Frail Elderly People*, OECD (forthcoming).

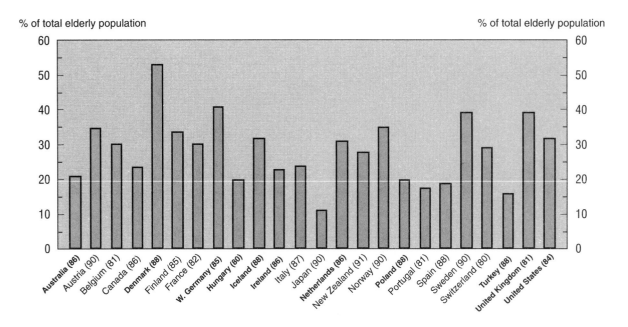

Chart 13. **Percentage of elderly (65+) living alone**

See Table 12.
Sources: Data for bold-type countries are from: *Caring for Frail Elderly People*, OECD (forthcoming).
All others from replies to the OECD questionnaire on the care of the frail elderly, 1992.

Chart 14. **Percentage of elderly (65+) living with their children**

% of total elderly population   % of total elderly population

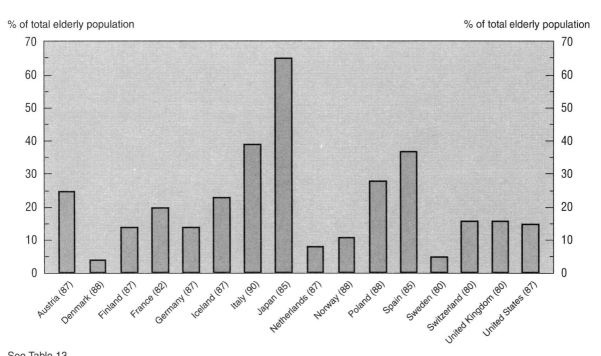

See Table 13.
Source: Caring for Frail Elderly People, OECD (forthcoming).

Table 14. Population structure in selected OECD countries, 1960-2040

(Millions)

	1960	1980	1990	2000	2020	2040
Australia	*1961*	*1981*		*2001*	*2021*	*2031*
0-14	3.18	3.66	3.74	3.84	3.66	3.63
15-64	6.44	9.49	11.44	13.23	14.69	14.59
65-79	0.76	1.18	1.53	1.81	3.08	3.68
80+	0.13	0.25	0.37	0.58	0.92	1.39
Total	10.51	14.58	17.08	19.47	22.35	23.28
Austria						
0-14	1.55	1.54	1.35	..	..	..
15-64	4.63	4.85	5.21	5.44	5.43	4.70
65-79	0.74	0.96	0.88	0.98	1.21	1.57
80+	0.13	0.20	0.29	0.28	0.42	0.62
Total	7.05	7.55	7.72	..	..	..
Belgium	*1961*	*1981*				
0-14	2.19	2.07	1.80	1.64	1.39	1.24
15-64	5.88	6.46	6.67	6.56	6.07	4.97
65-79	0.94	1.15	1.13	1.33	1.44	1.59
80+	0.18	0.27	0.35	0.36	0.52	0.71
Total	9.19	9.95	9.95	9.89	9.42	8.50
Canada	*1961*	*1981*	*1990 (est.)*	*2001*	*2021*	*2036*
0-14	6.19	5.48	5.56	5.33	4.83	4.45
15-64	10.66	16.50	17.97	19.46	19.87	18.43
65-79	1.16	1.91	2.42	2.93	4.77	5.46
80+	0.23	0.45	0.63	1.01	1.57	2.45
Total	18.24	24.34	26.58	28.73	31.03	30.79
Denmark						
0-14	1.15	1.08	0.88	0.95	0.78	..
15-64	2.95	3.31	3.45	3.47	3.22	..
65-79	0.41	0.59	0.61	0.58	0.76	..
80+	0.07	0.14	0.19	0.21	0.21	..
Total	4.59	5.12	5.14	5.21	4.97	..
Finland						
0-14	1.34	0.97	0.96	0.89	0.77	0.68
15-64	2.78	3.25	3.36	3.42	3.08	2.70
65-79	0.29	0.49	0.53	0.58	0.85	0.72
80+	0.04	0.09	0.14	0.17	0.21	0.30
Total	4.45	4.79	5.00	5.06	4.93	4.39
Japan						
0-14	28.44	27.58	22.81	19.28	19.62	18.41
15-64	60.47	78.83	85.90	86.19	75.32	65.64
65-79	4.72	9.03	11.94	16.94	22.96	21.61
80+	0.68	1.62	2.96	4.57	9.01	10.05
Total	94.30	117.06	123.61	126.98	126.90	115.71
New Zealand	*1961*	*1981*	*1991*	*2001*	*2021*	*2031*
0-14	0.85	0.85	0.78	0.90	0.80	1.19
15-64	1.41	2.01	2.21	2.48	2.77	2.34
65-79	0.12	0.26	0.30	0.33	0.52	0.63
80+	0.04	0.05	0.08	0.11	0.16	0.22
Total	2.41	3.18	3.38	3.81	4.25	4.39
Norway						
0-14	0.93	0.90	0.81	..	..	..
15-64	2.27	2.59	2.75	2.87	2.96	2.82
65-79	0.33	0.49	0.53	0.48	0.63	0.73
80+	0.07	0.12	0.16	0.19	0.18	0.27
Total	3.59	4.09	4.25	..	..	..
Portugal		*1981*	*1990 (est.)*		*2025*	*2035*
0-14	2.59	2.51	2.20	2.06	1.60	1.61
15-64	5.59	6.20	6.76	6.99	7.16	6.61
65-79	..	0.96	1.07	1.18	1.61	1.79
80+	..	0.17	0.28	0.33	0.68	0.76
Total	8.89	9.83	10.30	10.57	11.06	10.77

Table 14. **Population structure in selected OECD countries, 1960-2040** *(cont.)*

(Millions)

	1960	1980	1990	2000	2020	2040
Spain						
0-14	8.35	9.68	7.56	6.24	4.75	3.64
15-64	19.61	23.63	26.16	26.79	25.39	18.91
65-79	2.14	3.50	4.16	5.00	5.23	6.96
80+	0.43	0.73	1.12	1.35	1.65	2.04
Total	30.53	37.54	39.00	39.38	37.02	31.55
Sweden						
0-14	1.65	1.62	1.55	1.86	1.78	..
15-64	4.95	5.34	5.52	5.57	5.72	..
65-79	0.75	1.10	1.16	1.07	1.44	..
80+	0.15	0.26	0.37	0.45	0.45	..
Total	7.50	8.32	8.59	8.95	9.40	..
Switzerland						
0-15	1.37	1.34	1.21	1.22	1.07	0.98
16-64	3.44	4.12	4.46	4.53	4.45	4.04
65-79	0.47	0.71	0.73	0.81	1.06	1.10
80+	0.08	0.17	0.25	0.27	0.33	0.43
Total	5.36	6.34	6.65	6.83	6.92	6.55
Turkey					*2005*	
0-15	11.99	18.58	21.52	..	..	..
16-64	14.74	23.88	32.58	41.44	45.73	..
65-74	0.69	1.46	1.54	2.71	2.88	..
75+	0.29	0.66	0.83	0.96	1.28	..
Total	27.76	44.74	56.47	..	..	..
United Kingdom						
0-14	12.22	11.83	10.92	11.82	11.04	11.00
15-64	34.01	36.08	37.50	38.02	38.69	36.66
65-79	5.13	6.91	6.88	6.80	8.18	9.30
80+	1.01	1.52	2.11	2.41	2.76	3.60
Total	52.37	56.33	57.41	59.04	60.67	60.56
United States						
0-14	55.79	51.29	53.85	45.32	52.31	49.90
15-64	106.98	149.71	163.78	188.07	189.99	183.80
65-79	14.05	20.38	24.15	25.53	39.95	45.07
80+	2.51	5.18	6.93	9.36	12.11	23.04
Total	179.32	226.55	248.71	268.27	294.36	301.81

Source: Replies to OECD questionnaire on the care of the frail elderly, 1992.

Table 15. Population structure in selected OECD countries

(Per cent of total)

	1960	1980	1990	2000	2 020	2040
Australia	*1961*	*1981*		*2001*	*2021*	*2031*
0-14	30.23	25.09	21.88	19.73	16.36	15.60
15-64	61.26	65.11	66.97	67.99	65.74	62.65
65-79	7.27	8.07	8.98	9.30	13.78	15.80
80+	1.24	1.74	2.18	2.99	4.12	5.95
Austria						
0-14	22.05	20.40	17.43	..	..	..
15-64	65.73	64.18	67.45	..	..	..
65-79	10.44	12.74	11.43	..	..	..
80+	1.77	2.68	3.69	..	..	..
Belgium	*1961*	*1981*				
0-14	23.84	20.84	18.11	16.62	14.78	14.58
15-64	63.94	64.94	67.08	66.30	64.38	58.40
65-79	10.28	11.53	11.35	13.43	15.28	18.70
80+	1.94	2.69	3.47	3.65	5.55	8.33
Canada	*1961*	*1981*	*1990 (est.)*	*2001*	*2021*	*2036*
0-14	33.95	22.52	20.91	18.55	15.55	14.46
15-64	58.42	67.79	67.61	67.73	64.01	59.85
65-79	6.38	7.85	9.11	10.19	15.38	17.74
80+	1.25	1.85	2.37	3.53	5.06	7.95
Denmark						
0-14	25.09	21.11	17.15	18.25	15.68	..
15-64	64.27	64.54	67.27	66.54	64.80	..
65-79	9.01	11.57	11.92	11.10	15.23	..
80+	1.63	2.78	3.67	4.10	4.29	..
Finland						
0-14	30.14	20.16	19.29	17.58	15.72	15.40
15-64	62.49	67.78	67.24	67.51	62.47	61.52
65-79	6.45	10.25	10.59	11.42	17.18	16.30
80+	0.93	1.81	2.88	3.34	4.35	6.79
Japan						
0-14	30.15	23.56	18.45	15.18	15.46	15.91
15-64	64.12	67.35	69.50	67.88	59.35	56.73
65-79	5.00	7.71	9.66	13.34	18.09	18.67
80+	0.72	1.39	2.39	3.60	7.10	8.69
New Zealand	*1961*	*1981*	*1991*	*2001*	*2021*	*2031*
0-14	35.26	26.72	23.23	23.47	18.95	27.14
15-64	58.28	63.32	65.54	64.97	65.14	53.41
65-79	4.95	8.26	8.94	8.78	12.18	14.42
80+	1.51	1.70	2.29	2.79	3.73	5.03
Norway						
0-14	25.79	21.97	18.96	..	..	..
15-64	63.08	63.22	64.73	..	..	..
65-79	9.15	11.85	12.54	..	..	..
80+	1.98	2.96	3.76	..	..	..
Portugal		*1981*	*1990 (est.)*		*2025*	*2035*
0-14	29.16	25.51	21.36	19.54	14.50	14.92
15-64	62.87	63.04	65.57	66.19	64.79	61.35
65-79	..	9.74	10.34	11.18	14.58	16.64
80+	..	1.71	2.73	3.09	6.13	7.09
Spain						
0-14	27.35	25.79	19.38	15.85	12.83	11.54
15-64	64.23	62.95	67.08	68.03	68.58	59.94
65-79	7.01	9.32	10.67	12.7	14.13	22.06
80+	1.41	1.94	2.87	3.43	4.46	6.47
Sweden						
0-14	22.03	19.42	18.02	20.83	18.94	..
15-64	66.00	64.20	64.21	62.25	60.91	..
65-79	10.03	13.21	13.46	11.91	15.32	..
80+	1.94	3.17	4.30	5.01	4.83	..

Table 15. **Population structure in selected OECD countries** *(cont.)*

(Per cent of total)

	1960	1980	1990	2000	2020	2040
Switzerland						
0-15	25.52	21.12	18.19	17.82	15.49	14.96
16-64	64.20	65.01	67.07	66.39	64.33	61.60
65-79	8.73	11.21	11.05	11.86	15.35	16.83
80+	1.55	2.66	3.69	3.93	4.83	6.61
Turkey						
0-15	43.21	41.53	38.11	..	..	..
16-64	53.09	53.38	57.70	..	..	..
65-74	2.48	3.25	2.73	..	..	..
75+	1.04	1.46	1.46	..	..	..
United Kingdom						
0-14	23.33	21.00	19.02	20.02	18.20	18.16
15-64	64.94	64.05	65.32	64.39	63.77	60.54
65-79	9.80	12.26	11.98	11.51	13.48	15.36
80+	1.92	2.70	3.67	4.08	4.55	5.94
United States						
0-14	31.11	22.64	21.65	16.89	17.77	16.53
15-64	59.66	66.08	65.85	70.11	64.54	60.90
65-79	7.84	8.99	9.71	9.51	13.57	14.93
80+	1.40	2.28	2.79	3.49	4.11	7.63

Source: Replies to OECD questionnaire on the care of the frail elderly, 1992.

**THIS PAGE LEFT
INTENTIONALLY BLANK**

Table 16. **Employment/population ratios**

Averages	Years	Males			Females		
		Total	Full-time	Part-time	Total	Full-time	Part-time
Australia	1980-1991	78.53	73.23	5.30	51.63	31.96	19.66
Austria	1981-1990	67.22	66.29	0.93	40.11	32.85	7.26
Belgium	1981-1990 (–82)	68.02	66.80	1.22	37.82	29.44	8.38
Canada	1980-1991	76.62	70.91	5.71	57.10	42.76	14.34
Denmark	1981-1990 (–82)	81.19	74.34	6.85	68.50	39.95	28.55
Finland	1980-1991	75.56	72.23	3.33	69.26	61.48	7.78
France	1980-1991	70.05	67.94	2.11	49.62	39.00	10.63
Germany	1981-1989 (–82)	75.96	74.47	1.49	48.42	34.03	14.39
Greece	1981-1988 (–82)	73.84	71.70	2.14	36.31	32.71	3.60
Ireland	1983-1990	69.53	67.47	2.06	33.05	27.85	5.21
Italy	1981-1990 (–82)	72.32	70.21	2.10	34.23	30.78	3.45
Japan	1980-1991	84.15	77.52	6.63	55.24	38.29	16.95
Luxembourg	1983-1988	76.52	75.23	1.29	39.33	33.10	6.23
Netherlands	[a]	72.61	63.34	9.27	41.41	17.60	23.81
New Zealand	1980-1991	82.15	76.96	5.19	57.24	38.63	18.61
Norway	1980-1991	84.35	77.88	6.47	65.72	31.98	33.74
Portugal	[b]	82.99	80.15	2.84	55.20	49.30	5.89
Spain	1987-1991	64.31	63.14	1.16	29.11	25.53	3.58
Sweden	1980-1991	82.53	77.13	5.40	75.88	42.54	33.33
United Kingdom	1981-1990 (–82)	76.85	73.38	3.48	55.84	31.50	24.34
United States	1980-1991	76.78	68.98	7.80	59.65	43.86	15.80

Percentage point change	Years	Males			Females		
		Total	Full-time	Part-time	Total	Full-time	Part-time
Australia	1980-1991	–6.72	–9.34	2.62	7.67	2.10	5.57
Austria	1981-1990	–1.71	–0.82	–0.89	–2.57	4.32	–6.89
Belgium	1981-1990 (–82)	–4.73	–5.11	0.38	4.24	–0.36	4.59
Canada	1980-1991	–5.54	–7.39	1.85	9.01	5.82	3.19
Denmark	1981-1990 (–82)	3.26	–0.90	4.16	7.50	9.76	–2.26
Finland	1980-1991	–6.15	–7.38	1.22	0.99	1.18	–0.19
France	1980-1991	–9.32	–9.71	0.40	0.15	–3.08	3.22
Germany	1981-1989 (–82)	–3.41	–3.89	0.48	1.44	0.11	1.33
Greece	1981-1988 (–82)	–6.34	–7.01	0.66	3.35	1.72	1.64
Ireland	1983-1990	–3.80	–4.20	0.40	2.27	1.19	1.08
Italy	1981-1990 (–82)	–5.93	–5.45	–0.48	2.45	2.38	0.08
Japan	1980-1991	–0.09	–2.30	2.21	6.06	0.95	5.11
Luxembourg	1983-1988	–0.70	–1.43	0.73	3.95	4.07	–0.12
Netherlands	[a]	2.95	–4.66	7.61	15.40	–0.14	15.54
New Zealand	1980-1991	–20.82	–23.28	2.46	0.99	–3.04	4.04
Norway	1980-1991	–11.13	–12.33	1.20	4.28	4.88	–0.60
Portugal	[b]	9.97	8.54	1.44	17.51	17.59	–0.08
Spain	1987-1991	1.73	2.05	–0.31	2.63	2.72	–0.09
Sweden	1980-1991	–2.38	–3.57	1.19	6.62	8.01	–1.39
United Kingdom	1981-1990 (–82)	1.68	0.71	0.97	3.49	1.34	2.14
United States	1980-1991	0.19	–0.52	0.71	8.81	7.19	1.62

a) 1981 to 1991 excluding 1982, 1984 and 1986.
b) 1980 to 1991 excluding 1981 to 1985.
An employment ratio is defined as the sum of persons in employment as a percentage of the working-age population (15-64).
Change is defined as 1991 less 1980 unless otherwise specified.
Source: OECD employment duration data file.

Chart 15a. Employment/population ratios,[a] 1980-1991

Averages and percentage point changes[b]

Full-time   Part-time

MALES

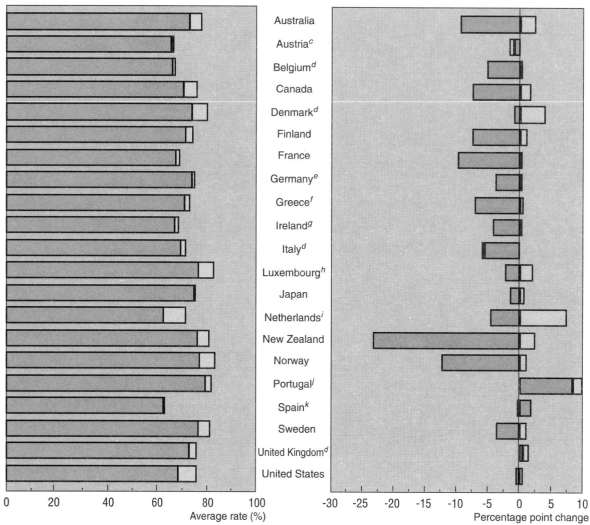

Australia	Austria[c]	Belgium[d]	Canada	

0   20   40   60   80   100
Average rate (%)

-30 -25 -20 -15 -10 -5 0 5 10
Percentage point change

a) An employment ratio is defined as the sum of persons in employment (part-time + full-time) as a percentage of the working-age population (15-64). It is calculated over the period 1980-1991 unless otherwise specified.

b) Change is defined as 1991 less 1980 unless otherwise specified.

c) 1981 to 1990.

d) 1981 to 1990, excluding 1982.

e) 1981 to 1989, excluding 1982.

f) 1981 to 1988, excluding 1982.

g) 1983 to 1990.

h) 1983 to 1988.

i) 1981 to 1991, excluding 1982, 1984 and 1986.

j) 1980 to 1991, excluding 1981 to 1985.

k) 1987 to 1991.

See Table 16.

Source: OECD, employment duration data file, 1992.

Chart 15b. **Employment/population ratios,**[a] **1980-1991**
Averages and percentage point changes[b]

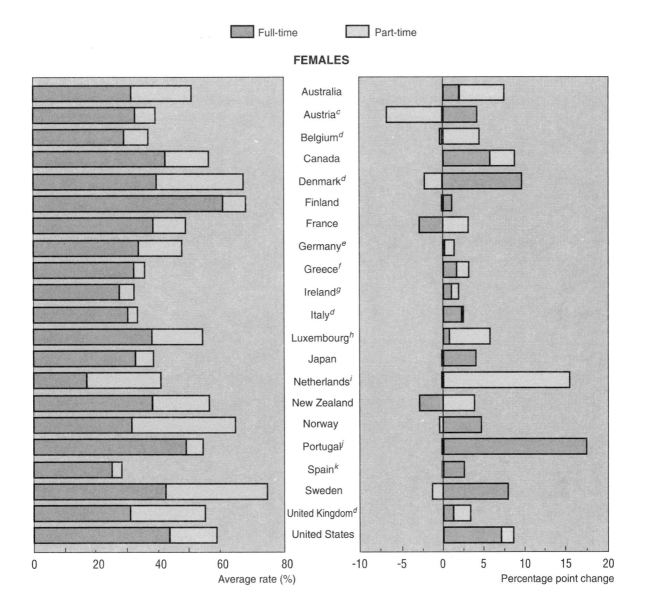

a) An employment ratio is defined as the sum of persons in employment (part-time + full-time) as a percentage of the working-age population (15-64). It is calculated over the period 1980-1991 unless otherwise specified.

b) Change is defined as 1991 less 1980 unless otherwise specified.

c) 1981 to 1990.

d) 1981 to 1990, excluding 1982.

e) 1981 to 1989, excluding 1982.

f) 1981 to 1988, excluding 1982.

g) 1983 to 1990.

h) 1983 to 1988.

i) 1981 to 1991, excluding 1982, 1984 and 1986.

j) 1980 to 1991, excluding 1981 to 1985.

k) 1987 to 1991.

See Table 16.

Source: OECD, employment duration data file, 1992.

Table 17. **Non-employment rates**

Averages		Years	Males aged			Females aged		
			15-24	25-54	55-64	15-24	25-54	55-64
Australia	Inactivity	1980-1991	26.0	6.6	63.9	35.0	40.8	89.4
	Unemployment		10.5	4.9	1.9	8.8	3.4	0.3
	Total		36.6	11.4	65.9	43.8	44.2	89.7
Canada	Inactivity	1980-1991	29.1	6.2	30.5	35.2	31.0	65.7
	Unemployment		11.7	7.0	4.7	8.6	5.8	2.3
	Total		40.8	13.2	35.3	43.8	36.9	68.0
Finland	Inactivity	1980-1991	37.3	6.9	49.2	46.5	14.2	57.1
	Unemployment		5.8	4.3	2.5	4.7	3.0	2.7
	Total		43.1	11.2	51.7	51.2	17.2	59.7
France	Inactivity	1980-1991	53.1	4.1	47.6	61.2	31.0	67.1
	Unemployment		7.5	5.1	3.2	10.1	6.4	2.4
	Total		60.6	9.3	50.9	71.3	37.4	69.5
Germany	Inactivity	1980-1989	37.6	6.1	37.9	43.3	40.5	74.1
	Unemployment		4.8	5.0	5.4	5.1	4.3	2.6
	Total		42.4	11.0	43.3	48.3	44.9	76.7
Ireland	Inactivity	1981-1989 (−82)	40.4	4.8	25.3	50.2	65.5	81.9
	Unemployment		14.8	14.9	10.1	9.3	2.7	1.3
	Total		55.3	19.7	35.4	59.5	68.2	83.2
Italy	Inactivity	1980-1991	52.2	8.4	62.6	59.1	54.9	89.3
	Unemployment		12.5	3.1	0.6	15.4	4.6	0.4
	Total		64.7	11.6	63.2	74.5	59.5	89.7
Japan	Inactivity	1980-1991	56.9	3.0	16.2	56.1	39.3	54.3
	Unemployment		2.0	1.7	3.7	1.9	1.4	0.8
	Total		58.9	4.7	19.9	58.0	40.7	55.1
Netherlands	Inactivity	1987-1989	38.4	6.6	54.2	40.7	43.1	84.1
	Unemployment		7.0	4.9	1.6	8.1	6.3	0.7
	Total		45.4	11.5	55.8	48.8	49.4	84.8
Norway	Inactivity	1980-1991	34.4	7.1	56.3	42.3	25.8	75.9
	Unemployment		5.0	2.0	0.7	4.8	1.9	0.2
	Total		39.3	9.2	57.0	47.1	27.7	76.1
New Zealand	Inactivity	1986-1991	25.7	6.5	39.8	35.7	31.0	68.2
	Unemployment		9.5	4.5	2.0	7.2	3.4	0.9
	Total		35.2	11.0	41.8	42.9	34.4	69.2
Portugal	Inactivity	1980-1991	30.9	5.8	32.4	41.8	36.6	68.2
	Unemployment		7.0	2.5	1.2	12.2	4.4	0.5
	Total		37.9	8.4	33.6	54.0	41.0	68.7
Spain	Inactivity	1980-1991	35.4	5.7	32.4	53.0	62.1	80.1
	Unemployment		20.1	10.7	6.4	20.1	6.2	1.0
	Total		55.5	16.4	38.8	73.2	68.3	81.1
Sweden	Inactivity	1980-1991	32.9	5.0	23.8	33.2	11.5	38.5
	Unemployment		3.5	1.6	1.9	3.6	1.5	1.6
	Total		36.5	6.6	25.7	36.8	13.1	40.1
United Kingdom	Inactivity	1980-1991	19.7	5.9	28.9	29.2	32.0	62.9
	Unemployment		15.2	8.8	8.8	9.8	3.2	1.7
	Total		34.9	14.8	37.7	39.0	35.2	64.6
United States	Inactivity	1980-1991	27.0	7.0	32.1	36.9	30.3	57.5
	Unemployment		9.7	5.1	2.9	8.0	4.0	1.6
	Total		36.7	12.1	35.0	44.9	34.3	59.0

A non-employment rate is defined as the sum of persons not in employment (unemployed + inactive) as a percentage of the age groups specified.

Table 17. **Non-employment rates** *(cont.)*

Percentage point changes		Years	Males aged			Females aged		
			15-24	25-54	55-64	15-24	25-54	55-64
Australia	Inactivity	1980-1991	5.9	1.6	8.0	0.2	–13.8	0.3
	Unemployment		4.5	4.4	1.8	1.5	1.8	0.2
	Total		10.4	6.0	9.8	1.7	–12.0	0.5
Canada	Inactivity	1980-1991	2.8	2.3	13.7	–2.5	–15.7	–2.0
	Unemployment		3.1	4.0	2.1	0.9	2.7	1.0
	Total		5.9	6.3	15.8	–1.6	–13.0	–1.0
Finland	Inactivity	1980-1991	6.0	0.0	10.7	1.8	–2.9	3.9
	Unemployment		4.3	3.9	1.4	0.9	1.2	–0.0
	Total		10.3	3.9	12.0	2.7	–1.7	3.9
France	Inactivity	1980-1991	14.0	1.1	23.9	11.6	–10.7	9.0
	Unemployment		1.1	3.0	–0.7	–1.8	3.6	0.1
	Total		15.1	4.2	23.2	9.8	–7.0	9.1
Germany	Inactivity	1980-1989	–1.3	2.6	9.6	–1.8	–6.0	3.5
	Unemployment		1.8	3.0	2.8	1.1	2.8	2.0
	Total		0.5	5.7	12.4	–0.7	–3.2	5.6
Ireland	Inactivity	1981-1989 (–82)	14.8	0.6	10.5	8.4	–10.5	1.3
	Unemployment		–0.2	3.9	2.6	1.6	0.9	0.3
	Total		14.5	4.6	13.1	10.0	–9.6	1.6
Italy	Inactivity	1980-1991	4.1	2.4	4.7	2.1	–10.0	1.0
	Unemployment		1.7	2.2	–0.1	1.4	3.2	–0.4
	Total		5.8	4.6	4.6	3.6	–6.8	0.6
Japan	Inactivity	1980-1991	–2.2	–0.2	0.9	–1.9	–8.4	–3.3
	Unemployment		0.4	–0.2	–0.6	0.5	0.2	0.3
	Total		–1.8	–0.4	0.2	–1.4	–8.2	–3.0
Netherlands	Inactivity	1987-1989	–2.3	–0.4	3.8	–3.6	–7.3	–0.2
	Unemployment		–1.5	–1.5	–0.4	–3.0	–1.1	–0.3
	Total		–3.8	–1.9	3.4	–6.6	–8.4	–0.5
Norway	Inactivity	1980-1991	5.5	1.4	15.5	–0.5	–10.0	0.3
	Unemployment		5.3	3.4	0.7	3.7	1.9	0.3
	Total		10.8	4.7	16.2	3.3	–8.1	0.6
New Zealand	Inactivity	1986-1991	8.4	7.6	10.4	3.3	–2.0	1.5
	Unemployment		8.3	5.4	2.3	5.4	2.8	0.8
	Total		16.7	13.0	12.7	8.7	0.8	2.3
Portugal	Inactivity	1980-1991	16.7	0.1	7.0	10.9	–16.2	–3.4
	Unemployment		–2.8	–0.1	1.3	–11.0	–0.6	0.3
	Total		13.9	–0.0	8.3	–0.0	–16.9	–3.1
Spain	Inactivity	1980-1991	16.6	1.1	14.4	2.4	–18.0	2.0
	Unemployment		–2.4	1.9	0.8	3.2	8.4	1.0
	Total		14.2	3.0	15.2	5.6	–9.6	3.0
Sweden	Inactivity	1980-1991	6.2	0.8	3.2	5.8	–7.6	–11.6
	Unemployment		1.2	1.2	0.3	–0.5	0.3	0.4
	Total		7.4	2.0	3.5	5.3	–7.3	–11.2
United Kingdom	Inactivity	1980-1991	–0.7	2.1	14.1	–0.6	–9.5	–0.1
	Unemployment		1.8	4.5	–1.8	–2.8	1.1	0.4
	Total		1.1	6.6	12.4	–3.4	–8.4	0.3
United States	Inactivity	1980-1991	4.0	1.1	4.9	–0.2	–10.2	–4.0
	Unemployment		–0.7	0.7	0.7	–0.3	0.2	0.2
	Total		3.3	1.8	5.6	–0.6	–10.0	–3.8

Change is defined as 1991 less 1980 unless otherwise specified.
Source: OECD, *Labour Force Statistics 1970-1991*, Paris, 1992.

Chart 16a. Non-employment rates,[a] 1980-1991
Averages and percentage point changes[b]

Inactivity   Unemployment

MALES

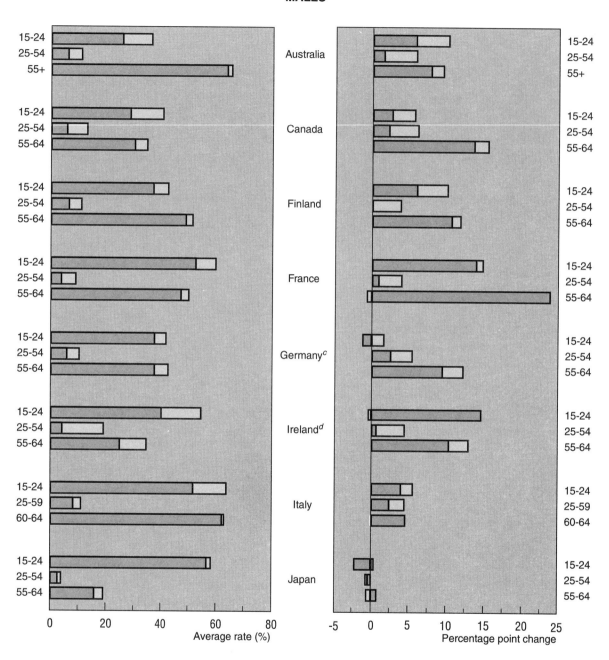

Average rate (%)   Percentage point change

a) A non-employment rate is defined as the sum of persons not in employment (unemployed + inactive) as a percentage of the population specified. It is calculated over the period 1980-1991 unless otherwise specified.

b) Change is defined as 1991 less 1980 unless otherwise specified.

c) Germany: 1980 to 1989.

d) Ireland: 1981 to 1989 excluding 1982.

See Table 17.

Source: OECD, *Labour Force Statistics 1970-1991*, Paris, 1992.

Chart 16b. **Non-employment rates,**[a] **1980-1991**
Averages and percentage point changes[b]

Inactivity   Unemployment

FEMALES

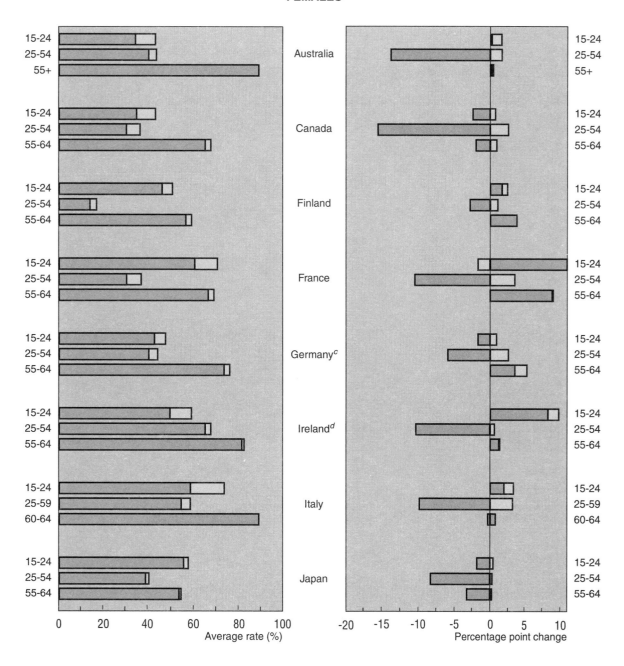

0   20   40   60   80   100
Average rate (%)

-20   -15   -10   -5   0   5   10
Percentage point change

a) A non-employment rate is defined as the sum of persons not in employment (unemployed + inactive) as a percentage of the population specified. It is calculated over the period 1980-1991 unless otherwise specified.

b) Change is defined as 1991 less 1980 unless otherwise specified.

c) Germany: 1980 to 1989.

d) Ireland: 1981 to 1989 excluding 1982.

See Table 17.

Source: OECD, *Labour Force Statistics 1970-1991*, Paris, 1992.

Chart 16a (cont.). **Non-employment rates,**[a] **1980-1991**
Averages and percentage point changes[b]

Inactivity   Unemployment

MALES

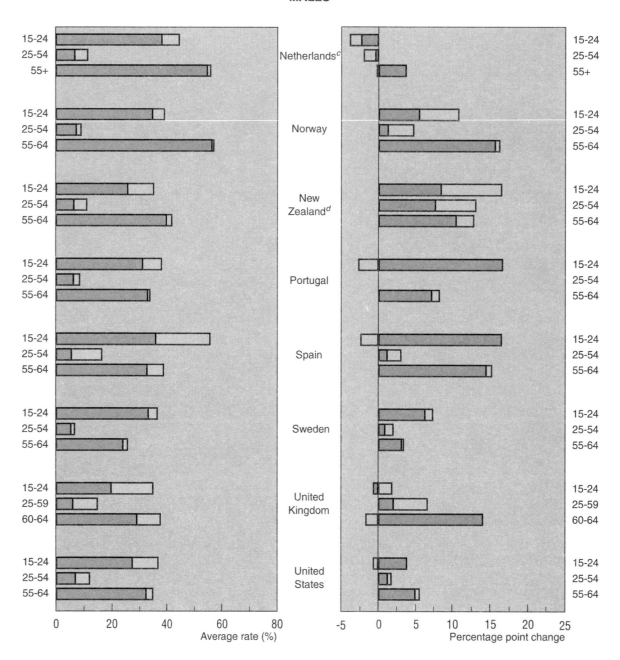

a) A non-employment rate is defined as the sum of persons not in employment (unemployed + inactive) as a percentage of the population specified. It is calculated over the period 1980-1991 unless otherwise specified.

b) Change is defined as 1991 less 1980 unless otherwise specified.

c) Netherlands: 1987 to 1989.

d) New Zealand: 1986 to 1991.

See Table 17.

Source: OECD, *Labour Force Statistics 1970-1991*, Paris, 1992.

Chart 16b (cont.). Non-employment rates,[a] 1980-1991

Averages and percentage point changes[b]

■ Inactivity   □ Unemployment

FEMALES

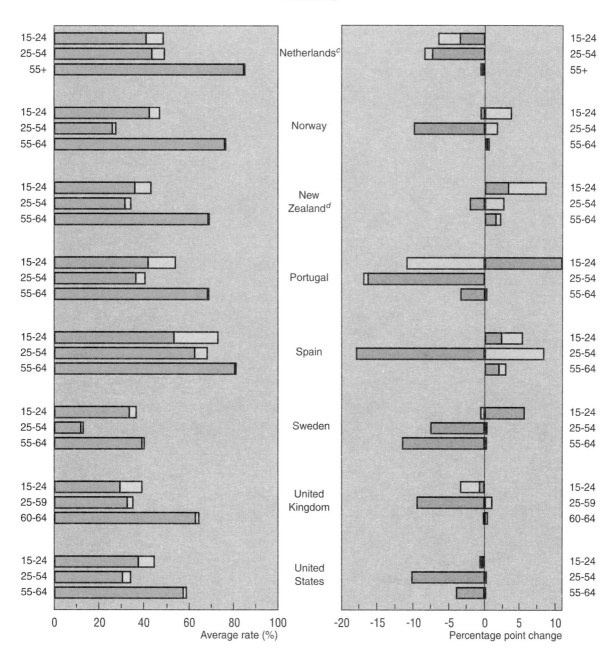

a) A non-employment rate is defined as the sum of persons not in employment (unemployed + inactive) as a percentage of the population specified. It is calculated over the period 1980-1991 unless otherwise specified.

b) Change is defined as 1991 less 1980 unless otherwise specified.

c) Netherlands: 1987 to 1989.

d) New Zealand: 1986 to 1991.

See Table 17.

Source: OECD, Labour Force Statistics 1970-1991, Paris, 1992.

Table 18. **Unemployment/population ratios, 1980-1990**

Averages		Years	Males aged			Females aged		
			15-24	25-44	45-64	15-24	25-44	45-64
Australia	Short-term	1980-1990	8.1	3.4	3.0	7.0	3.0	1.4
	Long-term		1.9	1.5	2.8	1.7	0.7	0.7
	Total		10.1	4.9	5.8	8.7	3.7	2.1
Austria	Short-term	1987-1990	3.3	4.2	1.5	3.3	3.3	0.8
	Long-term		0.1	0.6	0.6	0.1	0.6	0.2
	Total		3.4	4.7	2.1	3.4	3.9	1.0
Belgium	Short-term	1983-1990	3.2	1.4	0.6	4.6	1.7	0.3
	Long-term		3.4	3.6	2.7	6.7	7.4	1.8
	Total		6.6	5.0	3.4	11.3	9.1	2.1
Canada	Short-term	1980-1990	10.5	6.3	7.2	8.0	5.6	4.9
	Long-term		0.5	0.7	1.3	0.3	0.4	0.6
	Total		10.9	7.0	8.5	8.3	6.0	5.5
Denmark	Short-term	1983-1990	5.4	3.2	2.9	6.0	3.4	2.3
	Long-term		1.2	1.5	1.8	1.6	2.4	2.1
	Total		6.7	4.7	4.7	7.5	5.9	4.4
Finland	Short-term	a	4.1	2.7	0.6	4.1	2.1	0.6
	Long-term		0.6	0.6	0.3	0.2	0.6	0.3
	Total		4.7	3.3	0.9	4.4	2.7	0.8
France	Short-term	1980-1990	4.8	3.2	1.4	5.9	3.7	0.9
	Long-term		1.5	2.1	2.3	3.1	3.3	2.0
	Total		6.3	5.3	3.7	8.9	7.0	2.9
Germany	Short-term	1983-1988	3.2	2.3	2.6	3.5	2.6	1.9
	Long-term		1.4	2.2	3.7	1.6	2.1	2.8
	Total		4.6	4.5	6.4	5.1	4.7	4.7
Greece	Short-term	1983-1988	4.8	2.6	2.8	5.2	2.4	1.0
	Long-term		1.9	1.4	1.4	6.3	2.2	1.0
	Total		6.7	4.0	4.2	11.6	4.6	2.0
Ireland	Short-term	1983-1987, 1989	7.8	4.2	0.4	6.3	3.1	0.2
	Long-term		8.7	9.1	1.2	4.7	3.4	0.3
	Total		16.5	13.3	1.6	11.0	6.4	0.5
Italy	Short-term	1983-1987, 1989	4.6	1.1	0.6	5.2	1.5	0.4
	Long-term		7.9	1.8	0.6	11.0	3.4	0.5
	Total		12.5	2.9	1.3	16.2	4.9	1.0
Japan	Short-term	1980-1990	1.9	1.5	4.1	1.9	1.3	1.5
	Long-term		0.2	0.3	1.3	0.1	0.2	0.3
	Total		2.2	1.8	5.4	2.0	1.5	1.8
Netherlands	Short-term	b	4.8	2.2	1.5	5.0	2.9	1.2
	Long-term		2.7	3.7	4.2	2.5	3.1	2.3
	Total		7.5	5.9	5.7	7.5	6.0	3.5
New Zealand	Short-term	1986, 1988-1990	6.3	2.5	1.5	5.4	2.2	0.8
	Long-term		0.9	0.7	0.4	0.5	0.3	0.2
	Total		7.2	3.2	1.9	5.9	2.4	0.9
Norway	Short-term	c	4.0	2.0	1.4	3.7	1.7	0.9
	Long-term		0.3	0.3	0.4	0.2	0.3	0.2
	Total		4.3	2.3	1.8	3.9	2.0	1.1
Portugal	Short-term	1986-1987, 1990	4.5	1.6	0.9	4.8	1.7	0.5
	Long-term		4.0	1.5	1.0	6.3	3.1	0.5
	Total		8.6	3.1	1.8	11.1	4.9	1.1
Spain	Short-term	1980-1990	10.0	5.2	6.7	7.5	2.3	1.3
	Long-term		8.9	5.2	7.3	10.4	4.2	2.4
	Total		18.9	10.4	13.9	17.9	6.5	3.7
Sweden	Short-term	1980-1990	3.0	1.6	1.7	3.2	1.6	1.5
	Long-term		0.1	0.1	0.5	0.1	0.1	0.4
	Total		3.1	1.7	2.2	3.3	1.7	1.9
United Kingdom	Short-term	1983-1990	7.2	3.0	1.7	6.0	3.5	0.9
	Long-term		5.0	4.1	3.0	2.3	1.5	0.9
	Total		12.2	7.1	4.7	8.3	5.0	1.9
United States	Short-term	1980-1990	8.3	4.8	6.0	7.1	4.1	4.2
	Long-term		0.5	0.7	1.1	0.2	0.3	0.5
	Total		8.8	5.5	7.1	7.3	4.4	4.7

a) 1980, 1982-1987, 1989.
b) 1983, 1985, 1988-1990.
c) 1982-1985, 1987-1990.
The ratio is defined as the sum of the unemployed as a percentgae of the age group specified.

Table 18. **Unemployment/population ratios, 1980-1990** *(cont.)*

Percentage point changes		Years	Males aged			Females aged		
			15-24	25-44	45-64	15-24	25-44	45-64
Australia	Short-term	1980-1990	1.5	1.3	0.4	0.1	1.0	0.6
	Long-term		0.2	0.7	1.0	−0.4	0.2	0.2
	Total		1.7	2.0	1.4	−0.4	1.2	0.8
Austria	Short-term	1987-1990	−0.7	−0.2	−0.3	−0.3	0.3	0.2
	Long-term		−0.0	0.0	0.1	−0.0	0.1	0.2
	Total		−0.7	−0.2	−0.2	−0.3	0.5	0.4
Belgium	Short-term	1983-1990	−3.1	−0.8	−0.7	−2.9	−0.2	−0.3
	Long-term		−3.0	−1.4	−0.8	−4.7	−1.6	−0.7
	Total		−6.0	−2.2	−1.6	−7.6	−1.7	−1.0
Canada	Short-term	1980-1990	−0.4	1.6	0.8	−0.4	1.6	0.8
	Long-term		0.0	0.2	0.6	−0.1	0.1	0.5
	Total		−0.3	1.8	1.4	−0.5	1.7	1.2
Denmark	Short-term	1983-1990	−3.6	0.4	−0.9	−1.8	0.8	0.1
	Long-term		−1.1	0.3	−0.1	−1.9	0.3	0.5
	Total		−4.7	0.7	−0.9	−3.7	1.1	0.7
Finland	Short-term	*a*	−0.9	0.0	−0.1	−0.8	−0.7	−0.0
	Long-term		−0.5	−0.4	−0.6	0.0	−1.0	−0.7
	Total		−1.5	−0.4	−0.7	−0.8	−1.7	−0.7
France	Short-term	1980-1990	0.9	1.8	0.6	−0.8	2.0	0.5
	Long-term		0.2	1.4	1.2	−0.5	1.9	2.0
	Total		1.1	3.2	1.9	−1.3	3.9	2.5
Germany	Short-term	1983-1988	−1.0	−0.4	−0.3	−0.7	0.2	0.5
	Long-term		−0.7	0.1	1.4	−0.5	0.5	1.9
	Total		−1.7	−0.3	1.1	−1.2	0.7	2.4
Greece	Short-term	1983-1988	−1.7	−0.8	−1.7	−3.9	2.1	−0.0
	Long-term		0.5	0.4	0.2	4.9	−0.3	0.0
	Total		−1.2	−0.4	−1.5	1.0	1.8	−0.0
Ireland	Short-term	1983-1987, 1989	−5.5	−2.5	−0.3	−3.3	−1.6	−0.1
	Long-term		3.2	4.5	0.6	2.4	2.8	0.2
	Total		−2.3	1.9	0.3	−0.9	1.2	0.1
Italy	Short-term	1983-1987, 1989	−1.4	0.2	−0.1	−1.4	0.4	0.0
	Long-term		2.2	1.3	0.2	3.6	2.4	0.2
	Total		0.8	1.5	0.1	2.2	2.9	0.2
Japan	Short-term	1980-1990	0.1	−0.1	−0.8	0.2	0.1	0.7
	Long-term		−0.1	0.2	0.5	0.1	−0.1	−0.2
	Total		0.1	0.1	−0.2	0.3	−0.0	0.5
Netherlands	Short-term	*b*	−3.3	−2.0	−2.0	−0.5	1.2	0.3
	Long-term		−3.4	−1.5	−1.7	−2.7	0.1	0.6
	Total		−6.6	−3.5	−3.8	−3.1	1.3	0.9
New Zealand	Short-term	1986, 1988-1990	2.7	2.7	2.1	2.4	1.2	0.2
	Long-term		0.8	1.3	1.0	0.6	0.2	0.5
	Total		3.4	4.0	3.1	3.0	1.4	0.7
Norway	Short-term	*c*	1.7	2.0	2.5	0.5	1.0	1.5
	Long-term		0.6	0.9	1.3	0.6	0.8	0.9
	Total		2.3	2.9	3.8	1.2	1.8	2.4
Portugal	Short-term	1986-1987, 1990	−2.4	−0.9	0.0	−1.9	−0.4	−0.1
	Long-term		−4.4	−0.9	−0.1	−5.1	−1.3	−0.0
	Total		−6.8	−1.8	−0.1	−7.0	−1.7	−0.1
Spain	Short-term	1980-1990	−2.7	−0.4	−1.5	−0.1	2.5	1.5
	Long-term		0.8	1.9	2.5	5.1	3.2	9.4
	Total		−1.9	1.5	1.0	5.0	5.7	10.9
Sweden	Short-term	1980-1990	−0.7	0.1	−0.5	−1.5	−0.5	−0.0
	Long-term		−0.0	−0.0	−0.1	−0.0	−0.0	−0.0
	Total		−0.7	0.1	−0.5	−1.5	−0.5	−0.1
United Kingdom	Short-term	1983-1990	−2.7	−0.7	−0.7	−2.1	0.5	0.0
	Long-term		−5.4	−2.0	−0.8	−2.6	−0.8	−0.1
	Total		−8.1	−2.7	−1.5	−4.7	−0.3	−0.1
United States	Short-term	1980-1990	−2.0	−0.8	−0.2	−1.1	−0.6	−0.4
	Long-term		−0.1	−0.0	0.3	−0.1	0.0	0.1
	Total		−2.1	−0.8	0.0	−1.1	−0.6	−0.4

a) 1980, 1982-1987, 1989.
b) 1983, 1985, 1988-1990.
c) 1982-1985, 1987-1990.
Change is defined as 1990 less 1980 unless otherwise specified.
Source: OECD unemployment duration data file and demographic data file, 1992.

Chart 17a. **Unemployment/population ratios,**[a] **1980-1990**

Averages and percentage point changes[b]

Short-term   Long-term

MALES

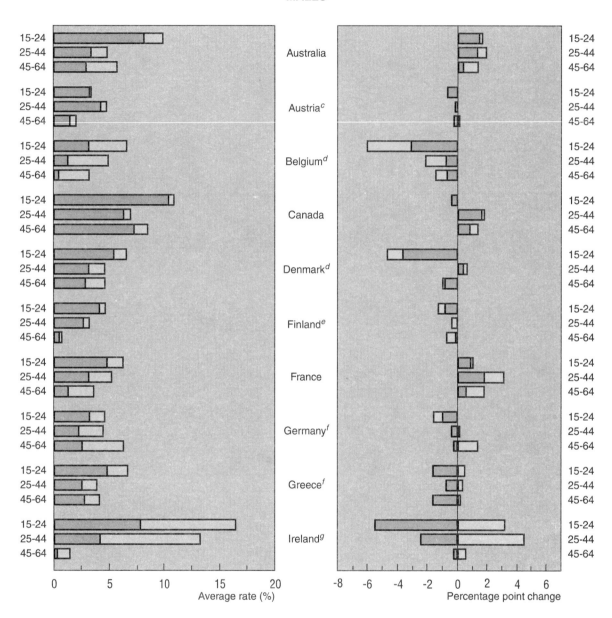

0   5   10   15   20
Average rate (%)

-8   -6   -4   -2   0   2   4   6
Percentage point change

a) An unemployment ratio is defined as the sum of unemployed persons as a percentage of the population specified. It is calculated over the period 1980-1990 unless otherwise specified.

b) Change is defined as 1990 less 1980 unless otherwise specified.

c) Austria: 1987 to 1990.

d) Belgium and Denmark: 1983 to 1990.

e) Finland: 1980, 1982 to 1987, 1989.

f) Germany, Greece: 1983 to 1988.

g) Ireland: 1983 to 1987, 1989.

See Table 18.

Source: OECD, unemployment duration data file, Paris, 1992

Chart 17b. **Unemployment/population ratios,**[a] **1980-1990**

Averages and percentage point changes[b]

■ Short-term   ▢ Long-term

FEMALES

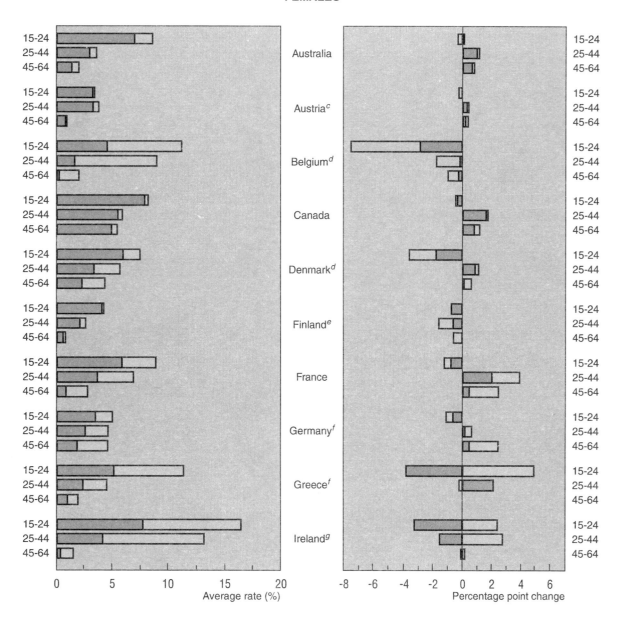

a) An unemployment ratio is defined as the sum of unemployed persons as a percentage of the population specified. It is calculated over the period 1980-1990 unless otherwise specified.

b) Change is defined as 1990 less 1980 unless otherwise specified.

c) Austria: 1987 to 1990.

d) Belgium and Denmark: 1983 to 1990.

e) Finland: 1980, 1982 to 1987, 1989.

f) Germany, Greece: 1983 to 1988.

g) Ireland: 1983 to 1987, 1989.

See Table 18.

Source: OECD, unemployment duration data file, Paris, 1992

Chart 17a (*cont.*). **Unemployment/population ratios,**[a] **1980-1990**
Averages and percentage point changes[b]

Short-term   Long-term

MALES

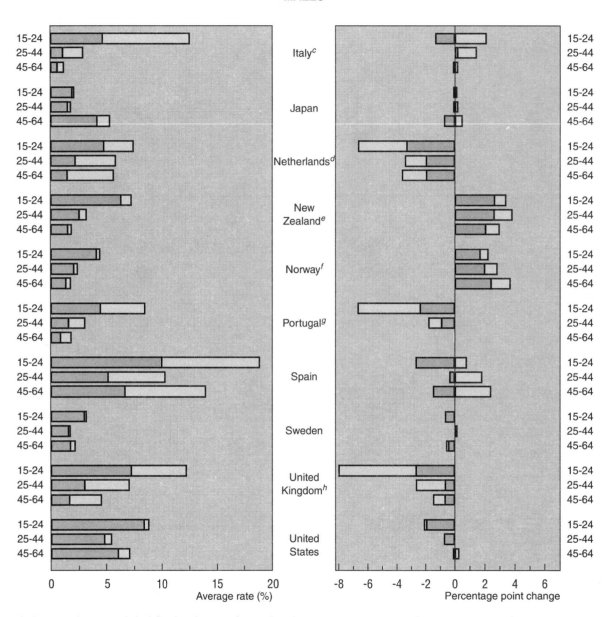

a) An unemployment ratio is defined as the sum of unemployed persons as a percentage of the population specified. It is calculated over the period 1980-1990 unless otherwise specified.

b) Change is defined as 1990 less 1980 unless otherwise specified.

c) Italy: 1983 to 1987, 1989.

d) Netherlands: 1983, 1985 and 1988 to 1990.

e) New Zealand: 1986, 1988 to 1990.

f) Norway: 1983 to 1985 and 1987 to 1990.

g) Portugal: 1986 to 1987, 1990.

h) United Kingdom: 1983 to 1990.

See Table 18.

Source: OECD, unemployment duration data file, 1992.

Chart 17b (cont.). Unemployment/population ratios,[a] 1980-1990
Averages and percentage point changes[b]

Short-term   Long-term

FEMALES

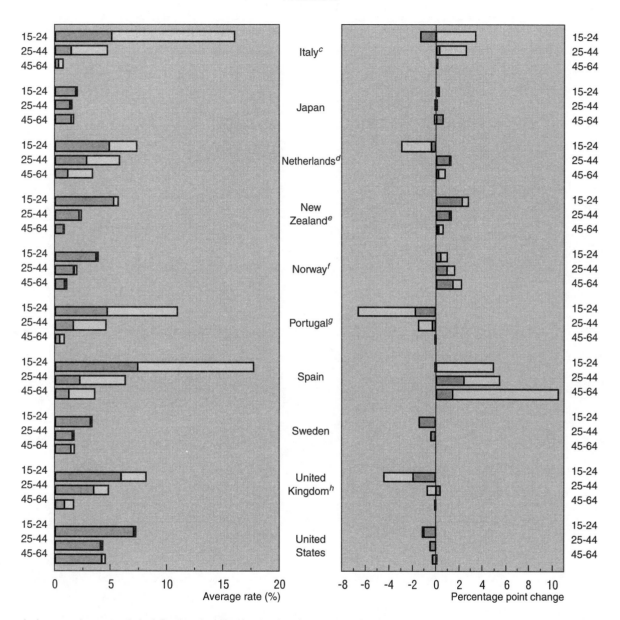

Average rate (%)   Percentage point change

a) An unemployment ratio is defined as the sum of unemployed persons as a percentage of the population specified. It is calculated over the period 1980-1990 unless otherwise specified.

b) Change is defined as 1990 less 1980 unless otherwise specified.

c) Italy: 1983 to 1987, 1989.

d) Netherlands: 1983, 1985 and 1988 to 1990.

e) New Zealand: 1986, 1988 to 1990.

f) Norway: 1983 to 1985 and 1987 to 1990.

g) Portugal: 1986 to 1987, 1990.

h) United Kingdom: 1983 to 1990.

See Table 18.

Source: OECD, unemployment duration data file, 1992.

MAIN SALES OUTLETS OF OECD PUBLICATIONS
PRINCIPAUX POINTS DE VENTE DES PUBLICATIONS DE L'OCDE

ARGENTINA – ARGENTINE
Carlos Hirsah S.R.L.
Galería Güemes, Florida 165, 4° Piso
1333 Buenos Aires   Tel. (1) 331.1787 y 331.2391
Telefax: (1) 331.1787

AUSTRALIA – AUSTRALIE
D.A. Information Services
648 Whitehorse Road, P.O.B 163
Mitcham, Victoria 3132   Tel. (03) 873.4411
Telefax: (03) 873.5679

AUSTRIA – AUTRICHE
Gerold & Co.
Graben 31
Wien I   Tel. (0222) 533.50.14

BELGIUM – BELGIQUE
Jean De Lannoy
Avenue du Roi 202
B-1060 Bruxelles   Tel. (02) 538.51.69/538.08.41
Telefax: (02) 538.08.41

CANADA
Renouf Publishing Company Ltd.
1294 Algoma Road
Ottawa, ON K1B 3W8   Tel. (613) 741.4333
Telefax: (613) 741.5439
Stores:
61 Sparks Street
Ottawa, ON K1P 5R1   Tel. (613) 238.8985
211 Yonge Street
Toronto, ON M5B 1M4   Tel. (416) 363.3171
Telefax: (416)363.59.63
Les Éditions La Liberté Inc.
3020 Chemin Sainte-Foy
Sainte-Foy, PQ G1X 3V6   Tel. (418) 658.3763
Telefax: (418) 658.3763

Federal Publications Inc.
165 University Avenue, Suite 701
Toronto, ON M5H 3B8   Tel. (416) 860.1611
Telefax: (416) 860.1608
Les Publications Fédérales
1185 Université
Montréal, QC H3B 3A7   Tel. (514) 954.1633
Telefax : (514) 954.1635

CHINA – CHINE
China National Publications Import
Export Corporation (CNPIEC)
16 Gongti E. Road, Chaoyang District
P.O. Box 88 or 50
Beijing 100704 PR   Tel. (01) 506.6688
Telefax: (01) 506.3101

DENMARK – DANEMARK
Munksgaard Book and Subscription Service
35, Nørre Søgade, P.O. Box 2148
DK-1016 København K   Tel. (33) 12.85.70
Telefax: (33) 12.93.87

FINLAND – FINLANDE
Akateeminen Kirjakauppa
Keskuskatu 1, P.O. Box 128
00100 Helsinki
Subscription Services/Agence d'abonnements :
P.O. Box 23
00371 Helsinki   Tel. (358 0) 12141
Telefax: (358 0) 121.4450

FRANCE
OECD/OCDE
Mail Orders/Commandes par correspondance:
2, rue André-Pascal
75775 Paris Cedex 16   Tel. (33-1) 45.24.82.00
Telefax: (33-1) 45.24.81.76   or (33-1) 45.24.85.00
Telex: 640048 OCDE

OECD Bookshop/Librairie de l'OCDE :
33, rue Octave-Feuillet
75016 Paris   Tel. (33-1) 45.24.81.67
(33-1) 45.24.81.81
Documentation Française
29, quai Voltaire
75007 Paris   Tel. 40.15.70.00
Gibert Jeune (Droit-Économie)
6, place Saint-Michel
75006 Paris   Tel. 43.25.91.19
Librairie du Commerce International
10, avenue d'Iéna
75016 Paris   Tel. 40.73.34.60
Librairie Dunod
Université Paris-Dauphine
Place du Maréchal de Lattre de Tassigny
75016 Paris   Tel. (1) 44.05.40.13
Librairie Lavoisier
11, rue Lavoisier
75008 Paris   Tel. 42.65.39.95
Librairie L.G.D.J. - Montchrestien
20, rue Soufflot
75005 Paris   Tel. 46.33.89.85
Librairie des Sciences Politiques
30, rue Saint-Guillaume
75007 Paris   Tel. 45.48.36.02
P.U.F.
49, boulevard Saint-Michel
75005 Paris   Tel. 43.25.83.40
Librairie de l'Université
12a, rue Nazareth
13100 Aix-en-Provence Tel. (16) 42.26.18.08
Documentation Française
165, rue Garibaldi
69003 Lyon   Tel. (16) 78.63.32.23
Librairie Decitre
29, place Bellecour
69002 Lyon   Tel. (16) 72.40.54.54

GERMANY – ALLEMAGNE
OECD Publications and Information Centre
August-Bebel-Allee 6
D-53175 Bonn 2   Tel. (0228) 959.120
Telefax: (0228) 959.12.17

GREECE – GRÈCE
Librairie Kauffmann
Mavrokordatou 9
106 78 Athens   Tel. (01) 32.55.321
Telefax: (01) 36.33.967

HONG-KONG
Swindon Book Co. Ltd.
13–15 Lock Road
Kowloon, Hong Kong   Tel. 366.80.31
Telefax: 739.49.75

HUNGARY – HONGRIE
Euro Info Service
POB 1271
1464 Budapest   Tel. (1) 111.62.16
Telefax : (1) 111.60.61

ICELAND – ISLANDE
Mál Mog Menning
Laugavegi 18, Pósthólf 392
121 Reykjavik   Tel. 162.35.23

INDIA – INDE
Oxford Book and Stationery Co.
Scindia House
New Delhi 110001   Tel.(11) 331.5896/5308
Telefax: (11) 332.5993
17 Park Street
Calcutta 700016   Tel. 240832

INDONESIA – INDONÉSIE
Pdii-Lipi
P.O. Box 269/JKSMG/88
Jakarta 12790   Tel. 583467
Telex: 62 875

IRELAND – IRLANDE
TDC Publishers – Library Suppliers
12 North Frederick Street
Dublin 1   Tel. (01) 874.48.35
Telefax: (01) 874.84.16

ISRAEL
Electronic Publications only
Publications électroniques seulement
Sophist Systems Ltd.
71 Allenby Street
Tel-Aviv 65134   Tel. 3-29.00.21
Telefax: 3-29.92.39

ITALY – ITALIE
Libreria Commissionaria Sansoni
Via Duca di Calabria 1/1
50125 Firenze   Tel. (055) 64.54.15
Telefax: (055) 64.12.57
Via Bartolini 29
20155 Milano   Tel. (02) 36.50.83
Editrice e Libreria Herder
Piazza Montecitorio 120
00186 Roma   Tel. 679.46.28
Telefax: 678.47.51
Libreria Hoepli
Via Hoepli 5
20121 Milano   Tel. (02) 86.54.46
Telefax: (02) 805.28.86
Libreria Scientifica
Dott. Lucio de Biasio 'Aeiou'
Via Coronelli, 6
20146 Milano   Tel. (02) 48.95.45.52
Telefax: (02) 48.95.45.48

JAPAN – JAPON
OECD Publications and Information Centre
Landic Akasaka Building
2-3-4 Akasaka, Minato-ku
Tokyo 107   Tel. (81.3) 3586.2016
Telefax: (81.3) 3584.7929

KOREA – CORÉE
Kyobo Book Centre Co. Ltd.
P.O. Box 1658, Kwang Hwa Moon
Seoul   Tel. 730.78.91
Telefax: 735.00.30

MALAYSIA – MALAISIE
Co-operative Bookshop Ltd.
University of Malaya
P.O. Box 1127, Jalan Pantai Baru
59700 Kuala Lumpur
Malaysia   Tel. 756.5000/756.5425
Telefax: 757.3661

MEXICO – MEXIQUE
Revistas y Periodicos Internacionales S.A. de C.V.
Florencia 57 - 1004
Mexico, D.F. 06600   Tel. 207.81.00
Telefax : 208.39.79

NETHERLANDS – PAYS-BAS
SDU Uitgeverij Plantijnstraat
Externe Fondsen
Postbus 20014
2500 EA's-Gravenhage Tel. (070) 37.89.880
Voor bestellingen: Telefax: (070) 34.75.778

**NEW ZEALAND
NOUVELLE-ZÉLANDE**
Legislation Services
P.O. Box 12418
Thorndon, Wellington   Tel. (04) 496.5652
                              Telefax: (04) 496.5698

NORWAY – NORVÈGE
Narvesen Info Center – NIC
Bertrand Narvesens vei 2
P.O. Box 6125 Etterstad
0602 Oslo 6   Tel. (022) 57.33.00
                              Telefax: (022) 68.19.01

PAKISTAN
Mirza Book Agency
65 Shahrah Quaid-E-Azam
Lahore 54000   Tel. (42) 353.601
                              Telefax: (42) 231.730

PHILIPPINE – PHILIPPINES
International Book Center
5th Floor, Filipinas Life Bldg.
Ayala Avenue
Metro Manila   Tel. 81.96.76
                              Telex 23312 RHP PH

PORTUGAL
Livraria Portugal
Rua do Carmo 70-74
Apart. 2681
1200 Lisboa   Tel.: (01) 347.49.82/5
                              Telefax: (01) 347.02.64

SINGAPORE – SINGAPOUR
Gower Asia Pacific Pte Ltd.
Golden Wheel Building
41, Kallang Pudding Road, No. 04-03
Singapore 1334   Tel. 741.5166
                              Telefax: 742.9356

SPAIN – ESPAGNE
Mundi-Prensa Libros S.A.
Castelló 37, Apartado 1223
Madrid 28001   Tel. (91) 431.33.99
                              Telefax: (91) 575.39.98

Libreria Internacional AEDOS
Consejo de Ciento 391
08009 – Barcelona   Tel. (93) 488.30.09
                              Telefax: (93) 487.76.59
Llibreria de la Generalitat
Palau Moja
Rambla dels Estudis, 118
08002 – Barcelona
               (Subscripcions) Tel. (93) 318.80.12
               (Publicacions) Tel. (93) 302.67.23
                              Telefax: (93) 412.18.54

SRI LANKA
Centre for Policy Research
c/o Colombo Agencies Ltd.
No. 300-304, Galle Road
Colombo 3   Tel. (1) 574240, 573551-2
                              Telefax: (1) 575394, 510711

SWEDEN – SUÈDE
Fritzes Information Center
Box 16356
Regeringsgatan 12
106 47 Stockholm   Tel. (08) 690.90.90
                              Telefax: (08) 20.50.21

Subscription Agency/Agence d'abonnements :
Wennergren-Williams Info AB
P.O. Box 1305
171 25 Solna   Tel. (08) 705.97.50
                              Téléfax : (08) 27.00.71

SWITZERLAND – SUISSE
Maditec S.A. (Books and Periodicals - Livres
et périodiques)
Chemin des Palettes 4
Case postale 266
1020 Renens   Tel. (021) 635.08.65
                              Telefax: (021) 635.07.80

Librairie Payot S.A.
4, place Pépinet
CP 3212
1002 Lausanne   Tel. (021) 341.33.48
                              Telefax: (021) 341.33.45

Librairie Unilivres
6, rue de Candolle
1205 Genève   Tel. (022) 320.26.23
                              Telefax: (022) 329.73.18

Subscription Agency/Agence d'abonnements :
Dynapresse Marketing S.A.
38 avenue Vibert
1227 Carouge   Tel.: (022) 308.07.89
                              Telefax : (022) 308.07.99

See also – Voir aussi :
OECD Publications and Information Centre
August-Bebel-Allee 6
D-53175 Bonn 2 (Germany)   Tel. (0228) 959.120
                              Telefax: (0228) 959.12.17

TAIWAN – FORMOSE
Good Faith Worldwide Int'l. Co. Ltd.
9th Floor, No. 118, Sec. 2
Chung Hsiao E. Road
Taipei   Tel. (02) 391.7396/391.7397
                              Telefax: (02) 394.9176

THAILAND – THAÏLANDE
Suksit Siam Co. Ltd.
113, 115 Fuang Nakhon Rd.
Opp. Wat Rajbopith
Bangkok 10200   Tel. (662) 225.9531/2
                              Telefax: (662) 222.5188

TURKEY – TURQUIE
Kültür Yayinlari Is-Türk Ltd. Sti.
Atatürk Bulvari No. 191/Kat 13
Kavaklidere/Ankara   Tel. 428.11.40 Ext. 2458
Dolmabahce Cad. No. 29
Besiktas/Istanbul   Tel. 260.71.88
                              Telex: 43482B

UNITED KINGDOM – ROYAUME-UNI
HMSO
Gen. enquiries   Tel. (071) 873 0011
Postal orders only:
P.O. Box 276, London SW8 5DT
Personal Callers HMSO Bookshop
49 High Holborn, London WC1V 6HB
                              Telefax: (071) 873 8200
Branches at: Belfast, Birmingham, Bristol, Edin-
burgh, Manchester

UNITED STATES – ÉTATS-UNIS
OECD Publications and Information Centre
2001 L Street N.W., Suite 700
Washington, D.C. 20036-4910 Tel. (202) 785.6323
                              Telefax: (202) 785.0350

VENEZUELA
Libreria del Este
Avda F. Miranda 52, Aptdo. 60337
Edificio Galipán
Caracas 106   Tel. 951.1705/951.2307/951.1297
                              Telegram: Libreste Caracas

Subscription to OECD periodicals may also be
placed through main subscription agencies.

Les abonnements aux publications périodiques de
l'OCDE peuvent être souscrits auprès des
principales agences d'abonnement.

Orders and inquiries from countries where Distribu-
tors have not yet been appointed should be sent to:
OECD Publications Service, 2 rue André-Pascal,
75775 Paris Cedex 16, France.

Les commandes provenant de pays où l'OCDE n'a
pas encore désigné de distributeur devraient être
adressées à : OCDE, Service des Publications,
2, rue André-Pascal, 75775 Paris Cedex 16, France.

2-1994

OECD PUBLICATIONS, 2 rue André-Pascal, 75775 PARIS CEDEX 16
PRINTED IN FRANCE
(81 94 02 1) ISBN 92-64-14056-5 - No. 46941 1994